Contemporary Public Budgeting

Contemporary Public Budgeting

Edited by
Thomas D. Lynch

Transaction Books
New Brunswick (U.S.A.) and London (U.K.)

The Bureaucrat, Inc.
Washington, D.C.

Library of Congress Catalog Number: 79-67062
ISBN: 0-87855-722-9
Printed in the United States of America

Library of Congress Cataloging in Publication Data
Main entry under title:

Contemporary public budgeting.

   Includes index.
   1. Zero-base budgeting—United States—Addresses, essays, lectures. 2. Budget—United States—Addresses, essays, lectures. I. Lynch, Thomas Dexter, 1942-
HJ2052.C66   353.007'2   79-67062
ISBN 0-87855-722-9

Contents

Acknowledgments

Grateful acknowledgment is made to the authors and publishers who granted permission to reprint selections from copyrighted material.

Graeme M. Taylor, "Introduction to Zero-Base Budgeting," from *The Bureaucrat*, Vol.6, No.1, Spring 1977, pp. 33–55.

Emerson Markham, "Zero-Base Budgeting in ACTION," from *The Bureaucrat*, Vol.7, No.1, Spring 1978, pp. 48–50.

Jerome A. Miles, "Fundamentals of Budgeting and ZBB," from *The Bureaucrat*, Vol.7, No.1, Spring 1978, pp. 41–44.

Nanette M. Blandin and Arnold E. Donahue, "ZBB: Not a Panacea, But a Definite Plus," from *The Bureaucrat*, Vol.7, No.1, Spring 1978, pp. 51–55.

Thomas P. Lauth, "Zero-Base Budgeting in Georgia State Government: Myth and Reality," reprinted with permission of the *Public Administration Review*, September/October, 1978, pp. 420–30.

Ernest C. Betts, Jr. and Richard E. Miller, "More About the Impact of the Congressional Budget and Impoundment Control Act," from *The Bureaucrat*, Vol.6, No.1, Spring 1977, pp. 112–20.

Linda L. Smith, "The Congressional Budget Process," from *The Bureaucrat*, Vol.6, No.1, Spring 1977, pp. 88-111.

James Davidson, "Sunset—A New Challenge," from *The Bureaucrat*, Vol.6, No.1, Spring 1977, pp. 159–64.

Steve Charnovitz, "Evaluating Sunset: What Will It Mean?" from *The Bureaucrat*, Vol.6, No.3, Fall 1977, pp. 64-79.

Harry P. Hatry, "The Urban Institute," reprinted with permission of *The Public Administration Review*, January/February, 1978, pp. 28-33.

Preface

Contemporary Public Budgeting is designed to complement this editor's earlier text, *Public Budgeting in America* (Prentice Hall, 1979). In a textbook, I found it impossible to present anything more than the basics of modern budgeting. This reader brings together articles published in *The Bureaucrat*, the *Public Administration Review*, and previously unpublished material. Each article was selected on the basis of helping the reader understand the contemporary nature of public budgeting. The authors, a blend of academicians and professionals, explain today's public budgeting in such a manner that the news stories have more meaning and the subject of budgeting becomes more relevant.

The field of budgeting is experiencing future shock. In writing a textbook, one is painfully aware of the explosion of new ideas, professional developments, new publications, and interesting research efforts in progress. This reader is an attempt to provide more depth to the recent developments in the field. It should help us, for a short time, to better appreciate the contemporary before it also becomes history.

Please note that an appendix contains study and review questions. These should help the reader reflect upon the chapters, and provide possible essay test questions for an instructor who might adopt this book for classroom use.

PART I

ZBB: A CONTEMPORARY BUDGET REFORM

Zero Base Budgeting is contemporary because as governor and then as president Jimmy Carter made ZBB a commonly heard expression. The general public knows little about ZBB, but they tend to believe that (1) ZBB saves taxpayer's dollars, and (2) ZBB involves completely rethinking the budget each year. ZBB is complex and the popular image is a gross oversimplification. In this section, the various articles help us understand:

- what ZBB is;
- how it worked in one federal department;
- some impressionistic evaluations of ZBB by those who must make it work;
- the changes attributed to ZBB based upon the Georgia experience; and finally,
- the very practical limitation of extending any sophisticated reform to the grass-root level of government.

ZBB is a current fad. One commonly sees it on professional conference programs, and hears politicians speaking its virtues. ZBB is a budget reform which focuses upon a way for the government to compile information and decide upon the important policy decisions implicit in any budget. ZBB is predicted on the rational decision-making model, and stress is placed upon the use of analysis. ZBB is a great deal of extra work. Interestingly, many commentators claim that the ultimate budget decisions are similar, using ZBB or the other approaches to budgeting. Thus, one wonders if ZBB is worth the extra work. Several authors in this portion of the book will help the reader decide this question.

In his "Introduction to Zero Base Budgeting," Graeme M. Taylor describes ZBB in the public sector. This particular article is a widely used introduction. Since it first appeared in *The Bureaucrat*, it has been used at various universities including the Harvard Business School and in numerous federal training sessions. The strength of the article is its readability, its insightful warnings about applying ZBB, and its stress upon considering a budget reform in the context of the present budget system. Taylor's article helps us to understand not only the

1

basics of ZBB, but how those reforms may or may not fit into the larger context of budgeting.

ZBB had a fast birth process in the federal government. The new president demanded that the entire federal budget be prepared with ZBB in his first year in office. That was done, and Ralph C. Bledsoe's "Zero Base Budgeting at HUD" is the story of its birth in one federal department. Often, case studies are self-serving public relations' stories. The Bledsoe case is a remarkably honest presentation of the difficulties of one department that took the president's mandate seriously. One can learn a great deal by reading about the pressure of deadlines, the problems of being in a new administration, and the challenge of making a foreign thought become a working reality. The birth had serious labor pains.

The people who must make ZBB work are the agency budget officers and the Office of Management and Budget (OMB) budget examiners. After one year of coping with this new baby, *The Bureaucrat* ran a forum titled "ZBB Revisited." That issue focused upon the subjective impressions of those who had to deal with the budget reform. Three short articles were selected from that forum to represent those impressionistic evaluations of ZBB. A student of public administration should especially enjoy the increased sophistication of these commentaries on ZBB. At first, most writers about ZBB were prophets of the new order. The recent body of literature reflects the complex political-administrative budget environment that much of the earlier literature ignored. In Jerome A. Miles's "Fundamentals of Budgeting and ZBB," the professional speaks as follows:

> ZBB is not the endless summer. We are not looking for the perfect wave. ZBB is a dynamic process and the structure has to be flexible enough to accommodate changes in programs as well as changes in policy staff preferences.

The role of OMB is explained in textbooks, but it is normally not appreciated by students. Nanette M. Blandin and Arnold E. Donahue give us the OMB perspective on ZBB, and they help us to appreciate the significance of OMB as an agency. Their appraisal of ZBB from their perspective is useful. The following quotes from their article illustrate some of the practical limitations of this technique:

> We suggest that the value of these ZBB features is yet to be fully realized, since they are admittedly difficult requirements.
>
> Yet there just aren't many incentives for a program manager to identify a real minimum funding level.
>
> Other areas of relative weakness were agencies' statements of program objectives, review of alternative means of accomplishing objectives, and programmatic evaluations of the impact of different funding levels.

The state government most associated with ZBB is Georgia. Was it successful? During President Carter's campaign for president, that question was asked many times by reporters, but there was little hard empirical evidence to support a pro or con position. Evidence is given in Thomas P. Lauth's "Zero Base Budgeting in Georgia State Government." Professor Lauth interviewed many state officials and examined several Georgia budgets. His conclusions are insightful and worth considering.

Reasoning from the claims of the ZBB supporters, one would conclude that a government should use ZBB. Daniel K. Wanamaker would question such a conclusion. In "ZBB is Light Years Away From Rural America," Professor Wanamaker helps us appreciate the extreme range of talent and expertise found in budgeting. He concludes that ZBB, as a budget reform, is presently impossible in most small local governments in this country. The reason for his conclusion is worth further reflection.

In the humor section of Volume 6, Number 1 of *The Bureaucrat*, David Snyder captured an important point which we often overlook. Consider carefully the following as you read the articles on ZBB.

> . . . whether or not zero-base budgeting is adopted will not depend upon its merits or its shortcomings, but rather on its overall image. If most people in the leadership of the executive and legislative branches are convinced that zero-base budgeting is a good thing, we will have zero-base budgeting. Then, it will be up to us to make the best of it we can.

1.

Introduction to Zero-Base Budgeting

Graeme M. Taylor

The term *zero-base budgeting* is not new. In the most literal sense, ZBB implies constructing a budget without any reference to what has gone before, based on a fundamental reappraisal of purposes, methods, and resources. This interpretation of ZBB has been roundly condemned as naive and impractical, if not downright mischievous. The U.S. Department of Agriculture's attempt at this sort of ZBB for FY 1964 was widely regarded as a failure. As Allen Schick has remarked, even a teenager doesn't have an identity crisis every year. Or, as Dean Acheson pointed out in another context, we can't have a foreign policy if we pull it up every year to examine its roots.

But there is another version of ZBB. Developed originally at Texas Instruments by Peter A. Pyhrr as a method of controlling overhead costs, and subsequently implemented by Jimmy Carter in the state of Georgia, this latter-day ZBB is simply the systematic application of marginal analysis techniques to budget formulation. It is this version of ZBB which is the subject of this article.

Although the basic concepts of ZBB as used at Texas Instruments and Georgia are indeed simple, putting them into practice is difficult, complex, and demanding. Many organizations, however, apparently believe the results are worth the effort. Within the past three years, at least one hundred major corporations have applied ZBB to portions of their operating budgets. A handful of states and several local governments have adopted ZBB. A few federal agencies have introduced ZBB on a limited basis within the past year.

Some of the growing popularity of ZBB must no doubt be attributed to presidential campaign publicity. But it would be a mistake to think that the bandwagon syndrome is the main reason for ZBB's adoption. The real explanation lies in certain intrinsic features of the process itself coupled, fortuitously, with the needs of the times.

Industry views ZBB as a more rational approach to the perennial problem of controlling overhead. The recent recession forced most companies to reap-

5

praise their discretionary costs, and many found ZBB an instrument ideally suited to the task.

In the public sector, the example of New York City looms like a severed head placed on a spike as an awful warning. Today, virtually everyone is a fiscal conservative. There is a growing realization that program initiatives to meet public needs must go hand-in-hand with sound financial management. As President Carter pointed out in *Nation's Business* (January, 1977): "There is no inherent conflict between careful planning, tight budgeting, and constant management reassessment on the one hand, and compassionate concern for the deprived and afflicted on the other. Waste and inefficiency never fed a hungry child, provided a job for a willing worker, or educated a deserving student."

Zero-base budgeting has come a long way since its origins at Texas Instruments and Georgia. These early models have been substantially improved upon and refined in later, less publicized applications, while still retaining the original fundamental principles. Experience indicates that there are almost limitless ways to adapt the basic ZBB concepts to the varying decisional needs of different organizations. This should come as no surprise. ZBB is, after all, a management-oriented approach to budgeting. It follows, then, that its basic principles must be adapted to fit each organization's unique management structure and culture.

This article will attempt, somewhat boldly, to summarize the state of a complex and rapidly evolving art. The writer's viewpoint is not that of a scholar, but rather a practitioner, one who has been actively involved in helping organizations design and implement ZBB. The reader will therefore not find much in the way of public administration theory, nor any glittering generalities to serve as a conceptual framework. If any apology is needed, it would be this: It is too early to predict the ultimate fate of ZBB in the public sector. It could evolve in many different ways to serve different needs in different government organizations. Many versions of ZBB could comfortably coexist in Washington, in the states, and in city halls. Different approaches may be quite appropriate even within the same government, at different levels and for different kinds of programs. No unified theory is likely to emerge; certainly none can be discerned at this time.

The basic principles and elements of ZBB, common to virtually all applications, are first summarized. Each of the elements of ZBB is then treated in more detail. Certain considerations affecting the design and implementation of ZBB are then reviewed, emphasizing the variety of possible approaches and the importance of tailoring the approach to the unique circumstances of each organization. Some differences between ZBB in the public and private sectors are then discussed, and results of a survey of corporate ZBB users are presented. The concluding section attempts to examine certain options for the application of ZBB to the federal government.

Principles and Elements of ZBB

The distinctive and essential hallmark of ZBB is its focus on the total budget request. The current spending level is not regarded as an inviolate base, immune from detailed scrutiny. Existing activities are examined along with proposed new activities.

In traditional incremental budgeting systems, all participants behave as if the relevant question were: At the margin, is an increment in Program A more important than an increment in Program B? Decision makers are forced to accept or reject a program increment, or to reduce its amount. Incremental budgeting effectively denies decision makers the option of trading off a requested increase in one activity against a reduction in another.

ZBB places a premium on offering decision makers a range of choices among alternate funding levels. The relevant budgetary question is: At the margin, is an increment in Program A more important than an increment in Program B or a previously funded item in Programs A, B, C . . .? It is explicitly *not* assumed that present activities must necessarily be continued. Given revenue constraints, an existing activity may be reduced or eliminated entirely to make way for new activities, or one program may be cut back to permit another to expand.

Basic Elements of ZBB

The three basic elements of ZBB are: (1) identification of "decision units"; (2) analysis of decision units and the formulation of "decision packages"; and (3) ranking. The decision units are the lowest-level entities for which budgets are prepared. One important requirement is that each decision unit have an identifiable manager with the necessary authority to establish priorities and prepare budgets for all activities within the decision unit.

ZBB calls for two kinds of analysis. First is the analysis which most truly deserves the name "zero base"—a reexamination of the purposes, activities, and operations of the decision unit. In this analytic phase, questions such as the following are addressed: What would be the consequences if the decision unit were entirely eliminated? How can the decision unit's purposes be achieved in a more cost-effective manner? How can the efficiency of the decision unit's operations be improved? Following the zero-base review of purposes, activities, and operations, the decision unit manager then segments the decision unit's activities into a series of "decision packages." The first package contains those activities, or portions of activities, deemed highest in priority. The second package contains the next most important items, and so on. The costs and consequences of each package are documented for higher-level review.

The third basic element of ZBB is "ranking," the process whereby higher-level managers establish priorities for all decision packages from all subordinate decision units. The priority-ordered set of all decision packages for the entire organization is then reviewed in light of the probable level of funding available to the organization. Packages which can be funded within the available total are included in the organization's formal budget request; those which fall "below the line" are dropped from the budget request—unless the organization chooses to seek an increase in the total funding level.

Decision Units, Decision Packages, and the Ranking Process

Identifying and Defining Decision Units

Decision units are the basic entities for which budgets are prepared. Decision units must be identified and defined as a necessary first step in implementing ZBB. This step is part of the initial design of the ZBB approach and need not be repeated in subsequent budget cycles, except to accommodate new activities or to improve the decisional usefulness of the budget structure. Decision units may be programs, functions, cost centers, organizational units or, in certain cases, line items or appropriation items.

A key consideration in selecting decision units is the organization's "responsibility structure." Decision units should generally be selected to parallel the flow of responsibility for budgetary decision making within the organization. To illustrate this point, consider an organization which operates a number of neighborhood health centers, each of which offers a variety of health services such as tuberculosis control, venereal disease control, lead poisoning control, maternal and child health clinics, and so forth. The decision units may variously be (1) each center, encompassing all health services provided within the center; (2) each separate health service provided in each center; or (3) each health service aggregated across all centers.

If each center has a manager responsible for resource allocation within the center, then the individual centers may be logically selected as decision units. If each health service within a center has an identifiable manager responsible for resource allocation within that service, each service within a center could be viewed as a separate decision unit. On the other hand, if resource allocation decisions within health services are made system-wide by identifiable managers at the organization's headquarters, then the individual health services, aggregated across all centers, would be logical decision units, The criterion is how responsibility for resource allocation decisions is distributed.

There is a fourth option: the entire organization may be considered a single decision unit. This option would make sense if all resource allocation decisions are made by the organization's chief executive, or if other considerations become important—such as the relative size of the organization with respect to the government of which it forms a part. For example, if an entire city is engaged in ZBB, then, from the standpoint of the mayor, the entire neighborhood health center program might be logically one single decision unit. Relative size, therefore, is a second important consideration in identifying decision units.

Availability of data often constrains the choice of decision units. The organization's accounting system may not provide reliable cost data for the "ideal" decision unit structure. Compromises may have to be made, or the accounting system may be modified so that something approaching the ideal structure may become feasible at a later time.

Analytic Emphasis

Some organizations emphasize a fundamental reexamination of each decision unit before its manager is permitted to proceed with the formulation of decision packages. In other instances, only perfunctory attention is paid to the questioning of objectives, activities, and operating methods, and decision packages simply reflect the status quo. The relative emphasis on each type of analysis is a matter to be decided by the architects and users of the ZBB system. Both types of analysis are useful, but considerations of time, practicality, and available analytic skills sometimes dictate that the former be sacrificed and attention concentrated on the latter.

Formulation of Decision Packages

The decision unit manager formulates, in priority order, a series of decision packages which together equal the sum total of his budget request for the decision unit. Each decision package consists of a discrete set of services, activities, or expenditure items. The first, or highest priority package addresses the most important activities performed by the decision unit, i.e., those which produce the highest priority services or which meet the most critical needs of the decision unit's target population. The cost of this first package is usually well below the current level of funding for the decision unit. The first, highest priority package is often thought of as the *minimum level* or *survival level* for the decision unit, the level of service and funding below which the decision unit might as well be eliminated.

In some cases decision unit managers are allowed complete freedom in determining the appropriate magnitude of the first package, subject only to the constraint that it cost less than the current funding level. In other cases, guidelines are provided in the form of a percentage of the current level, for example: "the first package should be less than 75 percent of current"; or "the first package should be between 40 and 60 percent of current." In most cases no firm rule is established for the total number of packages for each decision unit. In practice, the number can usually be expected to vary between a minimum of three and a maximum of around 10. Typically, packages are smaller and more discrete as their cumulative total cost approaches and exceeds the decision unit's current funding level. This offers decision makers a more practical range of flexibility in the subsequent ranking process.

The decision unit manager's analysis of decision packages is communicated on a series of forms, using a separate form for each decision package. Each form documents: (1) precisely what services are to be provided or activities performed, if this package is funded; (2) the resource requirements of the package and their cost; and (3) a quantitative expression of workload, output, or results anticipated if the package is funded. Usually, each form displays, in addition to the cost of the package, the cumulative cost of this plus all preceding (higher priority) packages in the series for the decision unit. Often the cumulative cost is also expressed as a percentage of the prior year's total for the decision unit. Similarly, the quantitative program measures are also usually cumulated and expressed as a percentage of the prior year's figure. In some cases, the decision unit manager is asked to identify additional information on each decision package form, such as "benefits of funding this package"; "consequences of not funding this package"; "present services which would not be provided if only this package and those which precede it are funded"; "support required from other decision units if this package is funded"; and the like.

The amount of cost and object class detail required on the decision package form can vary considerably depending on the requirements of the ZBB system's users. One approach is simply to record the package's total dollar cost and the number of positions involved. Or the dollar cost may be broken down into considerable object detail. A breakdown by source of funds can also be shown, if appropriate. In many cases it is helpful for the next level of management to conduct a preliminary review of proposed decision packages before the decision unit managers prepare the detailed forms. This review can help ensure that each decision unit manager and his superior agree on the priorities governing the formulation of decision packages before detailed cost estimates are prepared and forms filled out.

Ranking

Ranking is the process in which a manager reviews all decision packages (from all decision units reporting to him) and establishes their relative priority. A "ranking table" is prepared, listing all decision packages in descending order of priority. A running cumulative total is kept to indicate the total budget request for the sum of each package plus all preceding (higher priority) packages. Ranking may be performed in a variety of ways, for example, unilaterally by a single manager, or in a committee fashion where the manager meets with his decision unit managers. Depending on the size and complexity of the organization, a series of rankings by successively higher levels of management may be required to produce a single, consolidated ranking table for the entire organization. To avoid overwhelming higher levels of management with excessive detail, the ranked decision packages are often consolidated into a smaller number of "superpackages" for review and ranking by the next managerial level.

In the ranking process, attention is usually concentrated on those packages which lie within a reasonable range around the probable cutoff line, i.e., the expected funding level for the collection of decision units whose packages are being ranked. For example, if 40 packages are being ranked, it is usually not necessary to determine precisely the relative priorities among numbers one, two, and three, nor numbers 38, 39, and 40. It is more important to ensure that those packages which fall just above and just below the probable cutoff line are indeed in the order which properly reflects management's priorities.

Designing and Implementing ZBB

Before embarking on ZBB, an organization must carefully weigh several factors:

- What are the strengths and weaknesses of the existing budget process?
- What are the organization's objectives and expectations for ZBB?
- Who is the principal intended "consumer" of the information generated by the ZBB process?
- What implementation strategies shall be followed?
- What degree of linkage to existing management systems is appropriate?
- What particular ZBB "technology" shall be employed?

Any decision to launch ZBB should normally be preceded by a systematic appraisal of the strengths and weaknesses of the existing budget process. This review may be thought of as a "budget audit" during which managers assess the degree to which the current budget process serves or fails to serve the organization's planning, management, and control needs. Design of the approach to ZBB can then attempt to build on existing strengths and correct deficiencies in the current process.

The organization should next explicitly address the question of what it hopes to achieve by implementing ZBB. Different organizations may have quite different objectives and expectations for ZBB. Some of the more common are:

- Cut budgets rationally.
- Reallocate resources from lower to higher priority areas.
- Yield better information or more credible justifications to support budget requests.
- Forge a better link between budgeting and operational planning and control.
- Provide top management with better insights into the detailed workings of the organization.

- Create more substantive involvement by line managers in budget formulation.
- Achieve various "organizational development" objectives (such as improved communication between managerial levels, greater sense of participation, more identification with the organization's mission).
- Enable top management to evaluate the managerial capabilities of subordinate managers.

The design of the ZBB process may vary depending on who is to be the principal consumer of the information produced. The consumer may be the legislative body, the chief executive, the department head, or line managers—or all of the above.

Implementation strategies must be carefully considered. For example, should ZBB be applied to the entire budget or should certain activities or expenditure items be excluded? Should full-scale implementation be attempted immediately, or should a pilot test be first conducted? Should ZBB replace or supplement the existing formal budget process?

The organization must also determine the appropriate form and degree of linkage to management systems already in place. What should be the relationship of ZBB to current planning, control, and information systems? Can ZBB be appropriately meshed with an existing MBO system?

Finally, the organization must design the technical and procedural aspects of the ZBB process. Particular attention must be paid to the following:

- The logic by which decision units are identified and defined.
- The type of analysis to be emphasized.
- The particular forms, procedures, timetable, guidelines, and instructions to be used in implementing the process.
- The type and amount of training and technical assistance to be provided.

ZBB can take many forms and be used for many purposes. Existing public sector applications illustrate this variety. For example, the U.S. Navy, in response to a congressional mandate, is using a partial version of ZBB to provide more detailed justification of its FY 1978 Operations and Maintenance appropriation request. The Environmental Protection Agency has used ZBB principles to develop a FY 1977 operational plan for one of its programs. HEW's Data Management Center uses ZBB as part of a total management system, for manpower planning and project planning and control, as well as budget formulation.

ZBB need not rely on a "bottom-up" approach. In some cases a bottom-up approach may be entirely inappropriate. A structured "top-down" approach to ZBB is illustrated in the following example drawn from a large municipal hospital.

A framework of very specific and detailed planning guidelines, developed by the hospital administrator in conjunction with teams of doctors and other professional staff, was provided to all departments in the hospital. The guidelines consisted of, first, a series of "capacity" figures (e.g., varying numbers of in-patient beds), and second, a number of "service levels." Each service level was defined in terms of the medical and surgical specialties to be offered by the hospital at that level, and also in terms of the standards set for a number of "quality" proxies (e.g., nursing hours per patient-day). Each department head then developed estimates of resource requirements for every combination of capacity and service level. The departmental estimates were reviewed and then aggregated, producing a capacity/service level cost matrix for the hospital. This permitted the administrator to develop a budget which, in his judgement, reflected the appropriate balance between size, range of medical services offered, and standards of service. An alternative to the approach described above would have been the more traditional bottom-up ZBB process. Individual units, such as pathology and food service, would have independently formulated decision packages for subsequent ranking by division chiefs and then by the administrator. But this approach would have ignored critical interdependencies between units in providing service.

By linking dollar figures explicitly to service variables, at various possible funding levels, the administrator's budget presentation clearly demonstrated the service impact of increases or decreases in his recommended budget. This was useful in the case of this particular hospital, since it had undergone successive budget reductions but was still expected by the city government to continue providing the same level of patient care (what the "same level" meant was never precisely defined by the city fathers). The budget presentation made clear the consequences of further reductions—either wards would be closed, or the level of service would deteriorate, or both. Budget reductions could no longer be divorced from their service impacts.

In concluding this section on considerations affecting the design and implementation of ZBB, a number of issues will be listed. It is not possible, in the scope of this article, to give them the detailed discussion they deserve.

The users of ZBB must decide how to modify the process in the second and subsequent cycles following the initial year of implementation. Priorities may be reviewed to ensure that they are still relevant, decision units may be added or deleted as appropriate, new decision packages may be formulated to meet newly identified needs, and cost and output data may be refined and updated. But it is usually not necessary to repeat the considerable development effort normally required in the first year. Illustratively, the focus can shift to areas of the budget not included in the first year, or the process can be driven deeper in the organization, or the reliability of data can be improved, or the process can be more selective in concentrating analytic efforts on particular issues.

Other design and implementation issues might include the appropriate role of the computer, for example in reducing paperwork, aggregating data in various ways, helping decision makers ask "what if" questions, or aiding the formulation of decision packages by providing analytical modeling capabilities to predict cost/output relationships. The treatment of administrative support units deserves special attention; it is necessary to ensure that packages formulated for support units are consistent with packages formulated for the primary "mission" units. Another important design issue is the degree to which top management wishes to drive budgetary accountability deeper into the organization. Although the existing responsibility structure may be the starting point for identifying decision units, management may elect to delegate budgetary responsibility to lower levels—not merely for the purposes of ZBB, but as a means to increase management commitment throughout the organization.

Private Versus Public Sector Use of ZBB

The annual operating budget plays a less central role in the private sector than it does in government. Corporations employ a variety of management systems in addition to budgeting, to help set goals, acquire and allocate resources, and measure performance. Strategic decisions, such as decisions to enter new markets or launch new products, are usually completely divorced from the annual routines of budgeting. Formal business plans are prepared to set short-term goals for sales and profits and to monitor progress. The marketplace sends a variety of signals to the decision maker on the need to change direction or to shift resources from one venture to another.

In government, on the other hand, the budget process must generally serve many purposes. Certainly, many strategic policy decisions are initially made outside the budget, for example, through legislation or regulation. But the budget is the only conduit for funds to implement legislation or to enforce a regulation. It is only through the budget process, by appropriation or ordinance, that a president, governor, or mayor may legally draw from the public purse.

The budget process, in addition to its legal function in conferring authority to expend public funds, also serves, explicitly or implicitly, as the mechanism for establishing public priorities. Through the budget process, competing claims are resolved and expenditures brought into balance with revenues. Choices are made about which programs will expand and by how much and, less often, which programs will be cut back.

The public budget process also serves in lieu of a management control system. Unlike a private corporation which can point to growth, market share, and earnings, and despite a mounting clamor for "accountability," governments are rarely able to demonstrate the link between funding and results. For a government, simply living within its means is an achievement. The budget therefore carries with it strong sanctions to discourage deviations from its totals and subtotals; underspending and overspending are equally discouraged. Control is therefore exercised via inputs rather than outputs.

The different role and scope of budgeting in the two sectors partially explains a striking contrast in the application of ZBB in the private and public sectors.

Virtually all private corporations using ZBB have confined it to overhead expenses, whereas most government bodies employing ZBB have applied it to program expenditures as well as to support costs.

Another part of the explanation lies in the different determinants of manufacturing and overhead costs. In manufacturing, unit costs are largely determined by technology, the price of raw materials, and union contracts. Strong competitive pressures, reinforced by financial incentives, encourage managers to pursue a continual search for improved manufacturing methods, cheaper raw materials, and more productive ways to use labor inputs. Given unit costs, total production costs are then a function of sales volume.

Overhead costs are quite another matter. With respect to these costs, it is much harder to answer the central budgetary question: How much is enough? Management generally has much more discretion in funding overhead activities, and there is rarely any direct benefit-cost relationship to serve as a guide to appropriate expenditure levels. However, control of overhead costs is critically important. Excessive overhead undermines profit margins; savings are reflected directly in the "bottom line." Any budget process, such as ZBB, which offers a more systematic approach to control of overhead, is therefore likely to be warmly endorsed by private sector managers.

Corporate managers have found that ZBB has advantages other than overhead cost control, according to a survey of 54 private corporations which had recently implemented the process for the first time. All respondents were on *Fortune's* 1,000 list.[1] Respondents were asked by how much their operating budgets had changed from the prior year. Twelve percent reported a budget decrease of more than 10 percent; 30 percent reported a budget decrease of between 5 and 10 percent; 51 percent said that their budgets had changed (increased or decreased) less than 5 percent; and 7 percent of the respondents reported a budget increase of more than 5 percent.

Respondents were also asked to rate ZBB as (a) a tool to change total expenditure levels, and (b) a tool to reallocate resources from lower to higher priority areas. Results were as follows:

Respondents' Rating (percent)

	Excellent	Good	Fair	Poor	Not Ap.
Tool to change total budget level	28	46	20	0	6
Tool to reallocate resources	34	42	20	2	2

Respondents were asked for their overall evaluation of ZBB as a management planning and control system. Twenty-eight percent gave an "excellent" rating, 59 percent rated ZBB as "good," 13 percent gave only a "fair" rating, and none rated ZBB as "poor." In response to a question asking them to compare ZBB with other formal management systems, 67 percent of the respondents described ZBB as "better," and 33 percent said it was "about the same"; none described ZBB as "worse."

The following table shows how the respondents rated ZBB as a process to achieve a number of managerial purposes other than changing budget levels or reallocating resources.

Respondent's Evaluation of ZBB (percent)

	Excellent	Good	Fair	Poor	Not Ap.
Learn more about the organization	55	42	3	—	—
Manage overhead activities with more flexibility	20	54	23	3	—
Improve efficiency/effectiveness	18	58	18	3	3
Improve communications	16	47	29	3	5
Develop alternative methods of operation	15	46	36	3	—
Plan organizational changes	13	39	24	16	8
Evaluate staff performance	13	35	35	11	5

The Future of ZBB in the Federal Government

In this concluding section, some options for the application of ZBB to the federal government are discussed, employing the design and implementation framework described in a previous section. At best, this section can only present a partial and preliminary list of some issues and options. It was written before the inauguration, without the benefit of any inside knowledge of the plans of the new administration. The discussion may therefore be overtaken by events.

Strengths and Weaknesses of the Existing Federal Budget Process

The federal budget process works. It comprehensively reconciles the competing claims of a myriad of programs into a unified whole. Each party understands the rules of the game, and open conflict is kept to a minimum. The budget, quite properly, is a central and well-understood fact of life in both executive and legislative branches of government.

Some weaknesses are apparent. Budget justifications focus almost exclusively on increments—the additional positions and dollars requested above the ''adjusted base.'' Neither the president nor Congress are routinely provided the opportunity of examining whether objectives should be changed, or whether the same objectives could be attained more economically, or what would be the consequences of funding a given program at varying levels. Interagency trade-off opportunities, within the same general program area, are difficult to examine without special analyses. The link between costs and services provided is hard to discern. Often, cuts are imposed without any explicit recognition of which services will be reduced by what amounts. Agencies are frequently expected to absorb cuts and still somehow maintain the current level of operations.

Objectives for ZBB in the Federal Government

Objectives for ZBB should be formulated realistically, with due regard for the limitations of the process. Macro policy changes or changes in legislation might better emerge from the type of process envisioned in the so-called sunset bills discussed during the last session of Congress. Or within the executive branch, the kind of long-term policy, program, and organizational review that produced Elliot Richardson's ''mega-proposal'' for the restructuring of HEW might be more applicable to the design of fundamental changes in how public needs are to be addressed.

A tentative set of primary objectives for ZBB in the executive branch of the federal government might be as follows:

- Provide the president a range of choices within a given program area so that he can ensure that the total resources committed correspond to his policy preferences for that program area.
- Yield more credible budget justifications, at all levels within the executive branch, in support of total budget requests, and not merely with respect to proposed changes from the prior year. The information should be structured so as to illuminate the consequences of various levels of funding, both above and below current levels.
- Encourage agency operating managers to surface recommendations for improved methods of operation as part of the formal budget process.

Consumers

There are many potential consumers of the results of ZBB in the federal government; the Congress (its substantive, budget, and appropriations committees, as well as the Congressional Budget Office and the GAO), the president and his Office of Management and Budget, agency heads and their policy, planning, and budget staffs, and the several levels of operating ''line'' managers within each agency.

Implementation Strategies

The central question is to identify the most productive targets of opportunity for ZBB and then determine how best to implement the process in the selected areas.

Although the president's budget embraces virtually all federal expenditures, ZBB may not be equally appropriate for all types of expenditure. The interest on the national debt is hardly susceptible to annual zero-base review. A variety of income and other transfers such as social security payments, veterans' benefits, welfare payments, and general revenue sharing are controllable only in the long run and can be changed only if there is a significant shift in the political consensus. Other major expenditures have powerful constituencies; it would take more than a new budget process to significantly affect expenditures from the Highway Trust Fund or the various agricultural price support programs. Stability and credibility in national security and foreign affairs require a degree of continuity in the scale and distribution of resource commitment. Significant or abrupt changes in long-range procurement or construction programs, both civilian and military, could cause severe economic dislocations even if decision makers are persuaded to ignore such costs.

In the long run nothing is fixed. In the short run, much is, at least within the realm of practical politics. This is not to say that programs such as those cited in the previous paragraph should not be thoroughly reappraised from time to time. But the annual budget process may not be the proper forum for the debate. There are, however, several classes of federal expenditures ideally suited to the type of ZBB described in this article:

- The overhead agencies of government, i.e., those agencies providing services not to the public but to government itself (e.g., GSA, the Civil Service Commission, parts of Treasury and Justice, etc.).
- The overhead (administrative and support) activities of agencies, in Washington and in countless field offices. This is a very diverse category including a multitude of functions such as legal, ADP, personnel, training, accounting, research, planning, procurement, printing, communications, transportation, etc.
- Virtually all formula and project grant programs.
- Many operating programs of government, where the government itself acts directly as the provider of service, without any intermediaries. This group would include organizations such as the National Park Service, the Forest Service, the VA Hospitals, the Customs Bureau, the FAA, the FDA, and so forth.

A fundamental implementation issue to be resolved is the relationship of ZBB to the overall federal budget process. ZBB could be implemented as a supplement to the existing budget process, as a substitute for the existing budget process, or elements of ZBB could be incorporated into the existing budget process.

The first option would leave undisturbed the normal routines of budgeting, and therein lies both its advantages and disadvantages. Treating ZBB as supplementary to the existing budget process would cause the least disruption for both OMB and the agencies. True, it would generate an additional workload, but this could be accommodated. OMB and the agencies would in all likelihood set up special staffs to handle ZBB, effectively insulating it from the "real" budget process. This, of course, is precisely what happened to PPB.

The second option is only superficially a real option. The concept of "replacing" the existing budget process with ZBB is wrongheaded. In the first place, the budget process serves many purposes other than those for which ZBB is suited. Besides, a budget process is not an integrated circuit module which can be unplugged or reconnected at will.

The third option is real—the only one which makes sense. The basic principles of ZBB could be made an integral part of the agency budget formulation process and could form the basis for both the spring Preview and Director's Review. The formats of detailed supporting budget schedules need not necessarily be altered, but the schedules would probably be completed only after basic program allocations are made by OMB.

It is probable that at least three overlapping ZBB cycles would operate, each with a different focus. The first cycle would operate at the most detailed level within the agency. At this stage, operating managers would formulate zero-based budget requests which, through a successive ranking process, would flow upwards to the various line assistant secretaries. During the second cycle, the agency head would formulate the agency-wide budget and review it with OMB. The third cycle would involve OMB's own zero-base analysis and preparation of priority-ranked budget proposals for consideration by the president. In practice, the process would not be as simple and sequential as suggested above. Several iterations might be required, each cycle would operate within a framework of planning and policy guidelines, much as in the present process.

Remembering the bitter lessons of PPB, it is to be hoped that OMB will not simply issue a general "ZBB Circular," leaving it up to each agency to interpret the instructions as best they can. At the other extreme, OMB should not attempt to design and prescribe for all agencies a single, uniform set of forms and procedures. A more workable, middle-ground scenario might be as follows:

- OMB determines the most useful format for its analysis and presentation to the president of budget options, probably built around interagency program groupings.
- OMB negotiates, individually with each agency, the format for presentation of the agency's budget so that it is compatible with both agency top management needs and the requirements of presidential decision making.
- Each agency head is held responsible for development of an internal ZBB structure and process which most appropriately meets the agency's own management needs,

subject to the condition that it is compatible with the joint agreement on format for presentation of the total agency budget to OMB. The internal agency structure and process may well vary between bureaus to take account of differing kinds of programs and the varying decisional needs of lower-level management.

A major implementation issue concerns the form in which the budget will be presented to Congress. ZBB could be viewed solely as an aid to preparation of the president's budget, with the zero-base backup excluded from the justification material submitted to Congress. This would certainly conform to the stance adopted by previous presidents in dealing with Congress. It also agrees with the commonly accepted, some would say constitutionally mandated, view that the president must present and defend a single budget total for each appropriation requested from Congress. It is difficult to imagine any president, even one who believes strongly in the value of ZBB, presenting to Congress a rank-ordered list of decision packages and saying, "this is my recommended budget figure, but if you want to increase or decrease it, here's my priority list of possible increases or decreases." On the other hand, it is difficult to imagine a Congress refraining from demanding such material when it is known to exist, or from asking witnesses to explain those items which fell just above or below the president's cutoff line.

Linkage to Existing Management Systems

The budget, whether zero-based or not, will have to be capable of reconciliation with the Treasury's accounts. Various OMB reporting requirements, if maintained, will also have to be accommodated. However, unlike state and local governments, most of the federal government's management systems are not government-wide but are developed by each agency for its internal use. Since the most probable approach to ZBB in the federal government would be on a selective, agency basis, the question of linkage to existing management systems arises primarily at the agency level. To the extent possible, the design of the ZBB approach in each agency should take account of and build upon management systems already in place, such as planning systems, manpower management systems, specialized information systems unique to each program, performance measurement systems, and cost-accounting and other financial management systems.

ZBB Technology

As this article has attempted to emphasize, ZBB may be variously implemented for different reasons, in different ways, and to serve the needs of different users. The federal government is so diverse that no one ZBB "technology" can suffice. What constitutes a decision unit in one part of one agency will not apply in other parts of the same agency nor at different levels in the same agency, still less in other agencies. The decision variables governing the formulation of decision packages will vary within and among programs and agencies.

It would be possible, however, to develop models, standards, or guidelines to deal with similar classes of programs or activities commonly found throughout the federal government. Several agencies operate hospitals, for example; similar approaches to ZBB would probably be applicable regardless of the agency. Again, at a more detailed level, similar approaches could be used in different agencies to deal with functions such as maintenance, ADP operations, and the like. Within OMB, it would be desirable to develop a consistent framework to analyze programs from different agencies within the same general program area.

Conclusion

ZBB has proven, in diverse settings, that it can make a useful contribution to the art and practice of management. Whether it can be equally helpful if applied extensively in the federal government is an open question. Its success will depend on how it is conceived and presented, and on the political will to make it work. If, as seems probable, ZBB is launched on a broad scale, it is to be hoped that it will be viewed as an *approach* to resource allocation rather than a uniform set of procedures to be applied by rote regardless of the nature of the program, organizational level, or management's needs.

The ZBB approach will most likely be applied selectively, its purposes and technology geared to management's unique decisional needs, and building to the extent possible on systems already in place. The federal ZBB structure will probably not be a monolith, a gigantic pyramid with the president at the apex and agency branches, sections, and field offices at the base. Rather, the structure for ZBB will most likely be integrated and unified, if at all, only at the level of OMB for presidential decision-making purposes, and rather loosely coupled to the structures designed by individual agencies for their internal needs.

Tantalizing questions remain. How will responsibility for design and implementation of ZBB be distributed between OMB and the agencies? Who will conduct the necessary development and training? For what purposes will it be used? What parts of the federal budget will be included? Will it be applied to "tax expenditures"? To the entire revenue side of the budget? How will its results be communicated to Congress? What will be the administration's timing? How much will be attempted for the FY 1979 cycle?

Finally, what will be the lasting impact of ZBB? PPB is no longer a formal, government-wide system, but its effects are very much with us. The legacy of

PPB has been a demonstrable improvement in the amount and quality of policy, program and budgetary analysis, in the federal government and in state and local governments throughout the nation. Regardless of the ultimate fate of ZBB, the chances are that, after the next few years, budgeting will never be quite the same.

Note

1. The survey was conducted in 1976 by Paul J. Stonich of MAC, Inc. The results presented here are taken from his forthcoming book, *Zero-Base Planning and Budgeting: The State of the Art*.

2.

Zero-Base Budgeting at HUD

Ralph C. Bledsoe

During the presidential campaign of 1976, Jimmy Carter pledged to bring about many reforms in the operation and management of the executive branch of the federal government. Key among the changes proposed was the promise to implement a concept known as zero base budgeting, commonly called ZBB, for the examination and funding of federal programs. In fact, the promise to use ZBB was incorporated in the Carter-backed Democratic party platform, and was subsequently mentioned several times in speeches throughout the course of his successful campaign.

Within the federal government, the interest in ZBB increased as Carter was elected in November, and began development of his strategy for assuming office. During the transition, numerous agency budget officials initiated efforts to assess how ZBB might affect their organizations, and a few even undertook studies leading to development of ZBB approaches. Some departments, notably the Department of Agriculture in 1964, had previously attempted ZBB with little success. The Consumer Products Safety Commission already had one year of ZBB under its belt.

Training consultants and institutions in and around Washington began to advertise and conduct seminars on ZBB, charging large fees, and causing the Office of Management and Budget (OMB), the president's staff for financial and management advice and assistance, to caution agencies not to go too far with large investments in this area, until OMB was clearer about the directions that might be taken. Some career federal budget and management staff people hoped the president might lose interest in trying to implement ZBB in the federal government when he realized that the federal bureaucracy is so much more complex than Georgia state government, where he had found it useful. Their hopes were not to be fulfilled.

Ultimately, every political appointee and career federal government employee would learn that President Carter was serious about ZBB, and that he would be the prime "sponsor" of ZBB, federal-style. He was comfortable with it as governor of the state of Georgia, and he sincerely felt it would help him and others in his cabinet as they put together the federal budget each year. He particularly felt it aided him in learning about and understanding the many governmental programs for which he was responsible in Georgia, and that it would again be valuable for that purpose in the federal government.[1]

ZBB in the Federal Government

As many federal agencies increased their interest in and movement toward the ZBB concept during the early days of the Carter presidency, pressure began to mount on OMB for guidelines from the new administration. On February 3, 1977, at a meeting of cabinet-level officials, Bert Lance, then-OMB director, stated that ZBB would be implemented within the executive branch for preparation of the Fiscal Year 1979 (October 1, 1978 through September 30, 1979) budget. On February 14, 1977, the president issued a memorandum to all heads of executive departments and agencies (Figure 2.1) asking their use of ZBB and indicating that instructions would be forthcoming from OMB.

With these promises on the record, OMB staff members hurried to produce the detailed guidelines for the departments and agencies. Finally, on April 19, 1977, OMB Circular 77-9 was published, outlining the general instructions for utilizing a zero base budgeting technique in preparing the Fiscal Year 1979 president's budget. The annually produced OMB Circular A-11, *Preparation and Submission of Budget Estimates*, published in June each year, also incorporated ZBB terminology in its detailed instructions to the agencies on how to prepare materials for the president's budget. Budget examiners in OMB had been schooled on the ZBB process and interacted with agency management and budget personnel concerning how to incorporate the ZBB ideas outlined in the two OMB publications into their 1979 departmental and agency budget requests. While the general guidance and direction was provided centrally by OMB, federal departments and agencies were permitted to establish and proceed with specific procedures for costing and prioritizing programs and program levels as they saw fit.

HUD Preparation

During the November, 1976 to January, 1977, transition of the presidency from Gerald Ford to Jimmy Carter, the Department of Housing and Urban Development (HUD) was in step with the above developments. Career federal employees of the department had renewed and sorted out some of the problems experienced in HUD management under the prior administration, as well as the difficulties they anticipated in the implementation of a different budgeting

Figure 2.1
Memorandum from President Jimmy Carter to Heads of Executive Departments and Agencies, February 14, 1977

THE WHITE HOUSE
WASHINGTON

February 14, 1977

MEMORANDUM FOR THE HEADS OF

EXECUTIVE DEPARTMENTS AND AGENCIES

During the campaign, I pledged that immediately after the inauguration I would issue an order establishing zero-base budgeting throughout the Federal Government. This pledge was made because of the success of the zero-base budget system adopted by the State of Georgia under my direction as Governor.

A zero-base budgeting system permits a detailed analysis and justification of budget requests by an evaluation of the importance of each operation performed.

An effective zero-base budgeting system will benefit the Federal Government in several ways. It will

- Focus the budget process on a comprehensive analysis of objectives and needs.
- Combine planning and budgeting into a single process.
- Cause managers to evaluate in detail the cost-effectiveness of their operations.
- Expand management participation in planning and budgeting at all levels of the Federal Government.

The Director of the Office of Management and Budget will review the Federal budget process for preparation, analysis, and justification of budget estimates and will revise those procedures to incorporate the appropriate techniques of the zero-base budgeting system. He will develop a plan for applying the zero-base budgeting concept to preparation, analysis, and justification of the budget estimates of each department and agency of the Executive Branch.

I ask each of you to develop a zero-base system in your agency in accordance with instructions to be issued by the Office of Management and Budget. The Fiscal Year 1979 budget will be prepared using this system.

By working together under a zero-base budgeting system, we can reduce costs and make the Federal Government more efficient and effective.

Jimmy Carter

approach. They were to have a new secretary, Patricia Roberts Harris, who would surely possess a management philosophy and style different than that of her predecessor, Carla Hills. Jay Janis, the newly appointed undersecretary, also would bring different views as to how the administration should undertake the management of HUD programs.

Transition Activities

The HUD internal transition team was headed by a long-time HUD employee, Deputy Assistant Secretary for Administration Vincent J. Hearing. The Carter transition team was headed by Chuck Edson, a lawyer and editor of a housing publication, who was brought in to facilitate the changeover in an efficient manner.

During the transition, Hearing and Edson went over in great detail the operations of HUD, and many of the suggestions made by the career employees in the department, as well as some made by out-going appointees. Instrumental in these discussions was a 5-volume, several thousand page "briefing handbook" entitled *Review of Programs and Functions*, accompanied by a "pocket-size single summary synopsis" prepared for quick reference. The handbook was prepared by HUD career employees and appointees of the outgoing administration, specifically for the transition of authority.

Among the many aspects of HUD management that were covered in the briefing handbook, and discussed between Hearing and Edson during the transition (and later between other HUD careerists and incoming appointees), were two management tools—the HUD Regional Operating Planning System, and the budgeting process. The Regional Operating Plans contained descriptions of HUD goals and program activity in the field, and included assignments of staff resources and responsibilities, and procedures to be adhered to by HUD operating field units. The Operating Plans, which were a prelude to the preparation of the budget, had been put together for Secretary Hills by program assistant secretaries, and were reviewed by a group of headquarters and regional field appointees organized as a Program and Budget Working Group (PBWG), and chaired by a deputy undersecretary for management. The PBWG was a recommending body to the undersecretary, who in turn made recommendations to the secretary. Program assistant secretaries were provided with PBWG recommendations regarding the Operating Plans, and had the "right of response and appeal." As the budgetary process would begin, Operating Plans were sometimes modified, and in many instances drastically changed, as a result of program recommendations by this group. This was a rather cumbersome process in the eyes of some budget and staff personnel responsible for maintenance of the Operating Plans and preparation of the budget.

HUD Budget Experience

For the HUD budget staff, ZBB was not really a new idea. Al Kliman, HUD budget director, and Herb Persil, deputy budget director, had both been in the Department of Agriculture during the early 1960s when that agency had been directed by then-Secretary of Agriculture Orville Freeman to prepare a zero base budget for Fiscal Year 1964. Thus, Kliman and Persil had more than a passing knowledge of the concept. Bill Van Lowe, one of Kliman's branch heads had also been in agriculture during this period. As recently as 1975, James Lynn, then-secretary of HUD and later to become director of OMB under President Ford, had expressed interest in using zero base budgeting within HUD. This prompted the HUD budget staff to develop a paper outlining the pros and cons of ZBB. In the staff paper, it was pointed out that HUD currently was using a "zero base" approach in reviewing staffing and administrative expenses and program funds, but it was concluded that an all-out use of ZBB would require significant modification of HUD management practices, and major increases in budgeting and analytical staff. The staff paper included a recommendation that HUD might incrementally move into ZBB, but not enough interest was shown by Lynn to proceed with it any further before his departure for OMB.

When Jimmy Carter was elected president, the HUD budget staff dusted off the 1975 study, and began to prepare for the onset of ZBB, government-wide. Budget staff members, primarily Mel Roth and Bruce Conger, were asked by Kliman and Persil to create a ZBB file, and to keep their ears to the ground for detecting ZBB developments at OMB, the White House, Congress and within other federal departments and agencies, though they had an unwritten policy not to attend any of the many special seminars being offered by ZBB consultants. Their diligence in this effort paid off when Carter and Budget Director Lance initiated their ZBB approach on a federal government-wide scale.

HUD's Top Management Team

In his February 14 memorandum, President Carter instructed cabinet department and agency heads "to develop a zero base system within your agency in accordance with instructions to be issued by the Office of Management and Budget." In response to this directive, on February 23, Vince Hearing, then-acting assistant secretary for administration, recommended to Secretary Harris an improved process for "establishing goals, formulating the budget, and allocating and controlling resources." Key among his recommendations was:

> . . . that a new management entity be established to carry out the two functions (preparing the department's budget and identifying legislative proposals). This entity should be formally named and given a discrete charter. Its name should connote its function—such names as Board of Directors, Management Board, Council of Program Advisors, Management and Budget Review Committee, come to mind. I believe the entity should be constituted as follows:

> Undersecretary, Chairman
> General Counsel, Member
> Assistant Secretaries for Housing, Community Planning and Develop-
> ment, Fair Housing and Equal Opportunity, Policy
> Development and Research, Administration, and
> Legislative Affairs, Members
> President, Government National Mortgage Association (GNMA),
> Member
> Deputy Assistant Secretary for Administration, Director of Secretariat
>
> The Council or Board should be chartered to serve as ''decision recommenders''
> to you, specifically tasked and directed to carry out their work in a collegial way
> which intentionally forces the amalgamation of their delegated programmatic
> responsibilities into an integrated Departmental framework. They should deal in
> the areas of objectives and goals established, budget formulation and review,
> program and activity priority determination, operating plan resource allocations,
> and also, if you wish, as integrated policy developers and implementors.

It was Hearing's hope that this group would become HUD's ''top management team.''

Responding favorably to Hearing's recommendation, on March 8, a Management and Budget Review Committee (MBRC) was officially approved and established by Secretary Harris. On March 29, she issued the establishing memorandum describing in greater detail the ''management, budget, and legislative program review process'' and the role of the MBRC. It was to be chaired by Undersecretary Janis and consist of the following members:

- Assistant Secretary for Administration;
- Assistant Secretary for Community Planning and Development (CPD);
- Assistant Secretary for Fair Housing and Equal Opportunity (FH&EO);
- Assistant Secretary for Housing, Federal Housing Commissioner;
- Assistant Secretary for Neighborhood and Non-Governmental Organizations, and Consumer Protection[2] (NVACP);
- Assistant Secretary for Policy Development and Research (PD&R);
- General Counsel;
- President, Government National Mortgage Association (GNMA); and
- Deputy Assistant Secretary for Administration, Executive Secretary.

Added later as members were the following:

- General manager, New Communities Development Corporation;
- Counselor to the Secretary; and
- Executive Assistant to the Secretary.

While appointments still had not been made to several of the above positions, the size and makeup of the group was consistent with the intent of the incoming HUD administration to increase the power of the program assistant secretaries, in Washington, and to expand their participation in the overall management of

HUD. Secretary Harris handled the question of non-membership of other HUD managers by stating the following:

> For those of you not designated as members of the MBRC, this in no way diminishes your assigned authorities and responsibilities. Obviously, for any group to function, its membership must be within manageable limits. Your views will be solicited, and receive equal treatment in all matters under the purview of the committee.

Also contained in the memorandum were a very brief description of the ZBB process to be used, and a schedule for development of the Fiscal Year 1979 Budget and Legislative Program, and the Fiscal Year 1978 Operating Plan.

Early HUD ZBB Efforts

During the first few weeks following President Carter's inauguration, ZBB still had a relatively low priority within HUD. There was much speculation over who would be named to the key assistant secretary positions, and what their expectations would be. The budget shop was busy preparing modifications desired by the president to the Fiscal Year 1978 budget that had been submitted in January by the outgoing Ford administration. Al Kliman had been meeting with Secretary-designate Harris prior to January 20, with complete approval and encouragement by Secretary Hills, to acquaint the incoming secretary with HUD programs and its budget. But, he was in somewhat of an awkward position, since he could not violate a trust relationship with the current administration by revealing the detailed contents of HUD's part of the still-confidential 1978 presidential budget. Thus, the briefings for Secretary Harris were restricted to presentation of facts. Meanwhile, members of the Carter transition team at OMB were already at work on anticipated budget modifications.

Following the inauguration, Kliman and Persil and the HUD budget office began to work with the new secretary in earnest on both modifications to the 1978 budget, and in preparing her for the imminent appropriations hearings. The secretary soon found Kliman to be an invaluable information source and relied on him a great deal during these processes.

When the Fiscal Year 1978 budget modifications were completed, and the incoming appointees were prepared for their appropriations hearings, the HUD budget office was able to return its attention to ZBB and the Fiscal Year 1979 budget.

Budget Office Activities

On March 31, 1977, the HUD budget staff met with its OMB budget examiners, William Hamm and Ken Ryder, to discuss the tentative OMB guidelines for implementing ZBB (which were later issued in final form on April 19 as OMB Bulletin 77-9). Some of the HUD management developments and ideas for implementation were also discussed. This meeting represented essential advance work that takes place each year by the budget staffs, and was necessary for a running start with the new ZBB system.

Shortly thereafter, in early April, HUD received from OMB a list of several issues which were to be addressed in the Fiscal Year 1979 HUD budget request. Armed with this advance information from OMB about its concerns and the 1979 budget requirements, the HUD budget staff formulated and proposed to the secretary a detailed schedule that would allow for submittal of HUD's 1979 Budget and Legislative Programs to OMB by September 15, 1977. Receiving approval to proceed, the HUD budget staff on April 13 began meeting with budget officers from each major program area, to go over the procedures for preparing the HUD 1979 budget. On April 21, Hearing and Kliman briefed the MBRC on the schedule and the general approach to be followed, including the MBRC's overall role in the process. Various reactions to the whole ZBB process were received.

In housing, whose programs represent 65 percent to 75 percent of the overall HUD budget, the reactions were mixed. The Housing Management Office, headed by Paul Williams, an experienced HUD career employee, had gotten a head start on preparation for ZBB. They had begun reading about and studying ZBB during the presidential transition, referencing what little material existed at the time. Housing's Office of Budget had received an advance draft of the OMB Bulletin, and circulated it to all housing offices for comments and advance planning. By early April, the Office of Budget issued a draft "call" to housing program budget officers for ZBB-format submittals.

They met with housing's office directors and managers, to alert them that this process would not be an exercise solely done by "budgeteers," but would heavily involve program managers in making decisions regarding the various levels of funding to be requested. They urged office directors and managers not to take ZBB lightly. The general attitude among housing's management and budget staff was positive, though they realized the significant amount of additional work involved. The housing budget staff received good support from Lawrence Simons, assistant secretary for housing and federal housing commissioner, and Morton Baruch, deputy assistant secretary for housing and deputy federal housing commissioner.

Some of the newer special assistants in Housing were not so enthused about the ZBB approach, however. One or two felt that ZBB was not applicable to the federal government. Some felt that due to the complexity and size of housing's programs, its budget ought to be treated differently, and perhaps even separately from the rest of the department. Regardless of their differences, housing managers, for the most part, made the effort to go along with the ideas behind ZBB.

In Community Planning and Development (CPD), HUD's second largest budget component, the attitude among the budget staff and program managers during the transition was one of wait-and-see what OMB's directions would be. After it became official that ZBB would be used for preparing the Fiscal Year 1979 budget, Dave Brown, CPD budget director, and his staff began interacting with the HUD budget office. Their first meetings were in late March, in preparation for the April 13 orientations by the budget office. There was a high level of interest in ZBB on the part of CPD program office directors, and they actively participated in these orientations. This was a positive factor in the eyes of Brown, in that it got program officers more involved in the budgetary process. However, when many of them discovered the extent of the paperwork and detail involved, they lost a bit of their interest. Many did not attend the later-scheduled formal ZBB training sessions given by the HUD training office.

The CPD budget office briefed their assistant secretary, Robert Embry, on the ZBB process and the role he would be playing as a member of the MBRC. And, since one of his MBRC responsibilities was the development of objectives and issues, the budget staff worked with him in developing the possible budget issues, while program officers developed and worked with him on CPD's objectives.

Internal Training

During the months of April and May, more formalized ZBB training sessions were conducted for HUD personnel who would be involved in the preparation of the 1979 budget. Operational workshops were conducted for budget personnel by Mel Roth and members of the departmental budget staff. Budget personnel from all HUD program organizations participated in the workshops. Each workshop lasted one to four hours, and included discussion of ZBB procedures, the forms to be used, and detailed technical aspects of the HUD approach to zero base budgeting. About 250 people were involved in these sessions. In addition, Roth and his associates answered numerous individual inquiries from budget staff members.

Another round of training sessions was conducted during this period for HUD office directors and managers. For these sessions, which were coordinated by Judy Broida of the HUD Training Office, Management Analysis Center, Inc., a management research and consulting firm founded in 1964 by a group of Harvard Business School faculty members, was hired. Graeme M. Taylor, senior vice-president of MAC, Inc., who had written an article "Introduction to Zero-Base Budgeting" in the Spring, 1977 issue of The Bureaucrat, conducted six one-day sessions with 20 to 30 people in each, on "ZBB as a

Management Tool.'' In these sessions, Taylor described ZBB experiences in other organizations as well as how it might be used in HUD. Individuals from the HUD budget office and the organization and management information office supported this training effort, and sat in to help explain to office directors and division directors how ZBB was to tie in with other departmental management activities, such as HUD's work measurement system, the operating planning system, and program evaluation efforts. A notebook containing numerous charts, tables and examples of ZBB applications and procedures was provided each participant.

Reactions to this training were mixed, ranging from enthusiastic to apathetic. Some program areas, e.g., administration and housing, which had already conducted training sessions of its own, sent large numbers of office and division managers to these sessions, while other program areas came nowhere near using their assigned slots. The Training Office telephoned all of the ''no shows'' to ascertain their reasons for not attending. Lack of interest was most often cited, and primarily by those organizations with smaller budgets, and by individuals who felt ZBB to be simply another whim of an incoming administration which would surely pass as interest lagged or the usual obstacles were encountered. In at least one instance, that of CPD, the formal training came during a busy period in which they were already preparing their objectives and ZBB decision packages. Also, some of CPD's program officers felt they had learned enough in the earlier training sessions held within CPD and did not need additional preparation.

The HUD Training Office received good support from William A. Medina, the newly appointed assistant secretary for administration. Medina sent the invitations to the workshops, and made certain that the entire HUD administrative organization was involved in the ZBB process, including the offices of budget, training, personnel, systems development, ADP and organization and management information.

Terence Monihan, director of the HUD Training Division, reported the following results from the evaluations by HUD office and division directors who attended the ZBB training sessions:

1. the timing of the courses, depending on the particular office, was too late for managerial input into the ZBB budget process for this budget cycle;
2. in spite of some intense preliminary work by the consultants with the Office of Budget and Organization and Management Information, the participants generally preferred HUD instructors who would have been more familiar with HUD policies and organizational considerations;
3. the instructional format concentrated on lectures and a slide presentation by the consultants. As individuals became weary of this approach, they drifted away. In every session, the peak attendance level was reached prior to noon;
4. the sessions were originally designed for 180 HUD office and division directors. However, as it became increasingly clear this level of participation could not be

maintained, the base from which attendees were drawn was broadened; and
5. overall the participants rated the sessions as good. Particular days were rated better than others.

In retrospect, the in-house training workshops offered by HUD budget personnel appeared to be much more beneficial and well-received than those presented by the outside contractor.

Following the training sessions, HUD budget and program staff people shifted into gear to meet the July deadlines for budget requests.

The "Call" for Budget Estimates and Legislative Recommendations

On May 3, 1977, the official *Call for FY 1979 Budget Estimates and Legislative Recommendations* memorandum was issued by the undersecretary. This document contained the formal instructions "for the preparation of the FY '79 budget estimates on a zero base." Economic assumptions and estimates to be used in preparing budget requests were to be developed by HUD's policy development and research unit. HUD assistant secretaries and other top appointees were designated as program managers responsible for the 14 HUD program areas.

Proposals for legislation were to accompany budget estimates and were to include mention of any pending bills in Congress that may have an impact on HUD programs, and the program manager's recommendation as to whether the department should support or oppose the bill. The following were the key sections of the "call" document.

The Zero Base Concept

It was stressed that zero base budgeting should involve management at all levels of the organization in the budget process, and that all programs and activities must be justified. Further, various program levels were to be ranked in order of priority, evaluated, and alternative means considered for accomplishing the managerial objectives established. Program managers were to "begin immediately to develop processes which would involve their subordinate managers to the greatest possible extent." The memorandum encouraged program managers to use the formats prescribed by the HUD budget office, but indicated that "each program manager should develop those procedures which will best accomplish the preparation of the material required by these instructions and as may be appropriate for his or her organization and program." Due to the brief amount of time available, field organizations were not asked to formulate ZBB requests, but were to be consulted regarding program and staffing recommendations.

Legislative Assumptions

HUD's legislative recommendations were due to OMB on the same date as the budget estimates, September 15, 1977. Program managers were asked to "state explicitly if the enactment of legislation is assumed, including extensions of authorizations, additional authorizations, other legislative amendments affecting an existing program, or legislation authorizing a new program or activity." If program managers felt that any new legislation should be initiated, they were to include in their submittals:

> ... (1) a summary of the proposal; (2) the specific provisions of law to be amended; (3) a justification for the proposal; (4) a statement of any arguments you are aware of that might be advanced against the proposal; (5) cost and staff requirements and implications; (6) any other HUD officers, or other Federal agencies, that may have an interest, and the views of those offices or agencies, if known; (7) an indication of whether, in your view, an environmental or inflations impact statement is required for the proposal; (8) a statement as to any special timing considerations that may affect when the proposal should be submitted to the Congress; and, (9) any other background information which you believe may be helpful.

The Zero Base Process

The zero base budgeting process in HUD was more or less to follow the "typical" approaches used by other governmental and private organizations, and as generally prescribed by OMB. It was to include the following.

Identification of Decision Units. Decision units are programs or activities for which departmental budget decisions have to be made. A proposed list of decision units for each program area was recommended by the budget office and distributed for review by each program manager. After negotiation with each program manager, initial agreements were made to develop zero budget estimates for the decision units shown in Figure 2.2. The decision unit structure submitted later to OMB differed only slightly.

Preparation of Decision Packages. The decision package is a brief justification paper prepared for each decision unit. Decision packages were to be prepared for each level of funding associated with a program as follows.

Minimum Level Package. This is funding and performance at a minimum level for 1979; that is, a level below which it is not feasible or practical to continue the program or the activity because objectives could not be achieved. This level was to become the highest priority for the decision unit.

Current Level Package. This represents funding and performance for the current level of activity in a program area. This was to be an increment above the

Figure 2.2
Decision Units for Preparation of 1979 Budget Estimates

HOUSING PROGRAMS
Program Manager: Assistant Secretary for Housing

H-1 Annual Contributions for Assisted Housing (Consolidated)
H-2 Payments for Operation of Low Income Housing Projects
H-3 Housing for the Elderly or Handicapped (Section 202)
H-4 Urban Homesteading (In conjunction with Assistant Secretaries for PD&R and CPD)
H-5 FHA Fund
H-6 Section 235
H-7 Section 236
H-8 Rent Supplement Program
H-9 Housing Finance and Development Agencies
H-10 Nonprofit Sponsor Assistance
H-11 College Housing Loans
H-12 Public Housing Loan Fund
H-13 Emergency Homeowners' Relief Fund
H-14 Community Disposal Operations Fund
H-15 Revolving Fund (Liquidating Programs)
H-16 Disaster Assistance Fund
H-17 Housing Payments
H-18 New Program Recommendations
H-(last) Staffing (not in Decision Packages)

GOVERNMENT NATIONAL MORTGAGE ASSOCIATION (GNMA)
Program Manager: President of GNMA

GNMA-1 Special Assistance Functions Fund
GNMA-2 Emergency Mortgage Purchases Assistance
GNMA-3 Guarantees of Mortgage-Backed Securities
GNMA-4 Management and Liquidating Functions
GNMA-5 Participation Sales Fund
GNMA-6 Staffing

COMMUNITY PLANNING AND DEVELOPMENT
Program Manager: Assistant Secretary for Community Planning and Development

CPD-1 Community Development Grants
CPD-2 Comprehensive Planning Grants (Section 701) (Consolidated)
CPD-3 Rehabilitation Loans (Section 312)
CPD-4 Urban Renewal Grants
CPD-5 Staffing

NEW COMMUNITIES ADMINISTRATION
Program Manager: New Communities Administrator

NCA-1 New Communities Fund
NCA-2 New Communities Fund, Contract Services
NCA-3 Supplemental Grants
NCA-4 New program recommendations
NCA-(last) Staffing

FEDERAL INSURANCE ADMINISTRATION
Program Manager: Administrator, Federal Insurance Administration

FIA-1 National Insurance Development Fund
FIA-2 National Flood Insurance Fund
FIA-3 Flood Insurance Program
FIA-4 Staffing

NEIGHBORHOOD AND NON-GOVERNMENTAL ORGANIZATIONS, AND CONSUMER PROTECTION (NNOCP)
Program Manager: Assistant Secretary for NNOCP

NOCP-1 Housing Counseling Assistance
NOCP-2 Mobile Home Standards Program
NOCP-3 Interstate Land Sales Registration
NOCP-4 Neighborhood Activities
NOCP-5 Non-Governmental Activities
NOCP-6 Staffing

POLICY DEVELOPMENT AND RESEARCH (PD&R)
Program Manager: Assistant Secretary for Policy Development and Research

PDR-1 Research and Technology
PDR-2 Staffing

FAIR HOUSING AND EQUAL OPPORTUNITY (FHEO)
Program Manager: Assistant Secretary for Fair Housing and Equal Opportunity

FHEO-1 Staffing
FHEO-2 Special Contracts

FEDERAL DISASTER ASSISTANCE ADMINISTRATION
Program Manager: Administrator, FDAA

FDAA-1 Disaster Relief Fund
FDAA-2 Staffing

DEPARTMENTAL MANAGEMENT
Program Manager: The UnderSecretary

DM-1 Departmental Management Staffing

GENERAL COUNSEL AND LEGAL SERVICES
Program Manager: The General Counsel

GC-1 Office of General Counsel Staffing
GC-2 Field Legal Services

ADMINISTRATION
Program Manager: Assistant Secretary for Administration

ADM-1 Staffing
ADM-2 Automated Data Processing
ADM-3 Field Administration Staffing
ADM-4 Travel (Department Wide)
ADM-5 Consolidated Expense Items

Figure 2.3
Department of Housing and Urban Development
Decision Package

Organization (a)
Decision Unit (b)
Account Title and Numbers (c)

PACKAGE 1 of 3 -- MINIMUM LEVEL

RESOURCE REQUIREMENTS

	ESTIMATE 1977	ESTIMATE 1978	1979 ESTIMATE THIS PACKAGE	1979 ESTIMATE TOTAL CUMULATIVE
			(Dollars in Thousands)	

(Program activity items; units, number
of contracts, obligations for grants,
etc.) (e)

Obligations...........................			(g)	(g)
Contract authority...................				
Budget authority.....................				
Outlays..............................				
Staff-years..........................				

Five-year estimate: (f)

FISCAL YEARS

	1979	1980	1981	1982	1983
Budget authority......................	$	$	$	$	$
Outlays..............................	$	$	$	$	$

Activity Description:

(Describe the work to be performed or services provided with the incremental
resources specified in this package. If possible, this section should include
a discussion and evaluation of the significant accomplishments planned and the
results of cost/benefit analyses or other analyses that will help to support
this level. This section should be briefly stated -- two to three sentences.)

Short-Term Objectives:

(State the short-term objectives (usually achievable within one year) that would
be accomplished with the increment specified and the cumulative resources shown
in this package. Where possible, state the benefits to be derived. State the
results in quantifiable measures to the maximum extent. These objectives will
form the basis for Operating Plan determinations for FY 1979 and should be
stated in terms which are consistent with and usable for the operating
planning process.)

Impact on Major Objective(s):

(Describe the impact on the major objective(s) or goals of both the incremental
and cumulative resources shown in this package.)

Other Information:

Provide any other useful information which will assist in evaluating this package.
This should include, for example,

   --legislative implications or requirements;
   --impact or consequences of not approving the package;
   --for the minimum level package, the effect of zero-funding (i.e., elimination)
     of the program; and
   --other useful justification, stated briefly.

Figure 2.3 (Continued)

INSTRUCTIONS FOR PREPARATION OF DECISION PACKAGE FORM

NOTES

(a)   Enter the HUD organizational title (Housing, CPD, etc.)
(b)   Enter the name of the Decision Unit of which this Decision Package is a part.
      (See list of Decision Units.) Use the number and letter designation provided
      in Attachment 2; e.g., H-3, CPD-4, OIG-1, etc.
(c)   From the 1978 Budget Appendix, enter the 11-digit OMB account number and
      title which provides funding for this Decision Unit.
(d)   Enter the activity level for this Decision Package; e.g., "Minimum Level,"
      "Current Level," or "Improved Level." The "Current Level" would be
      "Package 2 of 3," etc.
(e)   Enter the relevant program and financial items. Usually these would
      include highlight data contained in the "Program Highlights" portion of
      individual 1978 Budget Justifications. This would include units reserved,
      grant obligations, numbers of contracts, etc. Note that this section may
      include additional information, especially staffing data for housing
      programs, data on reservations, starts and completions, etc.

      In all cases -- except for staffing decision packages -- enter information
      on obligations, contract authority, budget authority and outlays.
(f)   Five-year estimates must be provided for budget authority and outlays --
      except for staffing decision packages. These projections will reflect an
      extension of the programs and policies shown for FY 1979. Where the Program
      Manager determines that inflationary assumptions are an appropriate
      consideration, such assumptions may be included in estimates, but the
      assumption should be noted under "Other Information" on the second page
      of this form.
(g)   The amounts contained under "This Package" would reflect the full amount
      proposed in the "Minimum Level" package or the incremental amount proposed
      in the "Current Level" and "Improved Level" package. The "Cumulative
      Total" represents the total of the incremental amount of the previous
      column and amounts proposed in all preceding packages.

minimum level and was to be that level of activity, not necessarily funding, reflected in the Fiscal Year 1978 budget.

Improved Level Package. This is funding and performance at a desired level of expansion or improvement. This was to represent any increase above the current level and would usually reflect a desirable program level.

Intermediate Level. This represents funding and performance between either the minimum and the current levels, or the current and the improved levels.

Figures 2.3a and 2.3b contain the decision package format that was recommended, and the instructions on how to prepare a decision package form.

Preparation of a Decision Unit Overview. The decision unit overview was to identify the long-range goal of the decision unit, the major objectives, alternatives available for achieving them (including why the alternatives were not chosen), and other supporting information about the program. In addition, an outlay analysis was to be included in the overview (Figure 2.4a). Instructions for preparation of the decision unit overview are shown in Figure 2.4b.

Figure 2.4
Department of Housing and Urban Development
Decision Unit Overview

Organization (a)
Decision Unit (b)
Account Title and Number (c)

GOAL

(Identify the long range goal of the decision unit. The goal should be a brief
statement directed toward general needs, to serve as the basis for determining
the major objective(s) undertaken to work toward that goal.)

MAJOR OBJECTIVE(S)

(Describe the major objectives of the decision unit, the requirements that these
objectives are intended to satisfy and the basic authorizing legislation. Major
objectives normally are those of a continuing nature or take relatively long
periods to accomplish. The objectives should be measurable to the extent possible.
They should form the basis for identifying the short-term objectives stated in
the decision packages as well as a basis for subsequently evaluating the accomplishments of programs or activities. Consequently, the major objectives should be
stated in terms which can lead to the identification of more specific short-term
objectives which can be utilized in the operating planning process. This will
provide a managerial tool whereby specific short-term objectives in the decision
package can be integrated into 1979 operating plans.

(The statement of objectives should be kept brief, possibly two to three sentences.)

ALTERNATIVES

(This section should identify the alternative ways to accomplish the major
objectives and why they were not selected in favor of the alternative(s) reflected
in the decision packages. Here, too, brevity is essential, and the statements
should be limited to one or two sentences or a "bullet" style of presentation.)

SUPPORTING INFORMATION

(This section should provide, briefly, the necessary supporting data or background
information to an understanding of the program relevant to each decision package.
This would eliminate the need to repeat the information in each decision package.
The section may contain financial data, program data, and other explanatory materials
previously reflected in "justification" or provided as backup information.)

In addition, an analysis of outlay information should be provided as follows:

OUTLAY ANALYSIS

	1977 EST.	1978 EST.	1979 EST.	1980 EST.	1981 EST.	1982 EST.	1983 EST.
Outlays resulting from commitments on hand, September 30, 1976...............							
Outlays resulting from FY 1977 commit-ments..................................							
Outlays resulting from FY 1978 commit-ments..................................							
Outlays resulting from FY 1979 commit-ments:							
At Minimum Level......................							
At Current Level......................							
At Improved Level....................							
At Other Level							

Specific information requested for certain programs in Attachment 3 should be
included with this section or provided as an attachment.

Figure 2.4 (Continued)

INSTRUCTIONS FOR PREPARATION OF DECISION UNIT OVERVIEW

The decision Unit Overview must be prepared for each decision package series
(i.e., each set of three (or more) decision packages reflecting the minimum,
current or improved levels). These Decision Unit Overviews will replace the budget
justifications required in previous years for this stage of the budget process in
the Department.

The Overview is intended to provide an overview of the decision unit under discussion
and to provide information leading to a better understanding of the decision
packages themselves and provide data and information relevant to each package.

A Decision Unit Overview must be prepared for consolidated decision package series
as well as for the individual decision package series which form the basis for
the consolidated package.

A Decision Unit Overview need not be prepared for the "non-controllable" or
"non-discretionary" items where a decision package at the minimum level only is
provided.

NOTES

(a) Enter the HUD organizational title (Housing, CPD, etc.).

(b) Enter the name of the Decision Unit to which this Decision Unit Overview
     applies. (See list of Decision Units in Attachment 2.) Use the number
     and letter designation provided in Attachment 2; e.g., H-3, CPD-4, OIG-1,
     etc.

(c) From the 1978 Budget Appendix, enter the 11-digit OMB account number and
     title which provides funding for this Decision Unit.

Consolidated Decision Packages. For some major programs that included
several decision units, consolidated decision packages were called for, along
with the decision unit overview. For example, several programs were to be
consolidated in the decision unit on Annual Contributions for Assisted Housing, including Sections 8, 202, and 248.

Ranking Decision Packages. Program managers were asked to rank the decision units under their purview in priority order. No special procedures for this
ranking were prescribed. The only stipulation was that mandatory budget authority or outlay items were to be ranked highest, followed by discretionary
items. Also, the "minimum level" for any program was to be ranked higher
than the "current level" for that same program and the "current level" higher
than the "improved level." Figures 2.5a and 2.5b contain the summary ranking
sheet and instructions suggested by the HUD budget office.

Figure 2.5
Summary Ranking Sheet

Organization: _____   Date: _____

($'s in Millions)

RANK	Level	Title	1977 Estimate		1978 Estimate		1979 Estimate				Comments
							Decision Pkg		Cumulative		
			BA	SY	BA	SY	BA	SY	BA	SY	
(a)	(b)	(c)	(d)	(e)	(f)	(g)	(h)	(i)	(j)	(k)	(l)

Figure 2.5 (Continued)

INSTRUCTION FOR PREPARATION OF SUMMARY RANKING SHEET FOR DECISION PACKAGES AND
CONSOLIDATED DECISION PACKAGES

Each Program Manager will submit this completed Exhibit showing his or her priority ranking of each decision package for which he or she is responsible. In many cases, the Program Manager will be submitting this Exhibit twice: as a Decision Packages Ranking Sheet, and as a Consolidated Decision Packages Ranking Sheet where consolidated decision units have been identified among a manager's programs (see Attachment 2 for a listing of these).

(1) Decision Packages Ranking Sheet. When the Exhibit is used for this submission, it is a sequential ranking of all decision packages (including components of consolidated packages) for which the Program Manager is reponsible. It includes packages for "uncontrollable" or "nondiscretionary" programs, all other ("discretionary") packages prepared at "minimum," "current," and "improved" levels of activity, and packages reflecting staff years only.

The "uncontrollable" or "nondiscretionary" packages should be ranked first in the sequence.

The "discretionary" decision packages — those prepared at "minimum," "current," and "improved" activity levels — should then follow, ranked in the Program Manager's priority order. Note, however, that the first entry for any particular decision unit must always be at the "minimum" level. (This does not preclude the possibility of ranking a higher incremental level of one program above the minimum for another decision package, however.)

Decision packages reflecting staff-years only, such as those prepared for Headquarters staffing elements, should be included in the Exhibit. No budget authority estimates will be shown for these packages. (The "pricing" of such staff expense items will be developed by staff in support of the MBRC when overall Department rankings and consolidations are prepared.)

(2) Consolidated Decision Packages Ranking Sheet. When the Exhibit is used for this submission, it is a sequential ranking of those decision packages which comprise the consolidated decision package. It does not include all the decision packages ranked in (1) above, but only those component decision packages germane to this consolidation. (Note that these component packages are also ranked in (1) above, in a broader array.) The ranking process is otherwise as described above.

Figure 2.5 (Continued)

Column (a) : Enter the numerical ranking of each decision package in descending order starting with 1 until all decision packages under the individual program manager are listed.

Column (b) : Enter the level of the decision package, that is: M - minimum, C - current, I - improved, I(1) or I(2)) - intermediate.

Column (c) : Enter the title of the decision package.

Column (d) : Enter the estimated budget authority for the decision package in FY 77. (Except for staffing packages.)

Column (e) : Enter the staff years estimated for FY 77.

Column (f) : Enter the estimated budget authority for the decision package in FY 78. (Except for staffing packages.)

Column (g) : Enter the staff years estimated for FY 78.

Column (h) : Enter the estimated budget authority for the decision package for FY 79. (Except for staffing packages.)

Column (i) : Enter the staff years estimated for FY 79.

Column (j) : Enter cumulative estimated budget authority; that is, always take the amount of funds reflected in column (h), add the amount of the next decision package, and place that cumulative amount in column (j).

Column (k) : Enter the staff years estimated on a cumulative basis, using the same process as described for column (j).

Column (l) : Enter any pertinent written comments, or quantitative data, as desired.

Staffing. Estimates for staffing created the most confusion among program managers. Some staffing requests were to be included in the program decision units and some were to be submitted as separate staffing decision units. This area was later worked on for improvement prior to the 1980 budget cycle.

Changes in FY '78 Estimates. In addition to FY '79 budget estimates, any changes to the FY '78 budget originally submitted by President Ford, and subsequently modified by President Carter, any supplemental appropriations, or any reprogramming of funds were to be proposed, including a five year projection of the outlay impact.

Submission of Additional Materials. To facilitate the MBRC review and ranking process, any information not covered in the decision packages or decision unit overviews was to be submitted for special consideration.

Review by the MBRC. It was also pointed out in the "Call" that all materials were to be submitted to the MBRC, through the deputy assistant secretary for administration. The MBRC would then rank all programs and levels and present them to the secretary.

Preparation and Submission of Materials. Materials were to be addressed to the undersecretary, as chairman of the MBRC, and 30 copies were to be delivered to the Office of Budget no later than July 1, 1977.

Secretary's Retreat

Upon receipt of the *Call for Fiscal Year 1979 Budget Estimates and Legislative Recommendations*, HUD Program Managers began preparation of their estimates and recommendations. Secretary Harris scheduled and held a "retreat" for Saturday and Sunday, May 7th and 8th, at which major departmental issues were discussed, and HUD goals and major objectives were established for the coming year(s). These goals and objectives became the cornerstone for the ranking of programs subsequently accomplished by the MBRC. The goals agreed upon at the retreat were as follows.

I.   The central thrust of HUD's policies should be revitalization of urban areas.
II. HUD should use housing programs as an aid to revitalization and to provide necessary shelter for all citizens.
III. HUD should seek to provide freedom of choice for all persons.
IV. HUD should attempt to increase capacity of communities and neighborhoods to achieve revitalization.

Although the secretary considered the objectives under each goal to be quite "wordy," they nevertheless satisfied her need for some specificity of direction within each goal area.

This "retreat" was an important meeting because it was the first opportunity for the secretary's "top management team" to discuss together their overall views of HUD, its programs, and the needs and demands of the environment within which it and they must function. The history of federal housing efforts and urban development was reviewed, with special attention paid to the reasons why federal intervention may be needed. Some of the reasons were as follows.

1. Protection of the enormous capital investment we have in the cities.
2. The cities have large aggregations of the poor who cannot compete in the market in monetary terms. We must protect them and improve their environment.
3. We need to remedy conditions that exist now because we want to protect both our investment in human beings and our investment in the infrastructure.
4. This leads to our wanting to protect the poor where these problems exist. But this can also involve helping both the working poor and the middle class.

Given these justifications for federal intervention in the cities, much discussion occurred about HUD's role and the resources required.

While no specific, detailed strategy was articulated, the general philosophy that seemed to emerge was one in which:

> ... the basic direction of HUD is urban development and urban revitalization and preservation. For FY 1979, our concern is to utilize our housing and CD (community development) programs in a way to permit this. We do not believe this precludes giving attention to the needs of the middle income as well as the poor although we acknowledge a particular responsibility for the poor. We are troubled about increasing the amount of public housing in racially impacted areas though we recognize it can be done where there is a clear neighborhood stabilization value. We need something which improves construction for those currently aided by Section 8. We must continue to subsidize those projects we erect. We must provide management direction and continuity.

The assistant secretary for Policy Development and Research, Donna Shalala, was assigned the task of following up on the initiatives and issues arising from these weekend meetings—specifically freedom of housing choice, local "capacity building," inner-city rehabilitation strategy, commercial facilities for inner-city projects, an urban extension service, and a rural housing initiative. Program managers were asked by the secretary to develop issue papers pertaining to these, as well as other aspects of HUD programs around which controversy and differing views might exist.

Issue papers were to be submitted by June 1, 1977, with 1979 budget requests ready by July 1. The secretary closed out the meeting by stressing the importance of the deadlines established.

Preparation of ZBB Decision Packages

The preparation of decision packages was handled a bit differently within each HUD program area. In Community Planning and Development, for example, a special "budget call letter" was issued to its program offices on May 6, outlining the schedule for the legislative and budget review process. The schedule called for budget and legislative materials to be prepared by office directors and submitted to both the CPD Office of Management and the CPD Office of Policy Planning by May 27. Between May 30 and June 3 the Office of Management and the Office of Policy Planning were to put together the budget and legislative packages, with the ranking of CPD priorities to be done on June 6 by the CPD Budget Committee.

The budget committee recommendations were to be reviewed by Assistant Secretary Embry on June 13, following which the office directors were to prepare final budget and legislative materials for submittal on June 24. This left one week for the CPD budget office and the assistant secretary to get the materials into shape for delivery to the MBRC by July 1.

Throughout this process, which was completed according to schedule, the CPD budget office coordinated the development of issue papers, legislative proposals, and budget requests, and also worked with the office directors on setting CPD objectives, which became the basis for their ZBB program funding requests. Since little guidance had been provided about preparation of either issue papers or objectives, CPD budget and program staff developed some fifty issue papers. These were later reduced to twenty-seven, but even this was considered too many by the HUD budget office and MBRC staff. Also, some of the CPD objectives were rewritten by the MBRC staff to be more consistent with objectives submitted for other HUD programs.

In housing, a similar involvement of office directors and program officers occurred in the preparation of decision units. Though three weeks late in being submitted, the quality was considered to be quite good. One or two decision units were even added to the initially agreed-upon housing list. The housing budget staff relied heavily on the involvement of the program officers who were charged with deciding upon and developing the various levels of funding requests, and the determination of what could be accomplished within their very complex housing programs. In some instances program officers were somewhat concerned about the "minimum level" definition provided, and were reluctant to indicate that any reduction in their programs was possible. Many of their initial submittals contained identical figures for "minimum" and "current" funding levels and some even contained "minimum levels" that were higher than "current levels." Only after the budget staff asked program officers to re-package, were acceptable (at least according to OMB guidelines) "minimums" developed for these decision packages.

Another complication in housing arose around the development of substantiating data for the budget requests. Some of the housing staff cited insufficient time and lack of available computer support for analyzing 1977 housing data, as well as for projecting 1978 and 1979 data. They were forced to hand calculate many of these projections, and used this as one of the reasons for being late in their submittal to the HUD budget office. It was the opinion of some of the housing staff that 75 percent of the paper work could have been eliminated, what with it being necessary to repeat descriptions of programs, tables, objectives, etc. for each level of funding for each program. And, since housing had the lion's share of HUD programs and decision units to prepare, they felt justified in their concerns.

Upon completion of housing's decision packages and their submittal to the HUD budget office for distribution to other MBRC members, program officers and their deputies briefed the housing operations group, which is housing's policy committee. This group consisted of the assistant secretary for housing–federal housing commissioner, the deputy assistant secretary for housing–deputy federal housing commissioner, the deputy assistant secretary for insured and direct loan programs, the deputy assistant secretary for assisted housing, and the director of the Office of Policy Development and Evaluation. These briefings occurred daily between July 18 and 22, and lasted about two hours each. The policy committee then ranked all of the housing programs and sent this ranking to the MBRC. It might be noted that neither housing nor CPD utilized inputs from their field personnel, but they anticipated they would be more involved in the FY 1980 ZBB efforts.

Ranking of HUD Decision Units

HUD's "Ceiling Letter"

On July 22, Secretary Harris received HUD's official "ceiling letter," or as it is called by some, their "planning letter," from OMB. The letter contained "presidential policy guidance" for submittal of the Fiscal Year 1979 budget, and reminded the secretary of the September 15, 1977 deadline. It stressed the president's effort "toward a balanced budget for 1981," and indicated that the 1979 budget planning ceilings for HUD had been "determined by the president in accordance with his priorities, the anticipated availability of resources, the requirements of your Department, and the outyear effects of 1979 decisions." These and other more direct phrases represented a not-so-subtle way of telling the secretary that she should strive to accomplish as much as or more than had been accomplished in the previous administration, with the same or fewer resources. This is, of course, an oversimplification of the intent of the letter, but it was an attempt to caution departments and agencies against significant expansion of their previous year's budget. The letter also called for submittal or comment on any legislative proposals that might be made to the next session of Congress, and reviewed for the secretary the various requirements contained in OMB Circulars, and in the Congressional Budget Act of 1974, a major reform law passed in response to impoundments and other budgetary practices of former President Nixon.

Budget Year Issues

In addition to communicating the 1979 budget planning ceilings, OMB asked HUD to highlight in their decision packages the answers to sixteen issue questions. These answers were to assist the president in "analyzing the various options that will confront him for the budget year." The areas in which questions were raised by OMB included:

- rent-income ratios in subsidized housing;
- new construction;
- operating subsidies;
- modernization;
- Federal Housing Administration;
- loan management/property disposition;
- homeownership assistance;
- counseling;
- rehabilitation loans;
- community development block grants;
- community development;
- flood insurance;
- fair housing;
- staffing;
- elderly housing; and
- research.

Also, OMB "directed" that HUD "undertake longer range, in-depth studies" on a series of topics and "include, in your Fall budget submission status reports on progress made on the studies." These were to essentially be "Long-Term Zero Base Evaluations" in the following areas:

1. new construction;
2. nonprofit sponsors;
3. inventory management;
4. Section 223(f);
5. guarantees of mortgage-backed securities;
6. Tandem Plan;
7. community development block grants;
8. counseling;
9. fair housing; and
10. mortgage insurance.

In one regard, the OMB ceiling letter was timely in that it arrived just prior to the beginning of "MBRC Week," when the ranking of HUD programs was to be done. Thus, the ceiling figures were useful in making ranking decisions. However, the breadth and complexity of the budget year issues and the long term evaluations to be addressed were such that there was no way in which the necessary staff work could be completed in time for them to be completely

Figure 2.6
Proposed Schedule

```
Mon.
July 25      10:00 - 12:00    Overview                        2 Hours
                              -Introduction (Janis)      (30 Min.)
                              -Budget Overview (Budget) (45 Min.)
                                 Totals Requested
                                 Highlights (Budget)
                              -Procedures for Ranking
                                 Programs (Budget)        (45 Min.)

             2:00 - 5:00                                     3 Hours
                              -Legislative Strategy
                               and Outlook                 (1/2 Hour)
                              -Housing                     (2 1/2 Hrs.)

Tues.
July 26      1:00 - 5:00                                     4 Hours
                              -Remainder of Housing        (1 Hour)
                              -CPD                          (3 Hours)

Wed.
July 27      8:30 - 11:00                                  2 1/2 Hours
                              -Review Housing
                               and CPD Rankings            (1 Hour)
                              -GNMA                         (1/2 Hour)
                              -FHEO                         (1 Hour)

             3:00 - 6:00                                     3 Hours
                              -NCA                          (1 1/2 Hours)
                              -NVACP                        (1 1/2 Hours)

Thurs.
July 28      12:00 - 6:00                                    6 Hours
                              -FDAA                         (30 Min.)
                              -PD&R                         (1 1/4 Hr.)
                              -FIA                          (30 Min.)
                              -OIG                          (30 Min.)
                              -DM & Field Dir.             (45 Min.)
                              -OGC & Field Legal           (45 Min.)
                              -Admin, Travel, Special
                                 Contract Requests, Misc(1 3/4 Hours)

             7:00             -To Conclude

Friday
July 29      2:00 - 6:00                                     4 Hours
                              -Departmental Ranking
                              -Remaining Issues
```

included as a part of the ranking process. Some HUD careerists pointed out that many of the issues were holdovers from the prior administration and had been raised repeatedly by OMB in past years. Regardless, it was extremely late in the budget cycle for HUD to be receiving such a detailed request, and it consumed a great deal of management and staff time that ordinarily could have been devoted to the budgetary process.

In essence, OMB gave HUD the questions, and then revised them too late in the process to permit orderly use of them, causing confusion with HUD's schedule for preparation of budget materials.

"MBRC Week"

On Wednesday, July 20, MBRC members received the zero base budget requests for all the department's programs. These were to have been completed by July 1. This meant a minimum amount of time was available for reading the hundreds of pages in preparation for the week-long MBRC meetings that would begin on Monday, July 25. This late receipt of materials obviously was of major concern to MBRC members, and it became apparent that not all were able to read or digest in any great detail the objectives, justifications, alternatives, or even the funding levels submitted for each program.

"MBRC Week," as HUD Undersecretary Jay Janis labeled it, was a significant event in the HUD ZBB process, in that it was the point in time when all HUD programs were merged into a single priority listing for presentation to Secretary Harris. The proposed schedule (Figure 2.6) called for meetings each day, with final rankings and handling of remaining issues on Friday, July 29. Though the meetings ran over to Monday, August 1, a set of final rankings had been completed by the original target date. The additional meeting was to review and prepare a "cleaned-up" version of the computer-printed rankings.

"MBRC Week" began with presentation of the schedule and a series of ground rules by Janis. Key among the ground rules were the following.

- Rankings of decision packages would be compiled following coverage of each entire program area.
- All MBRC members were to participate in the rankings.
- Caution was urged as to "generosity" toward the earlier programs, keeping in mind that resources add up quickly, and there was an OMB "ceiling" to consider.
- Individuals from the HUD budget office were to act as "MBRC Staff" and would ask questions much like OMB or congressional committee staff members might ask.
- The undersecretary would take the rankings by the MBRC to the secretary, where he would present the majority views as well as his personal views.
- The undersecretary was to chair the meetings, with the deputy assistant secretary for administration, Vince Hearing, chairing when the undersecretary was absent.
- Herb Persil, deputy budget director would be the chief spokesman for the "MBRC Staff," with various members of the budget office doing most of the questioning of the program managers.
- MBRC Staff Recommendations had been prepared for each decision unit.

Persil began the substantive process by posting on the board the OMB planning figures, and the totals of the requests by the program managers. It was apparent that a great deal of cutting would be required, since the total of the budget requests at "improved levels" for all programs was more than twice the

OMB "ceiling" amount. Some discussion was held regarding the cutting process, or "how to squeeze a size 12 foot into a size 6 shoe." Once the OMB planning figures were understood and the differences between budget authority and budget outlays clarified, a process which took about 15 minutes, Persil handed out a description of the ranking procedures and explained its use.

The ranking procedures, which had been developed jointly by the HUD budget office and the Office of Organization and Management Information, called for each MBRC member to rank every decision unit. First, they were to score the decision unit as to its relationship to the four HUD goals:

1. revitalization of urban areas;
2. provide necessary shelter for all citizens;
3. provide freedom of choice in housing for all persons; and
4. increase capacity of communities and neighborhoods to achieve revitalization.

A 10 point scoring system was to be used. If a decision unit was considered essential to goal accomplishment, 8 to 10 points could be assigned. A decision unit considered to be supportive could receive 4 to 7 points; one marginally supportive could receive 1 to 3 points.

Secondly, MBRC members were to score each program as to its overall importance to HUD's "purpose and mission, value to constituencies, program impact, or other subjective factors." This was to be a single score, again on a one to ten scale. A total MBRC unit value was then computed for each decision unit, giving a 50 percent weighting to the score of the program manager whose program was being ranked, and a 50 percent weighting to the average scores of the other MBRC members. This gave more weight to the primary program manager, yet permitted some input from others on each decision unit. However, this also provided the opportunity for some "fudging" by program managers.[3]

The total numerical score for each decision package determined the relative position of that unit in the overall ranking of all HUD decision packages. This procedure, while not highly sophisticated, was considered statistically appropriate and produced what eventually proved to be a usable ranking, and one participated in by all MBRC members. However, the process took a bit of a beating and was referred to by some as a form of "bingo," and by others in even harsher terms.

Following the explanation of the ranking procedure, Harry K. Schwartz, assistant secretary for legislation and intergovernmental relations, discussed the department's overall legislative strategy and outlook, with comments about key presidential and congressional feelings and concerns. The basic thrust of his remarks was that HUD should look to consolidate programs wherever possible and clean up existing legislation to get rid of old unused program authorizations or programs that did not fit into the current HUD goals. By consolidating or eliminating programs, Schwartz said, HUD would be in line with the president's commitment to simplification of government.

Of importance to the ZBB process was his pointing out certain "gaps" in the proposed decision units that were certain to be identified by OMB, White House or congressional staff members. He pointed out that he hoped these would be picked up somehow as the process progressed. Janis suggested that these might be handled following the ZBB ranking. A separate process was later established and used to complete the HUD legislative proposal package before the submittal deadline of September 15th.

The morning session of the first day of "MBRC Week" was concluded with a short debriefing in Janis' office. Included were Kliman, Persil, Medina, Hearing, and Peter Kaplan, Janis' executive assistant. The main concerns were with the legislative "gap" problem, how to display goals to aid in the ranking process, and what to do about the extensive movement in and out of the conference room during the proceedings. It was decided to make a chart displaying the HUD goals and to put a "door monitor" outside the meeting room to deliver messages into and out of the room. The legislative "gap" problem was shelved for later resolution.

Gate Control

The afternoon session of the first day of "MBRC Week" began with an announcement by Janis of the "gate control," and placement of the goals charts on easels visible to the participants.

The 19-plus decision units for housing were then addressed. Persil introduced the MBRC staff members who would direct the questioning. The assistant secretary for housing, Lawrence Simons, waived any opening statements and proceeded directly to the concerns and recommendations of the MBRC members and staff. While he let it be known that he was not fully in favor of the ZBB process that had been developed, he nevertheless answered the questions and concerns of the MBRC members, and "educated" many of them on the complexities and poli ics of the various housing programs. In the end, though he still felt a better method was needed, Simons concluded that there was value to the MBRC going through and discussing all of the programs and budgets, and the process was more beneficial than he originally thought it might be. All in all, discussion of the housing decision units and budget estimates covered approximately four hours. This led Janis to recommend that rankings be completed after each decision unit, rather than after an entire program had been discussed. When his recommendation was not agreed to by the MBRC, he went along with the majority dissent.

As "MBRC Week" progressed, the members appeared to become more comfortable with the ranking process and with the questioning of each other.

Discussions included political as well as budgetary matters, and evoked considerable debate on both macro issues and details of some of the programs being proposed. The MBRC staff questions caused program managers to revise some of their estimates as did questioning by other MBRC members. Permitting deputy assistant secretaries and selected staff to attend improved immeasurably the technical quality of the discussions, though the program managers showed an excellent grasp of the details of their programs. Janis used great skill in facilitating the discussions, letting some proceed at length, cutting others when they ranged too far afield, and generally summarizing where the group was at appropriate points. At several junctures the process might have been in serious trouble had not the undersecretary been committed to producing a product, *and* ensuring the integrity of the MBRC as HUD's top management team.

Midway through the week, Janis, Simons and Embry accompanied Secretary Harris to meet with President Carter about several HUD management matters. Upon their return, Janis reported to the MBRC the president's interest when ZBB was mentioned, and his pleasure that HUD was using it as extensively as they were. This seemed to provide a bit of a spark to the remaining "MBRC Week" proceedings.

Following the housing and CPD rankings, the MBRC staff tried out their computer programs specially developed for merging the program levels in response to the MBRC scoring. With some very minor problems, the computer printed rankings were produced for each member in time for beginning the third day of "MBRC Week." Time was spent reviewing the rankings and the meanings of some of the columns, but almost all MBRC members were impressed with this quick turn-around capability and its potential.

One by one, HUD program managers presented their budget estimates, and the MBRC scored each according to the aforementioned process. Several things became clear as the sessions progressed, not the least of which was the interrelatedness of the HUD programs. Many of the appointees learned a lot about other HUD programs and capabilities. Some found out about administrative rules and regulations of which they were not previously aware, others learned of legislation that might affect their actions and policies, while still others found out about little publicized HUD services available to them. But perhaps of most importance, they were participating as a team in making major departmental decisions, and were becoming aware of each others' views and opinions on HUD, its programs, and its environment. Thus, the "educational" value was tremendous.

Upon completion of the scoring for each individual program area, all decision units were merged into an overall departmental ranking using the computer programs developed for that purpose. This was done during the evening of the fourth day, so that the final day could be spent reviewing the listings and making any changes before the MBRC recommendations were presented to the secretary. At first there was uncertainty as to exactly how to attack the lengthy listing. A few special anomalies were pointed out, such as very important programs being ranked too low, and certain ''political'' programs being below the OMB ''ceiling'' line. With little time to study the rankings, it was felt that quick decisions may not be desirable, and that the weekend should be used for further analysis. This was agreed and the undersecretary set Monday, August 1, for a ''cleaning up'' of the ranking sheet before MBRC approval.

On Monday, the MBRC met and made a number of changes to the rankings to be recommended to the secretary. The MBRC staff then took over and proceeded with production of the listings, working with the undersecretary in deciding on exact formatting and content.

"MBRC Week" Conclusions

In retrospect, the following might be concluded about the ''MBRC Week.''

Strong Points. The strong points were seen as follows:

- excellent leadership by the undersecretary;
- fairly good participation by MBRC members;
- good staff back-up to MBRC members;
- pretty good balance of rigor and flexibility in the ranking process;
- good role-playing by budget staff;
- good use of expertise of MBRC members and staff regarding potential reactions to HUD programs by external organizations, e.g., OMB, Congress;
- good attempt to stay with the process, even when tempted to change rules or relax rigor;
- good sharing of learning about the process as it progressed, e.g., ranking items after each decision unit was discussed, rather than lengthy coverage of an entire program area;
- good learning about availability of departmental support services, e.g., ADP support, special contracts, public relations capabilities;
- some learning about departmental regulations;
- the resultant budget was a more true reflector of departmental priorities;
- MBRC members and staff were more aware of, and understand, each others' programs, concerns and feelings;
- there were more integrated management responses to external demands as a result of the sharing that took place; and
- there was a great deal of ''educational'' value for the HUD top management team due to their participation.

Problems. The problems were seen as follows:

- the process was quite time consuming, but that is the price paid for more openness and wider participation;

- there was much movement about the room and noise that distracted the proceedings;
- attendance by program managers was spotty;
- there were some examples of poor meeting behavior, e.g., not listening, cutting speakers off, moving about the room, not being aware of pages being discussed;
- a number of stops were necessary for rule clarification or modification, but this is normal with a new process;
- there was perhaps a bit too much paper, both to review before MBRC Week, and in ranking the decision units;
- a great deal of staff work was required;
- some non-budgetary issues were raised, causing lengthy digressions from the budgetary process;
- discussions were sometimes too easily cut off by citing how external agencies might react, e.g., OMB, Congress, the president;
- there appeared to be uncertainty in how to handle legislative initiatives in the budget context;
- there was confusion on how to integrate personnel and staffing decision units with program decision units;
- there was not much consistency in the questioning of each program manager, or in the strategy discussions, except by the MBRC staff; and
- schedule changes caused some problems.

All in all, "MBRC Week" represented a serious attempt to incorporate management inputs into the HUD budget process, and to continue the building of HUD's top management team.

The Secretary's Decisions

Following "MBRC Week," the HUD Budget Office and Office of Organization and Management Information worked closely with Jay Janis and Vince Hearing in preparing the MBRC recommendations for presentation to Secretary Harris. In addition, they met with several of the program managers and their staffs to complete and reconcile staffing requests with budget requests. The original schedule had called for transmittal of both budget and legislative programs to the secretary on August 5, with her initial decisions to be made by August 9. Program managers were to make any appeals of her decisions by August 11, with her final decisions made on August 15, before she departed for a week's vacation. This schedule proved to be unacceptable to the secretary, since she wished much more time to deliberate over the many complex judgment "calls" she had to make. Also, the legislative proposals were not completely ready for her review on August 5.

Janis and the MBRC staff did meet with the secretary on August 5 and several times over the next ten days to present her with the MBRC budget and staffing recommendations, and to review the areas where her decisions were needed. She asked many questions about the individual view of MBRC members, the likely problems with OMB, the choices open to her, and several times about the last possible due dates for decisions. It was quite clear that she did not like having such a short time in which to make her decisions. The secretary continued to interact extensively with her own executive staff assistants, as well as with program managers in collecting information for use in making decisions, and took this information with her as she departed on her vacation. While the secretary was away, the HUD budget office continued to solicit materials from the program budget offices.

Meanwhile, at an August 17 meeting of the MBRC, the submission of legislative proposals was discussed. HUD General Counsel Ruth T. Prokop and Assistant Secretary for Legislation and Intergovernmental Relations Harry Schwartz were to jointly coordinate this effort. The May 3 HUD "call" memorandum was referenced as to the format to be used for submitting legislative proposals. OMB Circular A-19, which outlines the requirement for legislative clearance by OMB before proposals can be made to Congress in the name of the administration, was also mentioned. Lester Platt, of the Office of General Counsel, stated that proposed legislation would fall into one of three categories. Category I proposals were to be those that would be mentioned in the president's State-of-the-Union message or included in a special presidential message to Congress. Category II proposals were to include all other types ready for submission to Congress. Category III legislative proposals were to include those under consideration that may be ready sometime in the fall. Undersecretary Janis then led the MBRC discussion of some of the specific proposals. The discussion was quite active and pointed out more clearly the major differences in the views of the various HUD program managers, especially pertaining to treatment of some of the groups having interests in HUD programs, e.g., developers, poor people, landlords, tenants, minorities, lending institutions, welfare recipients, builders, and city mayors. Since these discussions were too important to cut short, Janis scheduled and chaired additional lengthy sessions to complete the legislative proposals and prepare recommendations for the secretary upon her return from vacation.

Secretary Harris returned to her office on August 23, and over the next three weeks made and revealed her decisions regarding FY 1979 HUD programs and the budget estimates to be submitted to OMB. Again, she worked through the undersecretary, her executive assistants, the MBRC members and the HUD budget office, so that they would be fully aware of her thinking, and be able to incorporate it into the September 15th submittal.

Submittal to OMB

The next major step in the process was the preparation of the transmittal letter to accompany the budget estimates. Working closely with the budget staff, a 30 page letter was prepared by the secretary. The letter outlined the goals and objectives established for the department, the ZBB process used, including the role of the MBRC, the legislative program, participation by public interest groups, and a general overview of each program area. Enclosures with the letter included the following:

- a list of department goals;
- the Zero-Base Budget Ranking Sheet;
- a comparative Summary of Program Budget Levels for Fiscal Years 1977, 1978 and 1979;
- the Budget Authority, by Program for Fiscal Years 1977, 1978 and 1979;
- Budget Outlays, by Program for Fiscal Years 1977, 1978 and 1979;
- Summary of Full-Time Employment in Permanent Positions, Fiscal Years 1977, 1978 and 1979;
- Summary of Subsidized Housing Programs (Reservations, Starts and Completions), Fiscal Years 1977, 1978 and 1979; and
- Property Acquisitions and Mortgage Assignment Activity for Fiscal Years 1977, 1978 and 1979.

The letter was signed by the secretary on September 14 and delivered to OMB on September 15, with "detailed budget decision packages to follow."

These decision packages were finally submitted on September 30, because the secretary wanted to study further certain areas. In addition, submissions for a decision unit on "Troubled Projects," and recommendations from the urban and regional policy group were late, creating confusion at both HUD and OMB. This pointed out one of the problems with any highly disciplined budgetary process involving interdependent steps. It is difficult to insert last-minute or late items without major impact on all of the preceding actions.

OMB Hearings

Because this was the first budget cycle of the Carter administration, OMB decided to schedule a series of hearings on HUD programs. These were to be conducted by the OMB examiners responsible for review of HUD's budget, with selected attendance by OMB's Associate Director for Economics and Government Dennis Green, in whose area the HUD budget is reviewed. To prepare for these hearings, the undersecretary scheduled a series of "mock hearings" for "certain program areas where we can expect the Office of Management and Budget to focus." This included housing, CPD, new communities administration, and neighborhood, voluntary action, and consumer protection. A panel of HUD executives was established to play the role of OMB examining panel and to conduct the questioning in the "mock" sessions. The panel consisted of Henry Hubschman, executive assistant to the secretary; Assistant Secretary Schwartz; Budget Director Kliman; Ray Struyk, deputy assistant secretary for Policy Development and Research; and Leslie Platt of the Office of the General Counsel. The undersecretary advised program managers that:

> It is essential that you be well prepared for these hearings and be able to justify and explain effectively the secretary's budget recommendations. For new program proposals, it is particularly important that we are able to explain the need for what we have recommended and how the programs will be carried out.

Several of the "mock" hearings were chaired by the undersecretary and most began with Kliman reviewing a few background items for the program manager. Some of these points were as follows.

- OMB has had "fact finding" sessions for the past several years, but has decided to pick up again on hearings because of some major policy issues to be discussed. In fact, the hearings will probably be more policy oriented than budget oriented.
- The examiners will probably ask if the prime witness has an opening statement. This is optional, but the recommendation is that unless there is really something special to report, it should be waived.
- In many instances the examiners will likely have preconceived notions toward certain programs they wish to focus on, so concentrate mainly on responding to questions rather than offering information about other programs.
- OMB will press for additional data or information, so do not promise it unless you can provide it.
- Two of the examiners are relatively new to the HUD budget process, but one or more experienced examiners may also be present.
- The examiners will be looking for disagreements between programs and for inconsistencies in statements and budget submittals, so study other HUD programs and the various budget submittals.
- HUD is going to OMB rather than the reverse, which occurred in the "fact-finding" years.
- The only people to speak for the department will be the program manager and the budget director. This was established by the undersecretary to limit the number of people involved in the hearings process.

Following discussion of these pointers, the questioning by the panel was begun. A comprehensive list of questions for each HUD program area had been prepared by the panel and HUD budget staff personnel. Many of the questions focused on supportive research for a policy or position, duplication or relationships between programs, and political implications of certain positions. Usually, after each response or series of responses to a question, the group paused and debriefed the answer(s). In some instances, it was decided that the answer was inappropriate, that certain words should be eliminated, that too much or too little information was included, or that the answer was probably about right. Before moving to the next question, closure was usually reached on the "correct" response. If no solution was decided upon, it was stressed that one should be developed prior to the actual hearings.

The consensus was that the "mock hearings" did serve a valuable purpose in preparing program managers for the hearings.

The formal OMB hearings on HUD's 1979 budget estimates began on September 26 with a review of neighborhoods, voluntary associations and consumer protection budget estimates. This was followed by hearings on the estimates and proposals for the government national mortgage association on September 27, community planning and development on September 30, fair housing and equal opportunity and policy development and research on October 3, housing on October 4, new communities administration on October 6, and departmental management on October 7.

The OMB hearings produced few "surprises," and were relatively subdued. Program managers answered most of OMB's questions directly, with only minor instances of having to offer to "get back to OMB" with more data, or to "evaluate in more detail" some situation raised by the OMB examiners. "Highlights" of each hearing were prepared by the HUD budget office both as a record of what was "promised," and for information in developing subsequent appeals or reclama of OMB decisions. In most cases, HUD program managers simply provided the OMB budget examiners with data they used when presenting and defending HUD's estimates within the OMB internal budget decision process. To a great extent, HUD had to rely on the ability of their examiners to adequately represent and justify HUD programs and budget estimates, when they began competing with other departments and agencies for a fair share of the total FY 1979 federal budget.

Upon completion of the OMB hearings, a major segment of the ZBB process was over for HUD managers. Outside of preparation and submittal of the budget presentation materials containing the detailed narrative and schedules for HUD programs and accounts, and some interactions between OMB examiners and HUD budget staffs on presentation formats, the next set of decisions were within OMB. OMB examiners engage in intensive interactions pulling together and reaffirming the totals to be incorporated in the president's budget. These are scrutinized carefully by political, economic and management advisers to the president, as well as by top OMB managers. Once their recommendations are made to the president, he decides what budget estimates will be submitted to Congress, both overall and for the various federal program areas. The acting director of OMB, James McIntyre, informed HUD that the president will begin this process in early November, with a "mark" possibly available by Thanksgiving. Departments and agencies have opportunities to appeal various decisions to OMB and the president, but until the FY 1979 budget estimates are presented to Congress in January, 1978, many do not know the exact amounts being requested. Then, of course, department and agency managers begin defense and elaboration of their estimates in appropriations—hearings held by the various congressional appropriations committees. These result in congressional decisions, hopefully by October 1, 1978, the beginning of the spending period. Meanwhile, work will already have begun on the FY 1980 budget within OMB and the departmental budget offices. And, HUD managers will have been involved in another cycle of discussions, debates, and decisions regarding HUD goals, objectives, policies, issues, legislation, priorities, staffing, accomplishments and funding.

Lessons Learned From the ZBB Process

What has been learned from all of this, other than that budgeting is a never-ending process, and that no matter what it is called, the techniques are similar and the result is the same, i.e., a budget is produced. Several things come to mind.

It Will Be Next to Impossible to "Zero-Base" an Existing Federal Program

The developers of ZBB felt that the basic idea ought to be that an organization should, for budgeting purposes, treat every program as a new one each year, and to build its budget from a base of zero. For a new program, yes, but for one with a history, many constituencies, and a current level of expectations and operations, there is almost no way. Even getting program managers to consider levels below the current ones, i.e., "minimum levels," required extra pressures from, and reassurances against dire outcomes by the HUD budget office. The learning from this is that if a true zero base approach is desired, i.e., treating every program each year as if it is a new one, great pressures will have to be exerted on program managers, and there will most likely be a heavy price to pay if this is done.

ZBB Will More Heavily Involve Program Managers in the Budgetary Process

In many organizations, budget staff members have been forced to assume responsibility for the detailed formulation of the major sections of the annual budget as a matter of routine, thus relieving the program manager of what may have become a time consuming incremental process. At HUD, the secretary and the undersecretary made the major budget decisions, with assistance from the budget staff. However, ZBB got the program managers into the act, because budget personnel did not wish or feel it appropriate for them to recommend decisions on the "minimum" or the "improved" levels of program opperations called for. The implications for top managers are that more policy decisions will be required, more interactions with program managers and staff will be necessary, and probably too little time will be scheduled for either of them. So, what else is new.

The ZBB Process Has Shown That the Merging of Programs and Program Levels Into an Organizational "Ranking" is a Very, Very Difficult Process

No matter what techniques are used, ranging from highly participative to highly autocratic, there is no easy way, and no one is ever completely satisfied. At HUD the ranking became especially important at the "mark," or the "ceiling" recommended by OMB. The game-playing around this point took many forms. Debates over which decision units or decision packages should end up above the line, and which below, were heated and numerous. There was a temptation to go with several "marks." Some managers proposed putting important programs below the line, thinking that during the subsequent steps of the approval process proponents would tend to move it above the line and not drop out an equal resource request. Others felt that this could result in "punishment" by the approving body for not recognizing the importance of the programs, and for placing it at such a low priority level.

The HUD budget office evaluation of the process found that:

> In addition, a substantial amount of time was spent by top staff in developing an initial ranking list which they could then work from for changes. It is possible that there was an overconcentration on the ranking procedure to the detriment of innovative thinking. A possibility here would be to have MBRC staff develop an initial ranking—perhaps using the 1979 rankings as a base—which the MBRC could then revise as desired.

No matter how difficult or time-consuming the ranking process, however, it is a most valuable activity. It mixes the "apples and oranges" into the "fruit salad" that departments and agencies must live with in today's complex society. This expression of programs and levels in priority order, which has been sorely lacking in many organizations because it calls for difficult choice-making, should give employees a clearer idea of management's intent, and, that might be a morale booster.

ZBB will Almost Surely Require More Paperwork

More paperwork is something we are all against, at least in principle. Describing a program three or more times, once for each level, is bound to produce a greater volume of reading material and more budget figures to digest. For the HUD ZBB process, the amount of paper produced was almost exactly double that produced for the 1978 budget process. About the only way to reduce this will be to have the program management and budget staffs identify only the most vital items of information to be required, and eliminate as much duplication as possible in the budget submittals for each program level.

In this area, the HUD budget office evaluation concluded the following:

> While an effort was made to minimize the amount of paper going to top staff, the ZBB process is structured so as to create a vast quantity of paper, much of it duplicative. To a large extent, this is caused by OMB instructions on the process. We hope to be making paper reduction suggestions to the OMB—which we hope will be accepted.

ZBB is a Time and Staff Consuming Process

(But, what important management activity isn't.) The number of staff and top management hours spent on the HUD 1979 ZBB process was perhaps three or four times that normally used. The preparation of alternative program levels, the review of the many programs, the ranking process, and the deciding on final budget estimates and rankings consumed significant amounts of time. The HUD budget office evaluation concurred as follows.

> The process consumed too much top staff time. While the collegial approach to decision-making and the number of MBRC sessions required served a useful educational purpose, the drain on the time of top Departmental staff was extremely heavy. An attempt should be made in the future to minimize the number of sessions requiring the attendance of MBRC members. One possibility would be to have staff sessions to resolve such time consuming issues as whether or not minimum and current levels are correct and whether or not there should be intermediate levels. Top staff could resolve those areas where staff is in disagreement.

The Attitude of Staff People Toward ZBB Will Be Most Important

The management and budget staffs throughout an organization must be willing to try to make ZBB work. At HUD, the ZBB process went as smoothly as could be expected, because the Budget Staff approached it with a positive, though not overly enthusiastic outlook. Al Kliman, HUD budget director, and Herb Persil, deputy budget director, maintained a positive attitude toward ZBB, and were supported in their efforts by Bill Medina, assistant secretary for administration, and Vince Hearing, deputy assistant secretary for administration. This was especially visible in their briefing and training of program managers, program budget staffs, and office managers and directors throughout HUD. They developed a "reasonable" set of guidelines consistent with OMB Bulletin 77-9, which all federal departments and agencies were to follow. They didn't "push," but they "gently nudged" the program budget staffs through the preparation process. They did the same to the Management and Budget

Review Committee (MBRC) during the ranking process, and even followed this pattern with the secretary during her deliberations on final ZBB rankings and decisions. At each stage of the process, they effectively integrated traditional budgeting practices with the ZBB processes, without losing sight of the ZBB intent.

The Organization and Management Information Office under Rod Symmes, and the Systems Development Office under Dave Albright provided positive support in developing a computer based ranking system. As concluded in the HUD budget office evaluation:

> The introduction of ADP assistance into the budget decisionmaking process was extremely useful. Without it, it is unlikely that the vast number of decision packages could have been handled and, without it, massive delays would have been built in while manual accumulations were laboriously prepared. A number of suggestions have been made for using ADP help more effectively during the 1980 process. We should start to review the basic systems used to determine if improvements are necessary and possible as well as determine whether or not more advanced equipment would aid in the process.

Consistent With the Above, Top Managers Should Also Approach ZBB With a Positive Attitude

They should honestly describe "minimum" program levels as well as "current" or "improved" levels. They should attempt to relate programs to organizational goals and rank each, whether it is their own program or not, in accordance with overall importance to accomplishment of organizational goals. They should work as a team in ironing out conflicts and developing a unified budget that would represent a sound expenditure of funds in each program area. In short, top managers must attempt to consider the superordinate organizational needs and goals if the organization's best interest are to be served. For the most part, this behavior prevailed during HUD's ZBB process.

ZBB Relates to All Other Management Systems That Demand the Time of Top Managers

ZBB is only one managerial responsibility, but it is closely tied to all the others. Personnel decisions are directly linked to budget decisions. Policy issue identification, analysis, and decision-making tie in to budget decisions. Legislative proposals and hearings affect the budget. Program evaluation, productivity, and work measurement outputs should be used in preparing budgetary requests. Organizational goal-setting and objectives-setting influence, and are influenced by the budget. In short, managers spend their time engaged in a number of managerial activities, and all too often the linkages between these are not totally understood.

At HUD the ties between ZBB and other management responsibilities became clearer during the ZBB process, and were developed for even greater clarity in preparation for the 1980 ZBB process. The HUD budget office evaluation addressed the following four associated managerial activities as follows.

> *Goals were set too late in the process.* In fact, because of time constraints and OMB requirements, we worked exactly backwards. First, we established decision units (since OMB wanted them quickly), then we set objectives for each decision unit (this was needed so staff could start preparing basic estimates), and then we developed our goals. In fact the process, ideally, should have been just the reverse. The result was that objectives and decision units had to be updated constantly to reflect the new goals.
>
> *Issue Papers.* The business of writing and rewriting issues papers was one of the most awkward, time-consuming, paper-producing, and least understood parts of the process. There were too many papers. There were papers being written on other non-MBRC processes—some of which related to the budget process and some of which did not. There was a tendency on the part of MBRC members to add ''favorite'' issues which only increased the workload and paper production without adding to the body of analysis necessary for knowledgeable decision-making. Of course, OMB added to the problem with its list of issues and subsequent changes. But, as a first priority, we must get our house in order on a logical, disciplined, limited, and integrated issues process.
>
> *Legislative.* While an attempt was made to integrate legislative considerations with budget review, the basic process of substantive legislative review did not occur until the very end of the process. The result was a hurried effort to develop a legislative program for submission to OMB. In addition, there appeared to be a confusion of roles between Administration, General Counsel, and Legislation and Intergovernmental Relations. For the 1980 process, a firm legislative timetable must be worked out, giving sufficient time for OGC staff analysis. It is also clear that, while the attempt to integrate legislative review into the budget process was nobly inspired, the technical problems of legislative development tend to be shunted aside by the exigencies of dollar determinations. It may be that a parallel—rather than an integrated—process is required.
>
> *Staffing.* The handling of the staffing packages caused much extra work because the program packages changed in scope and depth. The staffing on the program packages and the staffing-only packages had to be constantly adjusted. We will have to think about a smoother way of dealing with this matter.

Top Managers Must Know the Origins and Sponsorship of ZBB

Finally, top managers must know the origins and sponsorship of ZBB. All at HUD are now aware that President Carter is the prime ''sponsor'' of ZBB, federal-style, and is committed to its use. He was comfortable with it as governor of the state of Georgia, and sincerely felt it would help him and his cabinet as they put together the federal budget estimates each year. He particularly seemed to feel that it aided him in learning about and understanding the many governmental programs for which he was responsible in Georgia, and will again be valuable in that vein in the federal government. Some of HUD's newer managers also learned more about the role OMB plays as the president's key staff for budget preparation and stewardship over the ZBB process.

The HUD budget office evaluation contained a recommendation that would strengthen the "sponsorship" within the department as follows.

> *Involvement of the secretary.* Except for the secretary's involvement in the setting of goals and objectives, she was isolated from the basic review process. As a result, when MBRC recommendations were submitted to her, she was "cold" with insufficient background on the issues and recommendations to provide the quick response required by the timetable. In addition, items and issues which she wished considered were not included in the estimates. As a result, much backtracking had to be done to develop new information and estimates, thus adding to the delays in submitting materials to OMB and adding to the already heavy paper burden. A major priority consideration, therefore, in the development of the 1980 process must be a method of involving the secretary at all steps of the process, keeping in mind, of course, the other demands on her time.

The foregoing represents only a few of the things learned about ZBB at HUD. I suspect we shall know more about what we learned, and what we ought to learn, as experience is gained. The important thing is not to overlook or totally forget experiences with ZBB because we feel it will soon be replaced. It may be with us for awhile, like PPBS in the Defense Department.

It is suspected that these lessons are not earth-shattering and that many were indeed predicted. But they are valuable in that action was taken as a result. As was noted, steps were taken to improve the 1980 zero base budgeting process in HUD, and the general attitude seemed to be positive. HUD top managers were more concerned with ensuring that programs are funded adequately and managed well than they were with criticizing the processes and mechanisms used. At least, they appeared to feel that ZBB was workable at HUD.

Notes

1. For a more detailed description of the president's and OMB's thinking on ZBB, see Donald Haider's article, "Zero-Base: Federal Style," in *Public Administration Review*, Volume 37, No. 4 (July/August, 1977), pp. 400-07.
2. Title later changed to Assistant Secretary for Neighborhood and Voluntary Associations and Consumer Protection.
3. This occurred in one instance. A program manager assigned a 10 to all of his decision units. This was picked up by the undersecretary since each program manager had to identify himself or herself on his or her score sheet. After a private session with the program manager in question, at which the undersecretary "encouraged rule-following," the program manager changed his rankings to indicate appropriate differences in importance and relevance to HUD goals.

3.

Zero-Base Budgeting in ACTION

Emerson Markham

Describing very recent history—and the introduction of zero-based budgeting is very recent history—poses special problems. One is that the introductory period isn't over. Congress must pass the appropriation bills growing out of the process, and the departments and agencies must carry out the programs, i.e. execute the approved budgets. A second problem is the sensitive nature of this process, which could be obstructed if I were to give a full and frank disclosure of all the personalities and strategies employed in ACTION's first ZBB exercise. Therefore, I will attempt to describe only what transpired. If the *whys* and *whos* are not explicit—I must beg the reader's indulgence.

ACTION

ACTION is a relatively new federal agency. It came into existence on July 1, 1971, and included in one agency a number of the government's programs for sponsoring volunteer activities. The best known is undoubtedly the Peace Corps, previously an independent agency. ACTION also included Peace Corps' domestic counterpart, Volunteers in Service to America (VISTA), from the old Office of Economic Opportunity; the Foster Grandparent Program (FGP) and Retired Senior Volunteer Person's (RSVP) Program from the Administration on Aging in HEW; and the Senior Corps of Retired Executives (SCORE) and Active Corps of Executives (ACE) from the Small Business Administration.[1]

Subsequently, ACTION added two other significant programs, University Year in ACTION (UYA), which gave grants to colleges and universities to allow students to spend a year of their college career on a volunteer activity, and Senior Companions, which encourage older Americans to volunteer, through small stipends, transportation expenses and other support, to help other less able older Americans. In addition, ACTION engaged in a number of smaller activities, mostly experimental, to demonstrate the usefulness of volunteers.

Like other agencies with social programs, significant cuts were proposed in ACTION's last two budgets submitted under the Ford administration. Congress restored the funds in FY 1977 and the FY 1978 budget was amended by the incoming Carter administration to roughly its previous level.

The Structure of ZBB in ACTION

From the beginning, zero-base budgeting was inextricably interwoven with two key factors. The first was that it was a new process being implemented by a new administration eager to establish control over the course of events. The second was the determination of the ACTION director to shift the focus of attention in the agency from volunteers to the work the volunteers did for the people they served. This quickly became known as an emphasis on "basic human needs" (BHN).

These factors first converged in the consideration of the basic structure to be used in building a zero-base budget. Since ACTION's internal organization, its accounting system, and its information systems[2] are designed around its programs (Peace Corps, VISTA, etc.), these seem to be the logical ZBB building blocks. They met the definitions contained in OMB Bulletin A-11, so it was decided relatively early that they would be used in the presentation to OMB. However, since they did not adequately represent the new administration's goals, it was decided to build an internal system based on a categorization of the ways in which volunteer services meet basic human needs.

Two task forces comprised of those displaying interest were formed, largely on an ad hoc basis. One was in the international area, and one in the domestic area. Starting in late June and working into July, all projects were eventually amalgamated into a single structure containing nine major groupings:[3] Health and Nutrition, Food and Water, Knowledge and Skills, Economic Development Income, Housing, Energy and Conservation, Community Services, Legal Rights, All Other.

Policy Review

Starting in mid-July, a series of meetings was held to review the program proposals of the operating organizations. Each program was divided into basic human needs categories. The director presided, and all meetings were attended by the deputy director and the assistant director for policy and planning.[4] Appropriate staff members were present—typically there were 25-30 people at each meeting, representing all of the important players.

Two major types of questions were discussed, and to some extent resolved. Pressures were on the Peace Corps and the Older American Programs to plan for more projects in the areas of greatest need. Health and Nutrition became the preferred area of the new leadership, followed by Food and Water. Since a large part of the Peace Corps' program had been geared to Teaching English as a Foreign Language (TEFL), pressure was exerted to move away from this area. With respect to older Americans, it became apparent that Retired Senior Volunteer Program information was not readily available to determine the needs being served by these volunteers. A major telephone survey was used to obtain sample information, and the program was tagged for further review.

With respect to zero-base budgeting specifically, minimum levels were generally proposed at close to the current services level, and not taken seriously. Pressure by the Budget Division to reduce minimum levels resulted in the director establishing them at about 80 percent of current services, with some variations.

Current services were generally proposed at significantly higher dollars than planned for FY 1978. Here a strategy evolved. It was decided to hold current services at roughly the same dollar costs as in FY 1978 so that we could concentrate on incremental packages in discussions with OMB and the president.

Ranking Strategy

A number of agencies objected to OMB's (and the president's) insistence on ranking all agency programs against each other, particularly since OMB did not intend to interrank programs between agencies. In ACTION, this was accentuated by the desire to have Peace Corps ranked against other federal international programs. Since these were reviewed by a different part of OMB, the agency found itself urging that its programs be separated and reviewed in two parts of OMB. This would have corresponded to the congressional review process in which ACTION's programs are covered by two appropriations. The International Program (Peace Corps) is authorized by the Foreign Assistance Subcommittee in the Senate and the House Committee on International Relations, and its appropriations are approved by the Subcommittee on Foreign Operations in the House and the Senate. Its domestic authorization requests are heard by the Subcommittee on Economic Development and Regional Affairs in the House[5] and the Subcommittee on Child and Human Development in the Senate. Domestic appropriations are approved by the subcommittees for Labor-HEW in both the House and Senate. The number of committees involved for a small agency with approximately $200 million in appropriations appears unreasonable, but is rooted in committee jurisdictions established prior to ACTION's formation.

Needless to say, OMB took a dim view of our suggestion. However, an examiner from the International Division participated in OMB's review of the Peace Corps, and in the end, three rankings were forwarded to OMB: one for international programs, one for domestic programs, and a combined one for the entire agency.

In view of ACTION's stagnant funding history, it was apparent rather early in the process that the new leadership wanted substantial increases in the full-time volunteer programs as the highest priority in revitalizing the agency. As mentioned previously, current services were deliberately held at prior year levels to concentrate on the increments which would accomplish this. It was assumed that OMB would "mark-up"[6] the agency's requests at the current services level, and that the agency would appeal the next increments to the president.

The ranking process resulted in still another significant decision. A number of ACTION's offices serve both the international and domestic programs, notably by performing recruitment and administrative functions, and are split between its appropriations by formula. Budgets for these organizations were developed not only at the minimum, current services, and incremental levels, but also at 80 percent of current services level. When these were included in the rankings, they loomed so large that they were eliminated as separate units and were pro-rated over the programs. As a result, no support programs appeared in the rankings. The proration resulted in problems when OMB reductions were made since they did not accurately reflect support costs associated with the programs. In addition, these costs were not well understood and were therefore resented by program people.

Budget Preparation

The initial submissions of decision packages were made by the program offices in cooperation with the Office of Policy and Planning. Quality varied significantly. When questions could not be resolved between the program offices and the Budget Division, they were sent to the director's office for resolution.

The most glaring deficiency in this stage of the process was the lack of quantitative information and the lack of evaluations suitable for supporting policy decisions. A second problem centered around the difficulty of clarifying the differences in what would be achieved at the minimum, current services, and incremental levels.

Despite the fact that there was constant revision almost to the printing date, the budget was submitted to OMB on its due-date September 1. It consisted of 29 packages (another nine were considered but not requested) and 168 pages which was only 1 page more than the prior year. Little additional paper work, therefore, actually developed from the new requirements. However, this ignores the fact that later, in December, another submission of 40 decision packages and 134 pages organized by Basic Human Needs rather than programs was made. Also, in previous years the OMB submission had been a preview to the congressional submission. But, since ZBB was radically different, substantial additional work was required in January to prepare the congressional submission.

Presidential Review

ACTION, being a small agency, was usually reviewed early by OMB—the formal review (one-half day) was generally in the first week of October. This was preceded by a week, or so, of reviews within the agency. OMB's schedule was such that things moved faster for the FY 1979 budget. A formal review was held almost immediately in September, followed by two other reviews with OMB examiner personnel.

In early December, at the time the mark-up was received, two significant actions had taken place. The president had personally reviewed the agency's proposals along with OMB's recommendations and OMB examiners were permitted to attend.[7] It was made clear that a "reclama"[8] would be entertained. The mark-up utilized the ZBB ranking to an extent. One agency program was eliminated at the current services level despite the fact that the agency had ranked it ahead of proposed increments. The first incremental program was not granted, but a second increment was granted in part. In total the agency received a $4 million increase (roughly two percent) in the mark-up.

Reclama

The reclama was influenced by two factors. First, in the three-month period between the original submission and the president's mark-up a number of changes had taken place in ACTION. Three more presidential appointees, and a number of other important appointments had been made. Several programs had received substantial further consideration, reorganization decisions had been made, and new potential activities had been determined. Given the fact that reclamas couldn't be made on all programs, three major areas for appeal were decided upon. While they were all in the original proposal, their priority and character had changed. When presented to OMB, they were all relatively successful, and no further appeal to the president was necessary.

Preliminary Assessment

As far as ACTION is concerned, the sweat and gore shed during the ZBB process were not in vain, although some of the consequences are inseparable from the effects of a new administration.

1. For the first time since the agency's formation, significant increases are proposed in its budget—in excess of 10 percent. In addition, small supplementals were included for FY 1978.
2. The process represented the first opportunity to significantly refocus ACTION programs toward the meeting of basic human needs.
3. The ranking system focused the sense of priorities and at least two programs were sharply changed because of it.
4. Plans are proceeding to use ZBB at the lowest budget levels (by country, internation-

ally; by state, domestically) for internal operations in FY 1979, and as a basis for the preparation of the budget submission for FY 1980.

Notes

1. The latter two programs were transferred back to Small Business Administration in 1975.
2. ACTION's information systems were, and are, incomplete. However, volunteers can be associated with the appropriate programs and counted with reasonable accuracy.
3. There were no international projects in Legal Rights; no domestic projects in Food and Water.
4. These were the presidential appointees who were on board long enough to be involved in the process.
5. Authorizations for Older Americans are proposed by still another unit of the Committee on Human Resources: the Subcommittee on Aging.
6. "Mark-up" means to change an agency's submission, generally by reductions.
7. This is hardly a consequence of ZBB, but it does say something about the president's style. It significantly improved OMB feedback.
8. A "reclama" is the agency's appeal of a "mark-up."

4.

Fundamentals of Budgeting and ZBB

Jerome A. Miles

From the start of the republic in 1789 until the year of my birth, 1931, the federal government spent a total of about $100 billion. Thirty-one years later, in 1962, the federal government spent over $100 billion in a single year. Nine years later, in 1971, the federal budget broke the $200 billion barrier. In four more years, 1975, it reached the $300 billion mark and in 1977, federal spending exceeded $400 billion. Estimates for 1979 indicate that the government will spend over $500 billion.

It is not my purpose to comment on why federal spending has increased so rapidly in recent years nor to analyze the effect this level of spending has had on our economy. Rather, I would make the point that this tremendous rate of growth has generated numerous expressions of concern both inside and outside government.

Following World War II, a period when annual federal spending approached the $100 billion mark, a number of reforms were instituted. The first Hoover Commission made recommendations regarding the organization and management of the federal government. A Budget and Accounting Act was passed. This act mandated cost-based budgets. Sound, business-type accounting principles were thought to be the solution to the government's spending problems. But federal spending kept increasing.

In the mid-1960s, PPB (Planning, Programming, and Budgeting) was created. By this time the federal government had cracked the $100 billion mark. Economists were charged with putting the rein on federal expenditures. Later, as spending rolled over the $300 billion mark, a new administration instituted another business technique, Management by Objectives (MBO). Professional managers with business backgrounds were asked to slow the growth in spending. We are now in the age of zero-base budgeting (ZBB) and once again federal budget experts are charged with responsibility for balancing the budget by 1981.

It is not my intent to compare budget systems nor to comment on their

71

effectiveness. This brief history is intended to show the level of concern which has been demonstrated during the past 30 years over the cost of operating federal programs. There is, in the minds of many people inside and outside government, a way to control federal spending if only we can find the right tools. There is an implication that we are running programs which are not effective and which should be reduced or eliminated . There is general widespread acceptance of the fact that even those programs which are important to the public are not being run efficiently. Consequently, budget systems have been devised to curtail ineffective programs and to make government more efficient.

Simply stated, ZBB has the same intent. However, it can also be looked upon as a systematic way to produce a set of products. The set of products which we produced in the Department of Agriculture included our legislative program, our budget, and a study agenda—a list of programs and issues which need further analysis before the next budget.

There are certain fundamentals basic to any budget or management system. These fundamentals are also essential elements of ZBB. In this article I will discuss the fundamentals of budgeting and relate these to ZBB.

Budgeting Fundamentals and ZBB

First, any budgeting system requires a structure. The budget for a major agency is presented to Congress on an appropriation account basis. In most cases these accounts reflect the organizational units of a department. As budget reform occurred over the last 30 years, program budgeting became the rule, and appropriation accounts or budget activities within these accounts were normally based on operating programs of the organization. In PPB the basic line items were called program elements. In ZBB they are called decision units. The structure is important, but an agency can sometimes spend too much time trying to come up with a perfect structure, i.e., an ideal list of programs. In fact, any rational list of programs will work.

The key to the selection of appropriate decision units relates to the second fundamental of any budgetary process, the development of objectives for each program or decision unit.

A business has its balance sheet. Government agencies also have a type of balance sheet. While it does not show profits or losses, it can specify the achievement or nonachievement of objectives. These objectives must be expressed clearly and quantitatively. If Congress passes laws designed to feed needy people who are hungry, we should be able to find out how many such people there are and how many of this group we are actually feeding. If we have housing programs to move needy people out of substandard housing into adequate housing, it should not be difficult to state our objective and measure our progress toward the achievement of that objective. Any sound budget or management system must be built on this premise.

Third, there is generally more than one road to take between where we are and where we want to go. In ZBB we systematically look at alternatives. What is the best route a government agency can take to achieve its objectives? Current laws and administrative procedures can be changed and one of the outputs of a ZBB system should be legislative and administrative reform proposals.

Programs almost always can be operated at various dollar and manpower levels. In ZBB a formal system exists to describe minimum, reduced, current, and increased levels. Ironically, ZBB, which many feel provides a smooth curve from zero resources and zero outputs to maximum resources and maximum outputs, actually produces an incremental budget. The first increment should be below current spending and current output levels with successive increments to the recommended level.

The final fundamental of a good budget system is the setting of program priorities. In ZBB, decision packages are ranked from highest to lowest. In any budget system, however, if the requests exceed the total resources available, and they almost always will, policy officials must determine priorities. In the usual budget system, programs are either ranked in or out of the budget. In ZBB, the rankings form a comprehensive list of priorities.

The ZBB system then, incorporates the five fundamentals of a good budget system—structure, objectives, alternatives, levels, and priorities. When the process has been completed, however, it produces more than an annual budget.

ZBB and the Potential for Change

In considering alternatives which an agency recommends to achieve program objectives, we must look at possible changes in the law or in administrative regulations. Sometimes even different dollar levels require changes in the law or procedures, as in the case of so-called entitlement programs where the law dictates eligibility and the amount to be paid each eligible recipient.

Basically there are two types of authorizations. The first is an annual authorization which sets forth the level at which a program should be operated in the ensuing fiscal year. The development of proposals for such authorizations is not significantly different from the budget process itself. The second type of authorization involves changes in permanent or long-term legislation. Changes in such legislation are more difficult to achieve, since both the executive and legislative branches can choose to retain the status quo—always a powerful temptation. To successfully change legislation requires a thorough evaluation of existing programs, objective analysis of alternatives, and persuasive arguments for change. The ZBB process should produce the essential elements to effect changes in authorizations and appropriations.

A third and often overlooked output of the ZBB process is the study agenda for the next year. As soon as the budget process is completed and the secretary submits the budget to OMB, the agency should begin its next series of analyses. During the consideration of the budget and legislative programs, a number of promising alternatives will have been advanced but rejected because of weaknesses either in their analysis or presentation. Those which appear to be of merit should be targeted for consideration in the next year.

Budget analysis cannot be performed successfully after the budget is submitted for policy review. There is not enough time to do any kind of exhaustive analysis after the documents begin to flow. Program and budget analysis, if it is to be effectively carried out, must be done in those quiet months when the pressure of deadlines is less severe.

There is never an end to budget problems. The passage of an appropriation act does not end the budget cycle, but merely starts the phase which we call budget execution. Getting the right amount of money to each subunit of the organization after an appropriation is passed is a problem often overlooked in budget literature. Yet, bureau-level budget analysts spend most of their time allocating and reallocating funds, trying to get their agency's work done within the resources provided and at the same time meeting all the new problems that have developed since the budget was submitted more than a year earlier. Analysts involved in day-to-day budgeting cannot be expected to do the detailed program evaluation or policy analysis that must be carried out to make the ZBB process work. The ZBB system, then, should produce a legislative program and a study agenda in addition to the annual budget.

ZBB in USDA

I would now like to briefly evaluate the effectiveness of ZBB in the U.S. Department of Agriculture (USDA) during this first year. Insofar as the structure is concerned, the department has used a program structure for many years. In the mid-1960s, the department converted its internal budget structure completely to a program basis. Thus, for the past 10 or 12 years our budgets have been submitted to OMB using programs rather than organizations. For ZBB, we modified our program structure by combining some of the programs.

We reduced the 175 programs to 200 decision units at the secretarial level. However, this is still more decision units than a secretary and the top policy staff can be expected to handle. By next year we hope to reduce the number of decision units needing secretarial decisions even further. To do so, however, it is essential that agencies break each of the secretarial decision units into smaller components. The ZBB concept contemplates the development of decision units at the lowest level in the organization and aggregation of these units into larger packages as they move up the organization. This part of the system is not yet working well. The secretarial decision unit structure was largely developed by the central staff. Only a few agencies were able to disaggregate these units and apply ZBB processes at the lowest levels in their organization. This part of the system will have to be improved next year.

I suspect that it will be several years before we are able to develop a structure which is entirely satisfactory. I also caution agencies not to spend too much time on the development of structures. ZBB is not the endless summer. We are not looking for the perfect wave. ZBB is a dynamic process and the structure has to be flexible enough to accommodate changes in programs as well as changes in policy staff preferences. When one considers the average tenure of an assistant secretary in the government to be less than two years, the need for flexibility becomes obvious.

Further, although the decision unit structure will almost never coincide completely with an appropriation structure, cross walks can be easily developed if one is aware of the appropriation structure when developing decision units. Congress is slow to change its appropriation structure. Unlike the executive branch where one can expect a relatively rapid turnover in policy officials, changes in Congress are slower. Even with the new rules in Congress, congressmen generally do not become chairmen of committees or subcommittees until they have served for a number of years. Having served for a period of time on a committee, most congressmen are unwilling to spend much time and effort in restructuring the information submitted to them by the executive branch. Further, they tend to place a great deal of reliance on historical trends and incremental changes. They will undoubtedly continue to do so.

The next essential element of a budgeting system, the development of objectives, appears simple but it can be one of the most difficult to perform well. Most of us tend to express objectives in such general terms as improve, strengthen, coordinate, and other nebulous words which are impossible to quantify and which do not provide means for holding program managers accountable. If we are operating a housing program for needy families, we should be able to state the objectives of such a program in relatively precise terms without resorting to generalities. Consequently, the development of an adequate statement of objectives must be given a high priority in the ZBB process and is one which needs substantial improvement.

The third fundamental discussed earlier is the consideration of alternative means for achieving agency objectives. Here again a tremendous amount of work needs to be done if we are to successfully implement ZBB techniques. Government programs and policies require the concurrence of policy officials in many different political institutions. Generally agency officials, secretarial officers, central agencies such as the Office of Management and Budget, the Council of Economic Advisers, and Treasury, the White House, and finally Congress must all agree before a law can be changed. Once a bureaucrat has run this gamut and received an approved program plan, and the program has been audited by the General Accounting Office and his agency's internal audit staff, investigated by congressional investigators, and accepted by the editorial writers in the newspapers, he is not anxious to seek changes. Government officials are not, by and large, risk takers. The rewards for taking risks in the federal service are slight. Top salaries are frozen so promotions for ambitious executives are more for the ego than the pocketbook. Every mistake may be seized upon and made into a political issue. Unfortunately, although this is a very necessary and important part of our system, it tends to severely restrict initiative. Even elected or appointed political officials, once they have assumed office, become cautious about implementing the changes they so desperately sought when they were on the outside looking in. This environment makes the consideration of alternatives very difficult, yet this is one of the key elements of the ZBB system and one which must be rigorously pursued.

The next step in the process is the examination of different resource levels. Here again bureaucrats tend to be reluctant to seriously examine program levels below current levels. They realize that serious reductions in program levels will very likely be criticized, not only by the clientele groups which an agency serves, but also by the agency's own employees. Often the employees within an agency form the most powerful clientele group supporting the programs which that agency administers. Although government employees are subject to the Hatch Act, they can always write their congressman, and many congressmen are delighted to hear the inside story as told by a concerned bureaucrat.

Nevertheless, most programs can be operated effectively at a number of different levels. Programs can be stretched out to be completed over a period of 20 years instead of 10 years if resources are severely limited. Priorities can be established so that programs deal with the neediest or the most severe problems first. Some problems can be dealt with perhaps more effectively by state or local units of government. All of these options and many more can be examined to form the basis for different program levels. Again, however, this is not easily done. Tremendous pressures are exerted to maintain the status quo.

Finally, there is the matter of priorities and rankings. In USDA, we attempted to place our programs into four bands. These four bands were described in ZBB language as minimum, reduced, current, and increased bands. The minimum band represented those programs which it was felt must be carried on by the federal government and the levels at which they should be funded. There is no point in ranking programs at this stage since they share a common high priority.

However, the department did rank all programs above the minimum level. Before ranking them, they were divided into three other bands and the programs within each band ranked. We believe this gives decision makers sufficient flexibility to make decisions, especially since the total of our minimum band was well below current services.

In summary, the ZBB system is an orderly, systematic, management process. It includes all of the essential elements of an effective budget system. If properly carried out, it produces a budget, changes in policy—legislative as well as administrative—and the basis for determining analysis required in future years.

Its application for the first year was not wholly successful. However, its lack of success came about because of the time pressures within which it had to be installed, the problems attendant to changes in leadership, and the natural reluctance of the bureaucracy toward change. Each of these can be overcome. The system should be retained in its current form for a sufficient length of time to be properly implemented.

5.

ZBB: Not a Panacea, But a Definite Plus:
An OMB Perspective

Nanette M. Blandin and Arnold E. Donahue

It is obviously difficult to isolate one variable, in this case zero-base budgeting, and analyze the impact it has had on the Office of Management and Budget's review of the 1979 budget and on the final fate of the president's budget. There are too many other variables which influence these, including administration policies and priorities, fiscal restraints, new players in the budgetary arena, the political process, etc. Nevertheless, ZBB was a specific campaign promise, and ZBB is now a reality in the federal government. It is a discreet initiative that will no doubt be probed, evaluated, praised, and criticized for some time to come. Such assessments are healthy because they encourage practitioners and academicians to reflect on the process—what worked, what didn't, and why?—and because they can positively influence future change efforts.

We have approached ZBB from an analytic point of view and believe that it would be unfair at this point to render a final judgment. By the time ZBB was officially required as a basis for the preparation of the 1979 budget, many agency budgets were well under way. Thus, it cannot be said that all the 1979 budget submissions were 100-percent ZBB-conceived. Many were, in effect, hybrid documents—initially designed along traditional, incremental lines, and later reconfigured to conform to ZBB guidelines. Also, who is in the best position to make such a judgment is subject to debate. Budget decisions are not the exclusive domain of any one organization or any one person. They are made and influenced at various stages by different players, including program managers, agency budget officers, agency heads, OMB, the president, and Congress. Thus, we suggest that the extent to which ZBB was used by OMB and the president is an important ingredient in assessing ZBB's first year, but should not be prima facie evidence that ZBB either did or did not "work." We suggest that interim judgments and eventual verdicts on ZBB not be based on budget results, e.g., dollars saved, programs expanded, project funding reduced, etc., but rather on the value of the process to all concerned and on the quality of the decision-making process.

This article focuses on two major questions: (1) How did ZBB affect OMB's staff level review of agency budget requests? (2) How was ZBB utilized in the higher levels of OMB and in the presidential decision-making process? The majority of observations are based on our review of the National Foreign Intelligence Program. While there are some differences in the way OMB's Intelligence Branch operates, the budget review process is virtually identical to that of other OMB budget review units. While we have consulted with various OMB colleagues, this article does not represent an official OMB assessment of ZBB.

OMB Presidential Budget Review and Decision-Making: An Overview

To understand the OMB budget review process, it is important to understand OMB's role as an intermediary between the president and the departments and agencies. One of OMB's prime roles is to serve as a communicator of the president's expressed or implied policies and priorities—be they fiscal, pro-grammatic, or political—and the interests of the departments and agencies. Even when these are reasonably congruent, it takes detailed understanding of both to translate the president's objectives into specific agency activities or, conversely, to relate agency programs to the president's interests. OMB's role is a direct function of the president's need for a staff element that provides, in an independent and objective manner, information about, and analyses of, federal resource requirements and issues, particularly as they relate to presidential interests, and to see that these presidential interests are effectively carried out.

The fall budget season is a time when these processes merge—when agencies communicate their programs and interests to OMB in terms of resource needs, and when presidential policies and priorities are communicated in hundreds of specific decisions resulting in the executive branch's formal budget request to the Congress. Naturally, presidential and agency interests during the formula-tion stages are extremely diverse. OMB must, therefore, be prepared to analyze agency budget requests from a variety of perspectives, including fiscal/economic, outyear impact, program effectiveness and efficiency, object class, pricing, policy, cross-program, government-wide, intergovernmental, and so on. OMB's ability to perform its responsibilities is directly related to its ability to collect, digest, and synthesize information. Thus, information is an essential commodity to OMB. Collecting information is a year-long process, and OMB staff rely upon a multitude of information channels, including agency contacts, formal studies, briefings, informal surveys, publications, and agency docu-ments. The relative value of these information sources varies considerably. However, it is generally agreed that the agency's formal budget submission and the budget hearings which amplify on information contained in the submission are the most comprehensive sources of budgetary information, and, to the extent that the quality of information contained in them can be improved, OMB's ability to perform its responsibilities is enhanced.

While OMB budget examiners review agency budgets in considerable detail, the material which floats upward through OMB's leadership and to the president must, of necessity, be in an aggregated form. For example, for the Director's Review and the Presidential Review sessions, 10 consolidated decision units were presented for the National Foreign Intelligence Program. This is a reality at this stage of any budget process—at higher levels of review the scope is broader, and the need for aggregation is more important. This should be kept in mind, particularly as we discuss the influence of ZBB on presidential decision-making.

Impact of ZBB

Our view is that ZBB was an integral and important part of OMB's review of the 1979 budget. There were two major reasons for this. First, OMB approached ZBB with a generally positive spirit. This was due to the strong and persistent cues that the president was really serious about ZBB. Also, since OMB was given a major role in helping to implement ZBB, OMB staff felt responsible for ensuring it worked as effectively as possible. In all fairness, it should be noted that OMB staff members did not jump on the ZBB bandwagon without some skepticism. This skepticism was related to the organization's experiences with the ups and downs of past attempts to systemize federal budgeting (e.g., PPBS and MBO). As familiarity with ZBB, its terms, and its techniques grew, the skepticism seemed to dissipate rather quickly, and most people in OMB sincerely believed that the government had something to gain from ZBB. In large part, we attribute this to the flexibility built into the ZBB process, flexibility that is essential in so diverse and complicated an enterprise as the U.S. government. Second, most federal agencies took ZBB seriously and tried to implement it in a meaningful way. Thus, OMB received what the president wanted: 1979 budget requests based on ZBB. As ZBB gained momentum, a kind of synergism took place. Agencies which had invested time and interest in ZBB tended to become advocates of the process, creating an additional pressure that ZBB be used throughout the FY 1979 review cycle.

The most tangible ZBB outputs reflected in agencies' budget submissions were decision unit structures, decision packages, and agency-wide rankings. How each of these was utilized in the review and decision-making process is discussed below.

Decision Unit Structure

ZBB required that agencys' budgets be organized along programmatic lines, with decision units rather than organizational breakouts. This is not unique to ZBB, and, in fact, many agencies had previously used a programmatic format.

Nonetheless, ZBB did formalize and standardize this requirement. Also, because OMB had an early opportunity to endorse decision unit structures, we could better insure that certain program areas were given appropriate visibility in the budget, and the potential for cross-program analyses was enhanced. For example, in concert with the Intelligence Community Staff, OMB developed standard decision units for all National Foreign Intelligence Program Components. This helped examiners aggregate like programs for analytic purposes, and enabled presentation of increasingly aggregated decision units for internal OMB and presidential review where there was common understanding between OMB and the agencies. Indeed, after discussion and agreement on the structure and aggregation of decision units, there were—for intelligence—no disagreements from individual program managers up to the president. Everyone knew and accepted that activity X would be treated, compared, contrasted, and evaluated in terms of a known set of comparable activities. This was not uniform within OMB. Other branches felt compelled to restructure agency-submitted units into new aggregations, unknown to program managers when they prepared their rationale and justification.

Nonetheless, the decision unit structure, however formulated, provided OMB senior officials and the president an opportunity to see resource trends by major program activities and to better ascertain where possible trade-offs could be made.

Decision Packages

The use of decision packages, or different funding levels for a given decision unit, lies at the heart of ZBB. Ideally, it enables program managers and budget examiners to get a good feel for the impact of reduced and enhanced resources on the agency's ability to achieve programmatic objectives. Further, it encourages explicit articulation of a program's objectives and an assessment of alternative means of achieving these objectives.

We suggest that the value of these ZBB features is yet to be fully realized, since they are admittedly difficult requirements. Also, we feel compelled to point out that if agencies didn't achieve an exemplary performance in meeting these requirements, it was not the fault of ZBB. For example, the identification of a minimum decision package, or the funding level below which program objectives could not be pursued, is difficult both to conceptualize and to implement. But it is a critical ZBB building block. When an agency protects current resources in the minimum decision package, we're right back to incremental budgeting. To overcome this tendency, many agencies established arbitrary guidelines which defined the minimum at 80 percent or 90 percent of the current package. Clearly, this surrogate minimum does not conform to ZBB philosophy. Yet there just aren't many incentives for a program manager to identify a "real" minimum funding level. At OMB we have tried to discount the vulnerability factor. In other words, if a program manager develops meaningful decision packages, his/her program won't ipso facto be jeopardized. While this held true in our review of the National Foreign Intelligence Program, we cannot make any assertions about its validity throughout OMB. Unless specific incentives are provided, we suspect that time alone will sort this out. We continue to believe that meaningful decision packages hold the real key to ZBB's success.

Other areas of relative weakness were agencies' statements of program objectives, review of alternative means of accomplishing objectives, and programmatic evaluations of the impact of different funding levels. These are inherent difficulties with any budgeting system. The ZBB format, however, does tend to highlight these deficiencies.

Despite these problems, our assessment is that decision packages provided OMB with more and better information about agency programs, provided an improved analytic framework for many budget issues, increased OMB's focus on the agency's funding base, and deemphasized attention to year-to-year resource changes. Further, because OMB staff had an improved opportunity to review the impact of enhanced funding levels on the achievement of program objectives, we believe ZBB tended to downplay OMB's negative, budgetcutting image.

Decision packages were also of value in decision making, but their full potential was limited by two factors. First, unlike decision unit aggregations, the increasing aggregation of decision packages was a source of some conflict. While it was generally accepted that the minimum of all subordinate decision units did not necessarily equate to an aggregated minimum, there was significantly less common understanding on what new minimum, current, or enhanced levels should be. The different consolidation approaches used by the agencies, coupled with the difficulty of identifying "true" minimum levels, resulted in OMB staff having to construct aggregated decision packages. For example, the minimum level developed by OMB staff for the Intelligence Community's intelligence production programs in no way corresponded to a minimum package identified by the intelligence agencies, either singly or as a whole. This seems to have been the case widely in OMB and it caused some confusion between OMB and the agencies about what the various aggregated levels represented. Second, not all budget issues were automatically highlighted by decision packages. In these cases, traditional OMB issue papers were used, or the issue was forced into a ZBB format. Decision packages seemed to be most applicable to decisions about program level and to decisions on issues that had clearly definable funding alternatives. To the extent that other budget issues can be dealt with in the context of a broader decision unit, the decision-making process will gain further benefits from ZBB.

Ranking

While ranking doesn't pose the same technical difficulties as decision pack-ages, it probably was the ZBB requirement most difficult to implement from a bureaucratic/political point of view. The requirement to rank all decision packages precluded agencies from making the traditional argument that every-thing in their budget is equally important, and forced them, in an explicit and "public" manner, to prioritize all activities. This created considerable bureau-cratic struggles. But after the fact, many people, both in the agencies and OMB, believe that ranking was one of the more successful aspects of the first year's experience with ZBB.

In OMB, we believe ranking was of greatest benefit as a conveyor of information. Most examiners believe that the agencies' ranking reflected a fair, meaningful, and candid portrayal of priorities. Agency rankings were reviewed by OMB staff to ascertain major trends, to see where items of presidential interest were ranked, to see if any "Washington monuments" could be found, and generally to gain an appreciation of agency priorities.

Other uses of agency rankings are more difficult to pinpoint. Indeed, all budget decisions can be interpreted as a reranking or a modification to agency rankings. Our view is that the rankings were widely used as a major input to the decision-making process but were not by any means the sole decisionmaking focus. In some cases, the absence of agreement on decision package aggrega-tions meant that aggregated packages presented to senior OMB officials and the president were unranked, or rather were mixed-ranked packages, and it was difficult to convey the agency's true priorities as they related to budget issues. This, in turn, hampered, but was not the only factor that prevented, the development of cross-agency rankings that would have resulted in a com-prehensive national statement of budget priorities. Nonetheless, since the budget issues in a given program area were the primary focus of the process, the rankings at the margin were of considerable value to decision makers. When final budget decisions were being made, the rankings highlighted the implica-tions of alternative decision options.

There were also less visible benefits of ZBB. For instance, the active involvement of program managers in the ZBB process enhanced their ability to discuss budget requests and to respond to OMB's questions. And in many agencies, more people were involved in the budget process, thus broadening the range of inputs, encouraging greater attention to resource considerations, and promoting communication within the agency about program priorities and expectations.

As can be expected with any change effort of this magnitude, there were some negative aspects to ZBB. However, these related more to what ZBB did not do, rather than to problems directly caused by ZBB. For example, some OMB staff members believe that ZBB obscured the real budget issues. It would be more valid to say that ZBB did not automatically highlight all types of budget issues. We believe it is unrealistic to expect any budgeting system to neatly lay out all the issues. Also, many OMB staff members claim that ZBB did not provide sufficient output/productivity analyses. While we tend to agree that this kind of information was lacking or inadequate, we do not place the blame on ZBB. This is a general weakness of budgets and one which is more substance-than process-related. A negative comment about ZBB that we have heard rather frequently is that it increased the amount of materials the agencies were required to submit and that OMB was required to review. Thus, many believe that the workload, both in the agencies and in OMB, was greater because of ZBB. We believe this is probably a legitimate observation but do not necessarily regard it as a negative feature. Paperwork and workload factors need to be reviewed in context (i.e., did the additional materials improve the quality of the budget process?). OMB and the agencies have a mutual interest in balancing the need for meaningful information with the need to minimize paper and unnecessary work. Achievement of an improved balance in these areas will require a continuing dialogue between OMB and the agencies.

In summary, while no one we talked with believed ZBB to be a panacea, most OMB staff members agree that ZBB is a definite plus. The substantive input needs to be improved, as was the case pre-ZBB. Also, ZBB alone won't automatically meet all of OMB's information needs. Our view is that ZBB's inaugural year has demonstrated that ZBB is indeed applicable to the federal government, has been used effectively by the agencies, and has had a positive influence on the budget review process.

Further Improvements

We will take this opportunity to make some general observations about what we think can and should be improved in the ZBB process.

First, we believe agency and OMB staffs need to agree on both a decision unit structure and a structure of aggregation that both can live with and that will meet the president's needs. We do not mean to imply that this structure should be sacrosanct; obviously, as agency and presidential priorities and interests shift, adjustments will be required.

Second, agreement on reasonable minimum, current, and enhanced levels for packages and for aggregations of packages needs to be sought. We would tend to avoid a textbook definition of these levels, particularly at aggregated levels, but rather search for common understanding based on the tried and true principle of reasonableness.

Third, rankings at the aggregated package level are needed to minimize confusion. This is obviously heavily dependent on the package agreements mentioned above. In addition, we think the agencies, OMB, and the president would benefit from cross-department rankings. The budget decision process would benefit from knowing whether the president valued $100 million more in social security benefits greater than $100 million more in housing, defense, or foreign assistance.

Also, there needs to be better articulation on the part of the departments as to the rationale, criteria, or basis for their rankings, and on the part of OMB for their disagreement with them. It is not sufficient to know that the department ranked package X as high priority without also understanding why.

Finally, the agencies, OMB, and the president need to address other problems inherent in federal fiscal management that were highlighted by the ZBB process. For example, ZBB should promote better program evaluation within the agencies. More work is needed in developing output and productivity measures and in strengthening cost/effectiveness analyses, and OMB and the president should think creatively about ways in which ZBB can serve not only as a budget tool but as a program planning mechanism and as a vehicle for transmitting national priorities.

6.

Zero-Base Budgeting in Georgia State Government: Myth and Reality*

Thomas P. Lauth

Introduction

This article on zero-base budgeting presents an analysis of information obtained in a series of interviews with budgetary personnel in Georgia state government. Georgia was the first state to install zero-base budgeting,[1] and it is currently one of the states with the most highly developed ZBB process.[2] The Georgia system also gained national attention during the 1976 presidential campaign as the leading example of ZBB applications in governmental budgeting.[3] For these reasons the Georgia experience is an important source of information about the impact of ZBB on traditional budgeting practices.

Much of the early literature dealing with ZBB focused on defining it and describing its formal procedures.[4] Subsequent writings have assessed the adaptability of ZBB techniques to public organization,[5] speculated about their impact on those organizations,[6] and described the problems attendant to installing the system.[7] Advocates of ZBB have praised it as an innovative management tool,[8] while critics have expressed doubt that it represents much that is new.[9] Absent from the literature, however, is an empirical analysis of the impact of ZBB on budgetmakers and the budgetary process. This paper provides such an analysis.

The Myths and the Rhetoric

The initial claims made on behalf of ZBB were impressive but exaggerated, with promises far exceeding the likelihood of performance. The ZBB label was in many ways its own worst enemy. The label implies *tabula rasa* budgeting—an approach which would wipe the financial slate clean at the beginning of each fiscal year by assuming that an agency has no base from the previous year upon which to predicate its budget requests for the forthcoming year. According to such an interpretation each agency would build its budget requests from the bottom up without referring to the past as either guide for, or a constraint upon the future. Taken literally, a zero-base budget would seem to imply no base at all. Each program would be on trial for its life every year.[10]

While students of public budgeting easily recognized the absurdity of such a characterization, others seem to have been less certain about the extent to which proponents of ZBB actually expected budget decisions to be made by starting at point zero.[11] Confusion over the precise meaning of ''zero-base'' was unfortunately compounded by the statements of the then-governor of Georgia, Jimmy Carter—the leading public advocate of ZBB. In his 1971 Budget Message to the Georgia General Assembly Governor Carter stated:

> No longer can we take for granted the existing budget base and simply be responsible for reviewing proposed increases to continue programs and add new ones . . . . I will insist that the entire range of State services be re-examined and will cut back or eliminate established programs if they are judged to be ineffective or of low priority.[12]

On another occasion Governor Carter said: ''We stripped down our budget each year to zero and we start (sic) from scratch . . . we try to optimize the service delivered to our people compared to how much it costs.''[13] In 1976, presidential candidate Carter wrote: ''Zero-base budgeting starts from a very different premise (The comparison was with what he referred to as the traditional approach.) Rather than just incrementing the new on the old, the system demands a total rejustification of everything from scratch—from zero!''[14] While these statements can be dismissed as political hyperbole, they did lend credence to the most exaggerated caricature of ZBB. Thus, the combined effect of the ZBB label and the statements of Jimmy Carter both as governor of Georgia and as presidential candidate contributed to the misunderstanding about what ZBB entails for public budget-makers.

ZBB in Georgia: An Operational Definition

In actual practice ZBB is substantially different from its caricature. As operationalized in Georgia, ZBB is a set of budget preparation techniques designed to improve managerial control over agency funding requests so as to improve efficiency within the executive branch in the allocation of available resources. This is not a new objective; nor is ZBB the only set of techniques through which improvements in efficiency can be attempted. The uniqueness of ZBB is in the way in which it formats information.

In Georgia all departments of state government are broken down into activities which in turn are divided into programs. A program is the lowest organizational subdivision at which it is considered practical to maintain cost data. The budget request for each program is formulated in a series of decision packages which identify different levels of effort as well as alternate means for performing the same function. Decision packages are ranked in order of priority at each operating level within the organization. The manager at the next organizational level reviews the rankings and produces an aggregate ranking for all packages presented to him from below. This process continues until final rankings are completed at the departmental level.[15]

The underlying assumption of ZBB is that the ranking process for the forthcoming fiscal year will operate so as to focus attention on those packages at the margin—just above and just below the funding level of the current fiscal year. The corollary assumption is that with budget request information presented in this format there is a greater likelihood of some programs being decreased at the margin rather than increased.[16] The myths and the rhetoric notwithstanding, this is the crux of the ZBB approach in Georgia. One purpose of this paper is to analyze why there is such an incongruity between the caricature of ZBB and the claims made about it, and the operational reality which developed.

ZBB: An Alternative to Incrementalism?

While the ZBB label and the Carter statements tended to cloud rather than clarify the exact meaning of zero-base budgeting, neither are as troublesome as the assertions made by George S. Minmier that zero-base budgeting brought an end to "incrementalism" in budget-making in Georgia. Minmier's writings are the most widely referenced sources of information about ZBB in practice. In his otherwise useful studies of budget reform in Georgia he writes: "Prior to the change to the zero-base budgeting system Georgia had used an incremental budgeting system." Elsewhere the idea is repeated: "Under the former incremental system;" and " . . . the incremental budget system previously employed."[17] The clear implication is that at some point in time incremental decisionmaking stopped and a new mode of decision-making was installed.

That incremental decision-making played a very important role in the budgeting process in the state of Georgia prior to the advent of zero-base budgeting has been well documented by the research of Augustus B. Turnbull.[18] Minmier would have us believe, however, that incrementalism ceased after the installation of zero-base procedures. That is a dubious suggestion at best. Since "incrementalism" is not a set of budget procedures which are ever formally installed, but rather a concept which characterizes a set of practices used by budgetmakers to facilitate decision-making,[19] it is possible that despite the introduction of a new budget delivery process budgeters may continue to build budgets incrementally. A change in procedures does not necessarily alter behavior. Whether or not ZBB altered the behavior of budgeters is an empirical question. Thus, the second purpose of this paper is to assess the extent to which ZBB, a rational budget innovation, succeeded in penetrating the routines[20] of the traditional, incremental budgetary process in the state of Georgia.

Research Method

The research methodology employed was patterned after the approach used by Davis and Ripley in their 1965 study of U.S. Bureau of the Budget personnel.[21] Thirty-six interviews were conducted in 1977 with individuals actively involved in the budgeting process of the state of Georgia.[22] Respondents included the heads of both the Budget and Planning Divisions, Office of Planning and Budget; budget analysts and planners, Office of Planning and Budget; the Legislative Budget Analyst and the Deputy Legislative Budget Analyst; and the chief budget officers of twenty-eight executive branch agencies.[23]

Respondents were asked to reply to a series of openended questions about both their participation in the budget process and their interpretations of the working of the zero-base budget system. Since the ZBB approach operates almost exclusively during the preparation and submission phase of the budget cycle, the interviews focused primarily on matters related to that phase of the process. The same topics were pursued in every interview, but the precise wording of the questions and the order in which they were considered varied from one interview to the next. The length of the interviews ranged from 45 minutes to one and one-half hours. The average interview was one hour.

Defining the "Base"

If zero-base budgeting is a nonincremental approach to budgeting, evidence of the change from incremental decision-making practices to nonincremental practices should have been evident by 1977 in the way in which budgeters described their approach to the task of budget preparation. In zero-base budgeting the preparation of decision packages is the critical decision point where changed budgeting behavior would be expected. It is at this juncture that agency program needs are articulated and cost estimates assigned to programs.

In order to assess the extent to which budget requests were being built from the ground up with basic programs rejustified annually, agency budget officers were asked to describe the manner in which they proceed in the preparation of their annual budget requests. None of the twenty-eight agency budget officers interviewed described his/her approach in terms of a systematic reconsideration of existing agency programs and operations. The notion that budgetmakers start from zero or that programs and agencies are annually on trial for their lives was rejected by all of those interviewed. Without specifically using the language of incrementalism, most described an approach to budget preparation that is characteristic of the incremental approach to decision-making. Budgeters in Georgia tend to assume that agency programs will be continued at very close to, or slightly above, the current level. Ths following comments made by budget officers will serve to illustrate the point:[24]

> Zero-base is OK in theory, but I need to go back and find out where I am by looking at where I've been. I look at last year's budget and start from there.
>
> I look at the experience of last year's budget.
>
> We do "continuation" budgeting.
>
> I look at last year's budget. I rely on the auditor's report of actual expenditures, and figure in inflation. Then I figure in the number of people to be added, less the number of people to be separated; that gives you the number of people you need to pay. Salaries plus current expenses with inflation taken into account and you have it. After that we start to consider any new activities which we are not now doing.
>
> We look at last year's budget, figure inflation and required salary increases and try to anticipate likely increases in client requests.
>
> You have to do "continuation" budgeting because that is the way the legislature thinks.
>
> We calculate the amount we want . . . that is our best guess as to what the governor would be willing to recommend to the legislature . . . add in a little for the analyst to cut—he has a job to do, I understand that. Then we develop justification for the increase over last year . . . you don't have to justify what the legislature has already given you in the past—why should you?
>
> We start from scratch. By that I mean we use last year's expenditures as a bench mark. Then we begin to worry with what we will need to stay up with increased costs. After that we consider expansion of our operations. How else would you do it? Now under the new zero base system you have to do more justification for the "new or improved" levels of service.
>
> Except for the new forms, there has been no change in the way I make the budget.

Budgeters operate in a complex world of conflicting values and goals in which it is often difficult to sort out the interrelationship among policies, or predict the consequences of courses of action. In order to survive in such an environment budgetmakers in Georgia report that they have adopted strategies which aid them in making decisions. Rather than reconsidering their programs anew each year or attempting to consider the consequences of all alternative courses of action, they rely heavily on past experience. Even in ZBB the "base" is the historic base, not zero-base.

A unique feature of the zero-base budgeting format which also bears closely on the incrementalism issue is the ''minimum'' funding level. In Georgia, agencies are presently required to submit decision packages for each program at three levels of operations: minimum (less than 100 percent of the current funding level); current (continuance of last year's programs including increased costs); and new or improved (expansion of program objectives).[25] While no exact funding level is specified for the ''minimum'' in the budget preparation instructions given to agencies by the Office of Planning and Budget, the general consensus among both agency budget officers and OPB analysts is that the minimum level is approximately 85 percent of the current level. Information about the impact of the minimum level requirement is important to an understanding of the extent to which ZBB was able to penetrate the existing routines of budgeting because the very idea of recommending a funding level below the current level runs counter to the incremental strategy of protecting the base.

In order to assess the impact of the minimum level requirement on budget preparation and submission, agency budget officers were asked to comment on (1) the way in which they determine the minimum level, and (2) the impact of that requirement on the budgetary process. The following responses are indicative of the way in which budgeters view the minimum funding level requirement:

> The minimum is not very useful except that it may contribute to a more frugal attitude about the budget. I suppose that's why they have it. We have never had to live with anything close to the minimum level.

> We determine the current level first, then drop back to 80 percent or whatever the minimum level is supposed to be this year.

> The minimum level is not of much use . . . we work backward to get it.

> The minimum is a waste of time . . . no one looks at that. We determine where we want to be and work back to 85 percent.

> The minimum level is a pain in the ass. It is inconceivable that you would only fund 85 percent of current level.

> No one pays any attention to it. In 1975 when we had to rework our budgets because of the revenue shortage, we made cuts without any reference to the minimum. You certainly could not expect anyone to come up with 10 percent in each program. Some programs are untouchable. We would get 10 percent department-wide by taking most of it out of a couple of less important programs.

> The minimum level is worthless. We (Legislative Budget Office) don't look at it . . . the departments merely take their 'current' and lop off 10 or 15 percent to satisfy the requirement of submitting a minimum funding level.

> See that machine over there? (A desk calculator) I prepare my current level which to my way of thinking is not the same dollars as this year, but what it will take to provide the same level of services . . . then I hit those keys and multiply by .85 of the current to get the minimum.

The minimum is less threatening than you might think . . . the departments know that we (Office of Planning and Budget) don't intend to recommend that their programs be funded at that level. But, it makes them think about the possibility of a cut rather than always expecting more.

Another feature of ZBB which relates to the incrementalism issue is the ranking process. When ranking, managers usually give higher priority to the packages that satisfy essential operating requirements and lower rankings to more discretionary packages. In Georgia the "minimum" level is generally placed higher than the "current," and the "current" levels for the most activities tend to be ranked ahead of "new or improved" for any other activity. As a practical matter the ranking process concentrates on only a small segment of package rankings—those which might be regarded as marginal.

The budget format in Georgia makes available to decision-makers a cumulative total for each additional decision package entered into the rank order. Decision-makers know that if they recommend, for example, the funding of a thirteenth ranked package, then the cumulative total will be increased from perhaps 108 percent (at the twelfth ranked package) to perhaps 110 percent of last year's level. The consequences of recommending the thirteenth ranked package (which may actually be some "new or improved" level for a particular program) is thus known to be an increase of 2 percent over the next highest ranked package. It is also known that a recommended funding at the level will constitute an increase of 10 percent over the previous year's level for the department. The rankings depict incremental levels of effort.[26] The effect of this process is to reduce the number of packages receiving close consideration. An OPB official pointed out that in practice budget analysis is concentrated on those packages falling between 85 and 110 percent levels. Agency budget officers suggest that the range of OPB scrutiny is even smaller—somewhere between 95 and 110 percent levels.

In summary, agency budget officers reported that in building next year's budget the funding level of the previous year is a very useful starting point. Agency budgets are not reviewed as a whole every year for the purpose of reevaluating existing programs. In formulating budget requests agencies seek to protect the integrity of the existing base, and attempt to increase and expand the base by getting their share of whatever new funds are available. The requirement that a "minimum" funding level be identified seems to have little bearing on that budget preparation strategy, and the ranking process has facilitated rather than terminated marginal analysis. The budget preparation process in the state of Georgia conforms much more closely to Peter Pyhrr's idea that "a logical starting point for determining next year's needs is the current year's operation,"[27] than to former Governor Carter's notion that ZBB demands "total rejustification of everything from scratch—from zero."

Incremental Outputs?

The evidence obtained from interview sources strongly suggests that actors in the budgetary process in the state of Georgia continue to build budgets incrementally despite the procedural innovation called zero-base budgeting. However, as Bailey and O'Connor have pointed out, it is important to distinguish between incrementalism as a decision-making process and incremental budget outcomes. These are "separate but theoretically linked aspects" of the same concept.[28]

Incrementalism as a *process* characterizes the behavior of decision-makers, while incrementalism as *outcomes* refers to adjustments in existing policies. The former denotes a bargaining process among actors as well as individual intellectual responses to complexity.[29] The latter denotes marginal changes in agency funding levels from one year to the next. The literature often assumes that an incremental decision-making process will result in incremental budgeting outcomes, and that incremental outcomes are evidence of an incremental process. While that connection is intuitively compelling, it is not logically required.

Even though ZBB is essentially a managerial approach to budgeting which stresses efficiency and effectiveness of operations, rather than a planning approach which purports to redirect governmental goals and objectives,[30] the ever-present implication has been that ZBB could be expected to change budgetary outcomes in Georgia.

In order to assess the extent to which services were cut back and/or established programs eliminated because they were "judged to be ineffective or of low priority,"[31] budgetary outcomes for all agencies of Georgia state government between FY 1973 (the first year of ZBB) and FY 1978 were analyzed. Table 6.1 summarizes the annual percent change in appropriations for each department for the fiscal years through 1978.

When the most stringent definition of incrementalism is used—change in appropriation level of less than 10 percent—it is discovered that 49.3 percent of budgetary outcomes in the state of Georgia during the era of zero-base budgeting were incremental.[32] (If a less stringent standard of 15 percent is used, 65.0 percent of all budgetary outcomes were incremental. If Wildavsky's extravagant standard of 30 percent[33] is used, 87.1 percent can be characterized as incremental.) However, of those outcomes which can be considered nonincremental according to the most stringent definition (71 of 140 cases or 50.7 percent of all budgetary outcomes), only 16.9 percent (12 of 71 cases) were reductions in appropriation levels. In short, only 8.6 percent (12 of 140 cases) of the budgetary outcomes in the state of Georgia during the zero-base budgeting era were nonincremental reductions in appropriation levels. The remainder of the reductions in appropriation levels were "decremental" (or less than 10 percent).

Table 6.1
Summary of Percent Change in Departmental Appropriations FY 1973-1978

Number of Departments Per Fiscal Year

Percent Change	FY73 to FY74	FY74 to FY75	FY75 to FY76	FY76 to FY77	FY77 to FY78	FY73 to FY78	Cumulative Total
0-5%	3 (11.1)	11 (40.7)	8 (28.6)	20 (71.4)	6 (20.0)	48 (34.3)	34.3
6-10%	1 (3.7)	4 (14.8)	6 (21.4)	3 (10.7)	7 (23.3)	21 (15.0)	49.3
11-15%	3 (11.1)	3 (11.1)	5 (17.9)	0 (0.0)	11 (36.7)	22 (15.7)	65.0
16-20%	4 (14.8)	3 (11.1)	2 (7.1)	2 (7.1)	3 (10.0)	14 (10.0)	75.0
21-30%	8 (29.6)	4 (14.8)	2 (7.1)	1 (3.6)	2 (6.7)	17 (12.1)	87.1
31-40%	1 (3.7)	1 (3.7)	3 (10.7)	1 (3.6)	0 (0.0)	6 (4.3)	91.4
41-50%	1 (3.7)	0 (0.0)	0 (0.0)	1 (3.6)	1 (3.3)	3 (2.1)	93.5
51-100%	2 (7.4)	1 (3.7)	1 (3.6)	0 (0.0)	0 (0.0)	4 (2.9)	96.4
100%	4 (14.8)	0 (0.0)	1 (3.6)	0 (0.0)	0 (0.0)	5 (3.5)	100.0
TOTAL	27 (100.0)	27 (100.0)	28*(100.0)	28 (100.0)	30*(100.0)	140 (100.0)	

SOURCE: Compiled from data presented in State of Georgia, Office of Planning and Budget, *Budget Report - Volume I, Financial Display*, FY 1974, FY 1975, FY 1976, FY 1977, FY 1978, and FY 1979.

* Variation in the number of departments for which funds were appropriated each year is explained the following ways: beginning in 1975 the GBI was budgeted as an entity separate from the Department of Public Safety; beginning in 1977 the Department of Medical Assistance was budgeted as an entity separate from the Department of Human Resources; and beginning in 1977 the Georgia Franchise Practices Commission began receiving state appropriations.

Further evidence of the stability of budgeting outcomes in Georgia during this period can be seen from data presented in Table 6.2.[34] Departments have retained a rather consistent percentage of the total annual budget between 1973 and 1978. A comparison of the rank ordering of departments according to their percent of the total budget for the years 1973 and 1978 reveals very little difference (Spearman's Rank Correlation of 1978).

The data summarized in Tables 6.1 and 6.2 provide little support for the idea that zero-base budgeting enabled Georgia budgetmakers to effect substantial spending reductions through the elimination of programs. A caveat must be entered, however, regarding the use of departmental level budget output data as evidence of incremental budgeting. It is quite possible that within departments (at the division level) or within divisions (at the unit level) non-incremental changes occur from one year to the next. Indeed, Georgia OPB officials maintain that ZBB has enabled them to redirect funds at the micro-organizational level even though the savings achieved are not reflected in departmental budget totals due to the fact that the state was experiencing an overall growth in both revenue collections and expenditures between 1973 and 1978.[35] Zero-base budgeting is credited by those officials with slowing the rate of growth in the Georgia budget during that period.

There is, however, some additional evidence that suggests that departmental level data are not hiding significant spending reductions within departments. Minmier reported that through the fiscal year 1975 no apparent shift of financial resources could be identified which was attributable to zero-base budgeting. He pointed out that during the first three years of the zero-base budgeting system not a single instance could be identified where a function was funded at a level less than the previous fiscal year.[36] Eckert, using within-department budget categories, also suggested that ZBB did not significantly alter budget outcomes in Georgia through 1975.[37] Since there is no reason to expect that departmental level data are less reliable indicators for the 1975-78 period than they were for the 1973-75 period, it is unlikely that the departmental level data reported here misrepresent the impact of ZBB on budgetary outcomes in Georgia.

The Persistence of Incrementalism

In seeking an explanation for the continuation of incremental budgeting practices in Georgia despite the advent of zero-base budgeting, it is necessary to look at the political environment within which public budgetmakers operate. Budget preparation decisions are the products of political pressures and constraints exerted by actors and events outside the agency. At least six political constraints have been identified which operate to promote incremental approaches to budgeting in Georgia: (1) constitutional or statutory requirements; (2) public expectations that governmental activities will be continued at close to

Table 6.2

Departmental Appropriation as Percent of Total Appropriation—1973-1978

DEPARTMENT	FY 73	FY 74	FY 75	FY 76	FY 77	FY 78
Administrative Services	.737	.490	.562	1.106	1.445	1.368
Agriculture	.975	.984	.943	.845	.854	.824
Banking and Finance	.071	.069	.076	.086	.097	.097
Community Development[1]	.547	.672	.515	.953	.516	.473
Comptroller	.153	.169	.165	.178	.169	.144
Defense	.169	.130	.096	.088	.086	.112
Education	35.430	34.986	35.118	35.776	35.179	35.915
Employees Retirement[3]	-	-	.047	-	-	-
Forest Research Council	.038	.036	.036	.033	.031	.029
Forestry Commission	.553	.526	.529	.505	.512	.532
GBI	-	-	.398	.408	.393	.040
Franchise Practices Comm.	-	-	-	-	.002	.002
Financing and Investment Comm.[3]	-	-	-	-	-	-
OPB and Governor's Office	.316	.268	.302	.303	.301	.300
Human Resources	19.691	18.544	19.836	20.587	19.850	19.289[2]
Labor	.217	.138	.139	.182	.182	.181
Law	.106	.102	.116	.118	.118	.115
Merit System[3]	-	-	-	-	-	-
Natural Resources	1.404	2.384	1.776	1.586	1.478	1.352
Offender Rehabilitation	1.993	2.483	2.077	2.537	2.564	2.790
Public Safety	1.525	1.379	1.289	1.336	1.293	1.298
Public School Emp. Retirement	.184	.448	.431	.457	.448	.393
Public Service Commission	.073	.119	.121	.122	.120	.120
Board of Regents	15.137	15.004	15.145	14.712	14.726	14.916
Revenue	1.253	1.136	1.346	.997	.993	.999
Scholarship Commission	.394	.454	.489	.517	.529	.512
Secretary of State	.346	.333	.341	.325	.335	.350
Soil and Water Conservation	.038	.029	.024	.024	.019	.018
Teachers Retirement	.030	.135	.087	.107	.104	.068
Transportation	16.634	14.156	15.253	14.201	13.279	13.657
Veteran Services	.368	.367	.391	.342	.345	.315
Workmen's Compensation Board	.066	.061	.090	.098	.104	.017
Other	1.552	4.398	2.262	1.471	8.520	3.954

[1] Beginning with FY 1979 Department of Community Development divided into Department of Community Affairs and Department of Industry and Trade

[2] Beginning with FY 1977 Department of Medical Assistance budgeted as separate department. For comparison purposes Department of Medical Assistance combined with Department of Human Resources in FY 1977 and FY 1978, in this table.

[3] Merit System funded by assessments to other State agencies; federal funds; and employer/employee health insurance contributions. It receives no direct State appropriations. The Georgia State Finance and Investment Commission is funded by service fees and no State fund appropriations are required. The Public Employees Retirement System is funded from pension accumulation funds and no direct State appropriation is received.

existing levels; (3) demands from interest groups concerned with the funding of new programs or the protection of existing ones; (4) the differing roles of central budget office personnel and agency budget officers; (5) legislative budget practices and procedures; and (6) the requirements of intergovernmental grant-in-aid programs.

For example, the Georgia Constitution requires the General Assembly to appropriate to the Department of Transportation an amount for highway purposes not less than the previous year's receipts from the motor fuel tax. At least that portion of the agency's budget (approximately 84 percent of its state appropriation for the 1978 fiscal year) is protected from zero-base considerations. Statutory requirements were also cited as justification for the continued funding of programs by agencies charged with economic regulation or the administration of retirement and other entitlement programs. As one agency budget officer put it, ''We were established by statute to regulate _____; to cut back our program would reduce our effectiveness—that would be a violation of the law.'' Another noted, ''So much of our program is specifically required by law that I cannot conceive of any major phase of it being eliminated without closing out our agency completely.'' Those budget officers contended that so long as the legislature does not intervene to modify their agency's statutory authority, they are protected from budget cuts by other actors within the executive branch.

The second constraint is closely related to the first. Budget officers contend that public expectations preclude the reconsideration of the historic base each year. Certain functions of government, they believe, are simply not going to be significantly reduced (much less eliminated) for reasons of economic efficiency no matter how compelling the data and analysis. The level of public sector responsibility for ameliorating social problems and providing social amenities has evolved over many decades. The political costs of breaking faith with citizens on matters which are thought to have been resolved in the past are very high. ZBB has not altered that political reality. Those who participate in preparing the budget tend to assume that agencies will continue to do about what they have been doing because the public in some general sense expects the continuation of programs. While no precise figures are available, budgetmakers in Georgia assume that a significant portion of the budget is ''uncontrollable'' each year.

Perhaps the most troublesome counterclaim to this line of argument is the contention that 278 government agencies were eliminated during the first year of zero-base budgeting in Georgia. The most persuasive interpretation of those events, however, is that the Executive Reorganization Plan of 1972 (which, among other things, reduced the number of state agencies from 300 to 22) happened to coincide with the initiation of the zero-base budgeting system. It should also be noted that only 65 of the 278 agencies ''eliminated'' were actually being funded at the time of their discontinuation. One veteran budget officer contended that only one agency (the Georgia Educational Improvement Council) was actually eliminated; all of the others were subsumed as part of the reorganization plan. It was also the opinion of most of those interviewed that ZBB should not be given credit for ferreting out the need for reorganization. An agency budget officer who had served as part of the reorganization team in 1971 noted: ''We had already identified duplication and proliferation of agencies by the time the first ZBB packages were prepared in the summer of 1971—but the packages did reaffirm what had been identified by separate investigation.''[38]

Interest group activity is a third constraint. Although interest group activities are perceived by budget officers to be an important part of the budgetary process, they report very few direct contacts with interest group representatives. Interest groups in Georgia tend to concentrate their efforts within the executive branch on department heads or the governor's office, rather than with agency budget officers. Nevertheless, budgetmakers believe that interest groups play an important role in maintaining continued support for existing programs. The comment made by one agency budget officer captures the opinions expressed by several others: "Those people who depend on what we are doing here get with their representatives in a big hurry if it looks like our budget is in trouble."

The differing role orientations of agency budget officers and OPB analysts place an additional constraint on the zero-base budgetary process. While the precise relationship between OPB analysts and agency budget officers varies according to the personalities of the individuals involved, the nature of the relationship dictates that it will be characterized by both cooperation and conflict. These officials need each other—the analyst needs the budget officer in order to learn about the agency program, and the budget officer needs the analyst in order to interpret the governor's priorities as they relate to his department. Yet despite this mutual need, the overriding fact remains that the analyst's principal responsibility as a representative of the governor's budget office is to find ways to control agency spending by recommending cuts in requests put forth by the agency. The agency budget officer, on the other hand, is an advocate for agency programs and an interpreter of agency problems. The process of negotiation through which OPB analysts and agency budget officers reconcile the competing demands of their individual role requirements, tends to be marginal adjustment. Stated quite simply by one agency budget officer, "The analyst gets paid to cut—so I try to protect against that by making sure that there is something to cut . . . we trade around the edges."

The manner in which the General Assembly considers the budget places yet another constraint on the ability of zero-base techniques to alter budgeting practices in Georgia. The budget law of Georgia requires the governor to submit a draft appropriation bill along with the Annual Budget Report. After the bill is introduced in the House of Representatives, a "continuation" appropriation bill is substituted for the governor's recommended version. The difference between the spending level in the House substitute and the level proposed by the governor is an amount which the legislature can then redistribute, decrease or increase according to its own priorities. For the most part the legislature is guided by the governor's recommendations, and agency budget officials emphasize the importance of having their requests included in the governor's recommended funding level.[39] What finally emerges as the annual appropriation bill is an admixture of the priorities of the legislature and those of the governor. The significance of this process for an understanding of the impact of ZBB is that in the reordering of priorities the legislature focuses attention mainly on the categories of "new or improved." The legislative tendency is to fund established programs while negotiating with the governor to determine which of the new items will be funded.

In analyzing the budget, the Legislative Budget Office simply does not use ZBB. The "minimum" level information and the activity statements (which explain and support funding requests) are regarded by legislative budget analysts as "worthless." "We throw most of that stuff in the can," said one analyst. Agencies report that the LBO frequently requests information from them directly regarding their appropriation requests. The Georgia General Assembly does "continuation" budgeting and that strongly biases the total process in the direction of incrementalism in budget preparation.

Intergovernmental aid also constrains budgetmakers. For the 1978 fiscal year the Georgia Department of Labor obtained less than 5 percent of its funds from state appropriations; the Departments of Community Development and Human Resources received approximately half of their funds from state appropriations; while the Department of Transportation received slightly less than two-thirds of its funds from state appropriations. The balance of funds in each case came largely from the federal government. Program and matching fund requirements which are part of federal grants-in-aid limit the ability of budgetmakers to alter existing programs significantly from one year to the next.

In short, incremental budgeting continues amid the procedures of zero-base budgeting because it serves participants well as a useful decision premise when operating within a political environment. The pervasive characteristic of that environment is pluralism.[40] According to this interpretation of American politics, conflicts among competing interests over the distribution of socioeconomic benefits and burdens are frequently resolved by negotiated and partial accommodations with which the participants can live, at least temporarily. Many of those accommodations are recorded annually with the adoption of the budget. By assuming that existing programs will normally be continued, political accommodations arrived at on earlier occasions by previous actors are reaffirmed and the range of political conflict is restricted. By asking "How can we adjust what we are doing?" rather than abrogating prior agreements and asking anew each year "What should we be doing?" conflict over basic values and public purposes is minimized. Zero-base budgeting has had a difficult time penetrating existing budgeting practices precisely because those traditional practices have served the political interests of most of the participants in budgetary process. In one sense ZBB did successfully penetrate the routines of building and justifying a budget in Georgia. The format and procedures of ZBB were installed throughout the government during the first year with only minor difficulties. In a more important sense, however, ZBB has failed to fundamentally change the decision rules used by those who prepare budgets in the state of Georgia.[41]

The Achievements of ZBB in Georgia

It would be easy to take the caricature of ZBB at face value[42] and conclude that it is simply a "fraud," a "farce," or "a fantasy in someone's head" (to quote three of the more cynical budgeters in Georgia). However, as another agency budget officer said: "Too many claims have been made for zero-base budgeting that are not true; unfortunately that overshadows the good points about it." What are the good points?

The most frequently cited advantage of ZBB is that it has improved both the quantity and quality of information available to managers about agency operations.[43] The following comments will serve to illustrate that point:

> Zero-base is a useful management control device. The forms require people to organize and develop their information. Managers are better able, I think, to make decisions on the basis of an improved reporting system.

> It provides good, useable information for managers. It certainly is an improvement over the way we used to do things.

> I like zero-base. We used to make up the budget in this office with very little communication with the operating people. Now the budget format makes us reach to the lowest levels for information—that has advantages for everyone even beyond putting together a budget.

> Managers have better information—that is its strength.

> The biggest advantage is the visibility which we now get of what our people are doing.

> Zero-base may not be liked by everyone (I personally had doubts about it in the first year when we had to put together all that information which we did not have on hand) but it benefits the people of Georgia because it contributes to better management.

ZBB also requires greater justification for funding requests than ever before in Georgia. Although bargaining between OPB analysts and agency budget officers continues, agency officials believe that they now have a greater burden to demonstrate why existing programs should be continued at the current level or new programs funded. Prior to ZBB the burden tended to be on the budget analyst to demonstrate why new programs should not be recommended for funding. ZBB has shifted the burden of justification to the operating agencies as the following statements will indicate:

> Zero-base requires us to justify what we are doing—even justify continuation to some extent.

> On balance it (ZBB) is an improvement . . . more justification is required. I'm not

always convinced that its an 'improvement' when we are doing it, but I guess I think that it is.

The budgets have less fat in them ... tighter ... more justification for the requests.

A greater interest in evaluation is another development which can be partially attributed to ZBB. It was perhaps inevitable that an approach to budgeting so committed to achieving efficiency in government would eventually address the matter of performance evaluation. As part of the 1978 fiscal year budget preparation process state agencies were required to develop evaluation measures to be included in their decision packages. Two types of measures were developed: (1) program effectiveness—defined as the degree to which a program achieves its objectives; and (2) workload efficiency—defined as the degree to which the program economically manages the workload associated with its objectives. A considerable amount of difficulty has been encountered in formulating meaningful and operational performance measures during the first year. That is partially due to the lack of experience in some agencies in dealing with the performance evaluation concept. It is also due to the inherent difficulty in evaluating many of the kinds of things government agencies do.[44] Nevertheless, a beginning has been made. Agencies have been charged with the responsibility for developing and implementing performance measures through which managerial control can be effectively achieved. Most of the performance evaluation measures developed by the agencies are workload efficiency measures rather than program effectiveness measures. Since ZBB is largely a management approach to budgeting those measures are not inappropriate.

Finally, zero-base budgeting is, in addition to being a set of budget preparation procedures, also a state of mind. Many budgeters have acquired the habit of thinking about efficiency in on-going programs as well as alternate ways of achieving program objectives. This is perhaps best expressed by the budget official who said, "Zero-base is useful in that it causes us to think about what we are doing ... Many other approaches to budgeting might do that, but zero-base is the one we happen to be using."

Conclusion

Those who expected ZBB to result in widespread program elimination and/or substantial cost reductions in the state of Georgia have been disappointed. The effects of ZBB have been much more moderate and subtle. Incremental budgeting persists and zero-base budgeting innovations have taken place within that constraint.

However, the most important question which this research leaves unanswered is the extent to which the marginal analysis techniques of ZBB have been successful in, and directly responsible for redistributing resources within programs at the micro-organizational level. Some budget officials in Georgia, particularly those in the central budget office, are of the opinion that capacity for redirection is the essence of ZBB, and that significant redirections have taken place. Agency budget officers tend to be less convinced that ZBB has produced very much redirection of funds, and aggregate data analysis has been unable to reveal subtle shifts.

Before an adequate assessment of the impact of ZBB at any level of government can be made, it will be necessary to devise a research strategy to address this important question. That task should occupy a high place on our future research agenda.

Notes

*The author wishes to thank the budget officials of the state of Georgia who gave so generously of their time and information to this study. The research reported here would not have been possible without their cooperation.

1. On January 15, 1971 Governor Jimmy Carter in the annual Budget Message to the General Assembly announced his intention to install zero-base budgeting for all areas of State government. The zero-base budgeting system was first used in preparing the budget for the 1973 fiscal year.
2. Allen Schick and Robert Keith, *Zero-Base Budgeting in the States* (Lexington, Kentucky: The Council of State Governments, 1976), p. 5.
3. Governor Carter's interest in zero-base budgeting is reported to have been the result of his having read Peter Pyhrr's article in the November-December 1970 issue of the *Harvard Business Review*. In that article Pyhrr describes the use of zero-base budgeting by Texas Instruments, Inc. Pyhrr was subsequently hired as a consultant to the Georgia Budget Bureau for the purpose of installing the new budget system in State government.
4. Peter A. Pyhrr, *Zero-Base Budgeting: A Practical Management Tool for Evaluating Expenses* (New York: John Wiley and Sons, Inc., 1973); Peter A. Pyhrr, "Zero-Base Budgeting," *Harvard Business Review*, Vol. 49, (November/December 1970), pp. 111-121; Charlie B. Tyer, "Zero-Base Budgeting: A Critical Analysis," *Southern Review of Public Administration*, Vol. 1, (June 1977), pp. 88-107; and Graeme M. Taylor, "Introduction to Zero-Base Budgeting," *The Bureaucrat*, Vol. 6, (Spring 1977), pp. 33-55.
5. Peter A. Pyhrr, "The Zero-Base Approach to Government Budgeting," *Public Administration Review*, Vol. 37, (January/February 1977), pp. 1-8; Aaron Wildavsky, *Budgeting: A Comparative Theory of Budgetary Processes* (Boston: Little, Brown and Company, 1975), at pp. 278-296; and Aaron Wildavsky and Arthur Hammand, "Comprehensive Versus Incremental Budgeting in the Department of Agriculture," *Administrative Science Quarterly*, Vol. 10, (December 1965), pp. 321-346.
6. Walter D. Broadnax, "Zero-Base Budgeting: New Directions for the Bureaucracy?" *The Bureaucrat*, Vol. 6, (Spring 1977), pp. 56-66.
7. Donald F. Haider, "Zero-Base: Federal Style," *Public Administration Review*, Vol. 37 (July/August 1977), pp. 401-407; George S. Minmier, *An Evaluation of*

the Zero-Base Budgeting System in Governmental Institutions (Atlanta, Georgia: Publishing Services Division, School of Business Administration, Georgia State University, 1975); and George S. Minmier and Roger H. Hermanson "A Look at Zero-Base Budgeting—The Georgia Experience," *Atlanta Economic Review* (July/August 1976), pp. 5-12.

8. In addition to the writings of Peter A. Pyhrr, see: Herbert P. Dooskin, "Zero-Base Budgeting: A Plus for Government," *National Civic Review*, Vol. 66, (March 1977), pp. 119-121; 144.

9. Robert N. Anthony, "Zero-Base Budgeting is a Fraud," *The Wall Street Journal*, April 27, 1977.

10. For a more extensive discussion of zero-base budgeting see Wildavsky and Hammond, *op. cit.*, pp. 322-325.

11. See the Communications to the Editor from F. Ted Herbert and Peter A. Pyhrr which appear in *Public Administration Review*, Vol. 37, (July/August 1977), pp. 438-439.

12. Budget Message to General Assembly, January 15, 1971.

13. Address by Governor Jimmy Carter—Charter Property Casualty Underwriters, September 12, 1974, in Frank Daniel, Compiler, *Address of Jimmy Carter* (Atlanta, Georgia: Georgia Department of Archives and History, 1975), p. 277.

14. A campaign paper written in mid-1976 and published in Logan M. Cheek, *Zero-Base Budgeting Comes of Age: What It Is and What It Takes to Make It Work* (New York: AMACOM, A Division of American Management Association, 1977), p. 297. A slightly altered version of the same statement appeared in *Nation's Business* (January 1977), p. 24.

15. For a more specific discussion of Georgia's budget preparation procedures see: State of Georgia, *General Budget Preparation Procedures: Fiscal Year 1978 Budget Development*, June, 1976.

16. Allen Schick has written that despite the exaggerated claims, marginal analysis is the actual intent of ZBB. Allen Schick, "Zero-Base Budgeting and Sunset: Redundancy or Symbiosis?" *The Bureaucrat*, Vol. 6 (Spring 1977), p. 16.

17. Minmier and Hermanson, *op. cit.*, pp. 5 and 8, and Minmier, *op. cit.*, p. 135.

18. Augustus B. Turnbull, III, "Politics in the Budgetary Process: The Case of Georgia " (Unpublished Doctoral Dissertation, University of Virginia, 1967).

19. Two important works dealing with the topic of incremental decision-making are Charles E. Lindblom, "The Science of 'Muddling Through,'" *Public Administration Review*, Vol. 19 (Spring 1959), pp. 79-88, and David Braybrooke and Charles E. Lindblom, *A Strategy of Decision* (New York: The Free Press, 1970). Incrementalism as it applies to public budgeting is discussed in Aaron Wildavsky, *The Politics of the Budgetary Process*, Second Edition (Boston: Little, Brown and Co., 1974).

20. Allen Schick has pointed out the importance of "penetrating the vital routines of putting together and justifying a budget" if budgetary reform is to be successful. Allen Schick, "A Death in the Bureaucracy: The Demise of Federal PPB," *Public Administration Review*, Vol. 33, (March/April 1973), p. 147.

21. James Davis and Randall B. Ripley, "The Bureau of the Budget and Executive Branch Agencies: Notes on Their Interaction," *The Journal of Politics*, Vol. 29, (November 1967), pp. 749-769.

22. It is hoped that the interview technique used in this research will partially accommodate Peter A. Pyhrr's admonition that those who write about Georgia budgeting should "personally visit and evaluate the process as it actually exists in total

instead of spending their time in university libraries." Peter A. Pyhrr, "Communication to the Editor," *Public Administration Review*, Vol. 37, (July/August 1977), p. 439.

23. The term "agency" is used here in the generic sense to include all those executive branch entities which for budgetary purposes are accorded separate consideration. Fifteen are actually designated as departments, the remainder are designated as boards, commissions, or systems. During the period 1973-78 the state of Georgia budgeted for thirty-two executive branch agencies. The twenty-eight agencies included in this study are highly representative of all executive branch agencies since they received 99.4 percent of the total appropriations to the executive branch for the 1978 fiscal year and they employed 99 percent of all executive branch personnel as of 1977.

24. No notes were taken during interviews. All quotations were derived from notes made immediately after each interview. Although quotations may slightly paraphrase the words actually spoken during the interview, great care has been exercised to ensure the accuracy of the ideas expressed. Where doubt existed as to the accuracy of the quotation, it was excluded.

It should be noted that respondents were not consistent with each other in the way they referred to the base budget year. Some referred to it as "last year," while others called it "this year" or the "current year." For the purpose of clarity a uniform reference i.e., last year, has been adopted.

25. Prior to the 1978 fiscal year decision packages for four levels of operation were submitted: minimum, base (same dollars as last year), workload (same level of program activity with cost increases reflected), and new or improved.

26. Pyhrr, "Zero-Base Budgeting," *op. cit.*, p. 114.

28. John J. Bailey and Robert J. O'Connor, "Operationalizing Incrementalism: Measuring the Muddles," *Public Administration Review*, Vol. 35, (January/February 1975), p. 61.

29. For a discussion of the distinction between a management orientation and a planning orientation in budgeting see Allen Schick, "The Road to PPB: The Stages of Budget Reform," *Public Administration Review*, Vol. 26, (December 1966), pp. 249-253.

30. Bailey and O'Connor, "Operationalizing Incrementalism," *op. cit.*

31. Governor Jimmy Carter, Budget Message to General Assembly, January 15, 1971.

32. The 10 percent cutting point for incrementalism has recently been used by Steven A. Schull, "An Application of Budgetary Theory: Incrementalism Reassessed," *Georgia Political Science Association Journal*, Vol. IV, (Spring 1976), pp. 21-42.

33. Wildavsky, *The Politics of the Budgetary Process, op. cit.*, p. 14.

34. The format for this table was suggested by Turnbull's presentation of similar data. Turnbull, *op. cit.*, p. 131.

35. Net revenue collections by the Georgia Department of Revenue for the years 1973 to 1978 showed a percent average increase per year of 12.5 percent. During the same period the budget experienced a percent average increase per year of 12.4 percent. See: State of Georgia, Department of Revenue, *Statistical Report 1977*, (November 1977), and State of Georgia, Office of Planning and Budget, *Budget Report Fiscal Year 1974* and *Budget Report Fiscal Year 1979*.

36. Minmier, *op. cit.*, pp. 130-131; 154-155; and 173.

37. William Albert Eckert, "Evaluating the Impact of Zero-Base Budgeting," Un-

published paper presented at the Annual Meeting of the Midwest Political Science Association, Chicago, Illinois, April 20-22, 1978.

38. Peter A. Pyhrr has also written that the need for reorganization was recognized before the start of zero-base budgeting in Georgia. Peter A. Pyhrr, *Zero-Base Budgeting: A Practical Management Tool for Evaluating Expenses, op. cit.*, p. 113.

39. This is consistent with Sharkansky's findings regarding the reliance of legislatures on gubernatorial budget recommendations. Ira Sharkansky, ''Agency Requests, Gubernatorial Support and Budget Success in State Legislatures,'' *The American Political Science Review*, Vol. LXII, (December 1968), pp. 1220-1231.

40. For a discussion of the relationship between pluralism and the budgetary process, see Allen Schick, ''Systems Politics and Systems Budgeting,'' *Public Administration Review*, Vol. 29, (March/April 1969), pp. 137-151.

41. Allen Schick has recently made a similar assessment of ZBB in the federal government. Allen Schick, ''The Road From ZBB,'' *Public Administration Review*, Vol. 38, (March/April 1978), p. 178.

42. Allen Schick has discussed the strategy of caricature as it was applied to PPB. Allen Schick, *Budget Innovation in the States* (Washington, D.C.: The Brookings Institution, 1971), pp. 200-201.

43. This amounts to a confirmation of similar findings reported by Minmier and Hermanson, *op. cit.*, p. 11.

44. For a discussion of this problem see: Harry P. Hatry, et al., *Practical Program Evaluation for State and Local Government Officials* (Washington, D.C.: The Urban Institute, 1973).

7.

ZBB Is Light-Years Away from Rural America

Daniel K. Wanamaker

A number of articles about zero-base budgeting (ZBB) have been accepted in academic and practitioner-oriented journals in the last two years (McGinnis; Minmier and Hermanson; Pyhrr; Rehfuss; Scheiring; Singleton, Smith, and Cleaveland; Tyer). Probably as a result of the Carter nomination and election, the topic of ZBB has been "selling like hotcakes." However, the idea of ZBB is light-years away from small town, rural America. In fact, ZBB like PPBS may pass from the governmental scene before the idea reaches the hinterlands. One reason for this is that governmental change in rural America is slow. As the former director of the Bureau of Intergovernmental Personnel Programs of the U.S. Civil Service Commission (currently Office of Personnel Management) commented, "Some people forget that an agenda for the city council meeting may be a governmental innovation in some communities" (Robertson). Unfortunately, this level of understanding of governmental activities in small cities is the exception rather than the rule. Many federal, state, and university officials do not recognize the problems connected with innovation in rural areas.

Difficulties to Face

Besides the problems of resistance to change, which are common in most organizations, small local governments face additional difficulties. First, many proposed changes are often difficult for local officials to understand. For example, some of the first revenue-sharing forms sent by the federal government were thrown away or misplaced, since some mayors did not know why the forms were sent (Stansbury). In other cases, local governments did not initially receive all the revenue-sharing funds for which they were eligible, since they did not keep all legitimate tax records in a form that they readily could identify these funds as "local tax effort" (Lodgson).

Second, most federal and state regulations and guidelines are written in a bureaucratic language that is beyond the comprehension of local officials. As a result, many federal and state programs have to be "explained" to local officials (Sundquist). For example, much of the time of circuit riding city managers employed by councils of governments or development districts is spent interpreting government programs for local officials (Wanmamaker, Stansbury).

Third, small town administrative personnel are often poorly paid. For instance, a recent salary survey in Kentucky found that the average salary for city clerks in cities between 2,500 and 5,000 population was $6,610 per year, while the average salary for postmasters in those same cities was $19,205 per year (Combs, Davis, and Roederer; Ryan). In cities between 500 and 2,500 population the average salary for city clerks was $5,631 while the average salary for postmasters in those cities was $18,383 (Combs, Davis, and Roederer; Ryan)[1] All of these factors, combined with the possibility of both political and personality clashes, contribute to the problems that often make governmental change in smaller communities difficult.

A Case Study

The following case study illustrates the problems of implementing and retaining the first formalized budgeting and accounting system in a small town. An appropriate title for this case is "ZBB Is Light-Years Away" or "How Can a City Use a Budget When the City Clerk Does Not Know How to Replace a Fuse?"

The Central State Council of Government (CSCOG), a cooperative association of local governments, had recently received a grant to hire a "roving city manager" to assist local governments in the CSCOG with their capital improvement programming. The executive director of CSCOG was enthusiastic about adding a new staff member who could provide a broad range of management services to the local governments in this nonmetropolitan area. Within a few months, Frank Scott was hired to be the new "circuit riding capital improvement specialist." Frank was well qualified for the position, as he previously had worked for two cities in the capital improvement area. In addition, he held a master's degree in public administration from a well-known university.

Frank was eager to begin his work in capital improvement programming; however, he soon found there were major obstacles in his way. Few, if any, of the small towns had a budget. Only the city of Harmon, which had both a professional city manager and finance director, had a formal budget. Hence, the adoption of an annual financial plan seemed to Frank to be needed before any small city could consider adopting a capital improvement budget.

Most of the smaller communities operated on the "shoebox system." Taxes and other forms of revenue such as income from water bills were collected at city hall and deposited in the city's checking account. All bills for office supplies, equipment and other expenses, including salaries, were put in a shoebox and paid by check on a first come, first serve basis. Frequently the city might discover midway or near the end of the "fiscal year" that there was not enough money in the city's bank account to pay the employees. This financial crisis was solved by the city fathers by going to the local bank and borrowing against the net year's anticipated tax receipts. This process of deficit financing for current operating expenses was common. Although most local officials in the area would have been suspicious of any ideas from New York City, they knew that "their" method of financing worked.

Frank Scott proceeded to discuss the advantages of instituting budgeting and accounting procedures with several city governing bodies in CSCOG. Some city council persons listened patiently, while others were not interested in the idea at all. Since Frank was not a native of the state and some of his ideas were from the "outside," Frank decided to try to find one community in the area that would adopt a city budget. This city could then serve as a local model for the other towns.

A Test Case

Finally, Frank Scott found a city council that was interested in developing a budget. Mapleton, a city of 1,200 population with a very small work force, was an ideal test case, since the new city clerk, Melba Furlong, liked the idea of having a town budget. Melba had had some bookkeeping courses in high school and Frank felt that she could understand both the purposes of the budget and its internal mechanics. Frank knew that he could piece together the budget based on what few records the city had kept in the past. However, he decided to talk over the idea with Tom Osborne, city manager of Harmon, a community of 50,000 population in CSCOG. Tom quickly called in his city finance director, Gene Wiley, to discuss the idea of developing a budget for Mapleton. After several meetings the three agreed that Frank would gather all the financial records he could from the city clerk, Melba Furlong. City Manager Osborne and Finance Director Wiley would develop a simplified budget and accounting system that they thought would work for a city the size of Mapleton, and one that the city clerk could understand.

Within a month the preliminary budget for Mapleton was developed. City Manager Osborne, Finance Director Wiley, and roving manager Scott made the presentation to the Mapleton City Council. After some discussion the city council decided to wait until the next meeting to decide what to do. The city council asked Frank to work with the city clerk to help her understand all aspects of the new system. Frank spent considerable time working with City Clerk Furlong between then and the next meeting. He also discussed the budget with the mayor to gain his support for its adoption. As a result, the city council adopted the new budget at the next meeting.

Frank Scott began to talk with other city and county officials in CSCOG about the budget in Mapleton. However, he found that this one-to-one approach "did not get the word out fast enough"' Frank decided to talk with a public administration professor at a nearby state university about developing a workshop for small town mayors and city clerks. After some discussion, a workshop was planned and developed. One major portion of the session was devoted to Mapleton's new system. The workshop was well attended; some local officials in other cities seemed interested in the idea of developing a budgeting and accounting system for their towns.

Frank Scott's plan for encouraging needed changes in local government was working. One small city had adopted a budget and it looked like others might follow. However, trouble soon developed. In the next city election, a different group of city councilmen were elected in Mapleton. Only the mayor, who was elected for a four year term rather than a two year term, remained from the previous city council. The new city councilmen, who had complained about the high cost of local government in their campaigns, decided to take action. They fired the city clerk, Melba Furlong, who "was paid too much," and rehired the old city clerk at a lower salary than Furlong was paid.

Frank was worried about what was happening in Mapleton. He had remembered that Melba Furlong had shown him a number of "cold checks" that were stuffed into one of the desks at the Mapleton City Hall. Although every city gets some "cold checks," these checks were made out to the Lucht County Rural Electric Cooperative. Melba had told Frank (and this had been verified by the mayor) that the old city clerk (now rehired by the city) would take the checks down to the bank and deposit them in the Lucht County REA's account. Although the city received a small fee for taking payments at City Hall for the REA, these fees were minimal, and did not cover the "cold check losses." Frank went to see the newly hired city clerk on a routine visit. She did not appear interested in this new budget system. "After all, I have my own system which has worked well in the past," she told Frank. Although he was discouraged, Frank decided not to give up in Mapleton; he was determined!

Several weeks later Frank was invited to attend the next city council meeting. During the week before the meeting there had been several major thunderstorms in the area. These storms never lasted over an hour and were accompanied by rain which was much needed in this farm area. As Frank drove to Mapleton, he kept thinking about what he might tell this new city council so that they would be as enthusiastic as the previous one had been about the budget. Finally he had it figured out. The budget was a way to cut costs—to keep down the expenses. This approach would be well received with this cost-conscious city council.

When Frank arrived at the Mapleton City Hall, the sky was dark, as night had come. However, he was surprised that the City Hall was dark too. He could see several figures inside the building. As Frank entered the building, he met the mayor, who seemed confused. There were six men groping around the dark building. Finally, one city councilman struck a match and found the fusebox. He replaced the burned out fuse with one he found on the top of the box. As he did the lights came on and so did the copy machine, which began to produce copies, "swish, swish, swish." Frank looked at the electric clock; it was three o'clock. Obviously the city clerk had been running the copy machine when it blew a fuse. She did not check the fusebox; she simply closed up the City Hall and went home to get out of the "electrical storm." Frank was perplexed. He did not know how this city could utilize ZBB or *any* budget when the city clerk did not know how to replace a fuse. Do you?

Note

1. The average salaries for city clerks were taken from Combs, Davis, and Roederer, while the average salaries for postmasters were computed from data given by Ryan.

References

Combs, Paul E., John W. Davis, and Paul D. Roederer. *Personnel Data for Kentucky Municipalities, Fall 1976.* Lexington, Kentucky: University of Kentucky, 1976, p. 45.

Lodgson, Ed, County Judge of Edmonson County, Kentucky. "Community Speaks." Interview, WBKP-TV, Bowling Green, Kentucky, October 24, 1976.

McGinnis, James F. "Pluses and Minuses of Zero-Base Budgeting." *Administrative Management,* 37 (September, 1976), 22-23 and 91.

Minmier, George S., and Roger H. Hermanson. "A Look at Zero-Base Budgeting—The Georgia Experience." *Atlanta Economic Review,* 26 (July/August, 1976), 5-12.

Pyhrr, Peter A. "The Zero-Base Approach to Government Budgeting." *Public Administration Review,* 37 (January/February, 1977), 1-8.

Rehfuss, John. "Zero-Base Budgeting: The Experience to Date." *Public Personnel Management,* 6 (May/June, 1977), 181-187.

Robertson, Joseph M., Director of the Bureau of Intergovernmental Personnel Programs, U.S. Civil Service Commission. Interview, Miami, Florida, November 26, 1974.

Ryan, Ed. "Postmaster is Often one of the Best-Paid in Town." *Louisville Courier-Journal and Times,* 24 (July, 1977), A1 and A16.

Scheiring, Michael J. "Zero-Base Budgeting in New Jersey." *State Government,* 49 (Summer, 1976), 174-179.

Singleton, David W., Bruce A. Smith, and James R. Cleaveland. "Zero-Based Budgeting in Wilmington, Delaware." *Governmental Finance,* 5 (August, 1976), 20-29.

Stansbury, Paul, Management Specialist, Bluegrass Area Development District, Lexington, Kentucky. Interview, Lexington, Kentucky, October 22, 1976.

Sundquist, James L. *Making Federalism Work*. Washington, D.C.: The Brookings Institution, 1969.
Tyer, Charlie B. "Zero-Base Budgeting: A Critical Analysis." *Southern Review of Public Administration*, 1 (June, 1977), 88-107.
Wanamaker, Daniel K., and Paul Stansbury. "Riding the Circuit with the Kentucky Public Administration Specialist." *Public Administration Review*, 37 (May/June, 1977), 290-293.

PART II

LEGISLATIVE BUDGETING

Contrary to popular opinion, legislatures are very much involved in budgeting. Different labels are used, but legislatures make the key budget decisions. Prior to the 1970s most budget reforms were addressed to the executive branch, and, in fact, were designed to strengthen the executive branch. In contemporary times, there are two significant reforms involving the legislative branch: the 1974 Congressional Budget and Impoundment Control Act and sunset legislation.

Many astute observers of government consider the 1974 Congressional Budget and Impoundment Control Act as one of the most significant pieces of legislation that Congress has passed in this century. When legislation changes the fundamental rules of the game of institutional decision-making, you then have significant legislation. There were two major motivations behind the 1974 act: one, to revise the de facto impoundment process so a president could not veto by impoundment the will of Congress; and two, to create a unified comprehensive budget deciding process rather than maintain the fractional decision-making, which was subject to intense presidential and media criticism.

Linda Smith's "The Congressional Budget Process: Why it Worked this Time" should be considered a classic in the literature on budgeting. The rules of the game have changed in Washington as noted in the following quote:

> If President Carter wants an immediate tax cut, he must convince the Budget Committees of Congress to approve it. If President Carter wants to stimulate the economy through increased federal spending, he must first persuade the Budget Committees to accept this.

Smith's article explains the complex set of reforms that have altered the power relationships with the Congress and between the president and Congress. These reforms are extremely subtle and reflect a remarkable understanding of the internal maze of Washington decision-making. Students must not rush through this article. Instead, each reform must be carefully examined and reflected upon in terms of how that reform contributes to the major purposes of the legislation.

The 1974 act reflects artistry of the highest quality and Smith's article helps one appreciate that achievement.

The Betts and Miller article ("More About the Impact of the Congressional Budget and Impoundment Act") complements Smith's article. At the time Linda Smith wrote her article, she was a professional on the House Budget Committee. Her perspective helped her assess the nature, significance, and viability of the act. Betts and Miller are former agency and department budget officers with an important, but different, perspective on the 1974 reforms. They help us understand the administrative confusion caused by the pre-1974 budget procedures, and the total demands placed upon budget officers with the 1974 act, as well as other reforms. Also, they help us understand the challenges that still exist after the reform.

Sunset legislation is a popular reform topic in the Congress and various state legislatures. The concept is simple. Every few years the legislature reconsiders existing legislation. If they do not act to renew the legislation, it "sunsets" or dies. Thus old unneeded legislation can be culled out. This especially applied to the authorization section of legislation. Edmund Muskie has been the federal advocate of sunset and his aide, James Davidson, "makes the case for sunset" in "Sunset-A New Challenge." The appeal of sunset legislation is strong, but there are reasons for caution. Steve Charnovitz explains the complexities and probable consequences of sunset laws in his article, "Evaluating Sunset: What Would it Mean?" Government is complex. Charnovitz helps us appreciate those complexities and reflect upon them in light of a popular budget reform.

8.

The Congressional Budget Process: Why It Worked this Time

Linda Smith

If President Carter wants an immediate tax cut, he must first convince the Budget Committees of Congress to approve it. If President Carter wants to stimulate the economy through increased federal spending, he must first persuade the Budget Committee to accept this. If President Carter wants to balance the federal budget by 1980, he will have to work continuously with the Budget Committees to reach that goal.

The reason why is there now is a congressional budget in effect for fiscal 1977 which reflects Congress' present tax policy and establishes a federal spending ceiling. Increasing federal expenditures or lowering tax revenues will require a change in this budget—a change which the Budget Committees of Congress must first approve. This budget exists because the 94th Congress has successfully implemented a process for setting national fiscal and tax policies and for determining federal budget priorities. It has done so under the provisions of the 1974 Congressional Budget and Impoundment Control Act (P.L. 93-344). The successful operation of the budget process in 1975 and 1976 marks the advent of an economic and fiscal policy that is distinctly that of the Congress—not the president.

This point is a crucial one for Mr. Carter. The president, of course, will continue to propose both an economic policy and a set of priorities in his own annual budget which will appeal to and may be embraced by the Democratic majorities of Congress. Congress, in turn, will continue to exercise its authority under Title I, Section 9 of the Constitution to initiate all appropriations for the expenditure of federal monies. For the first time, however, Congress has a proven mechanism to challenge the president's budget policies and priorities and establish its own. This mechanism takes on added importance when we realize that a majority of the members of Congress have never served with a Democratic president in the White House and will be reluctant to relinquish their heightened fiscal powers. President Carter's budget will be a "starting point," but it no longer will be viewed as the definitive budget statement of the United States government.

Understanding the new congressional budget system is important for government administrators, because it will affect the growth and development of all federal programs. To understand this new process, why it succeeded, and its potential impact on the programs you administer, it is helpful to look briefly at the events that gave birth to the Budget Act, to survey its key provisions, and to examine how well it functioned during its first two years.

Genesis

Contrary to popular opinion, Congress did too much, not too little, budget work in the years prior to 1974. What it lacked, however, was an overall framework to establish fiscal and tax policy and to set budget priorities.

Congress recognized this as long ago as 1921 when it passed the Budget and Accounting Act. The aim of the 1921 act was to abolish the practice, begun in the first Congress, of each federal agency submitting its own budget to Congress, unrelated to the budgets of other agencies and to any overall spending priorities. The 1921 Act vested in the president the sole authority to consolidate agency budget requests and to present to Congress an overall recommendation.

In the ensuing years, however, the number of federal agencies and programs, as well as the size of the federal budget to support them, exploded. With little advance preparation, Congress received a 200-page budget accompanied by a 500-page appendix organized in a complicated accounting format, supplemented by thousands of pages of agency explanations. Even more critical than this sensory overload was the problem that the president's budget had become a vehicle designed to persuade Congress, not to inform it. There was no discussion, for example, of spending alternatives or the long-range consequences of particular budget decisions.

Facing these problems, in 1946 Congress enacted the Legislative Reorganization Act requiring the preparation of its own *legislative budget*. The task, however, was given to an ad hoc joint committee of nearly 100 members of the House and Senate with no special arrangements for staff support or for expert analysis of the budget. It is small wonder that in 1947 the Congress failed to adopt a spending ceiling; it did not abide by its 1948 ceiling; and the whole process was dropped in 1949. In 1950, the Congress enacted an omnibus appropriations bill covering all of the regular bills usually acted upon separately. Again it abandoned the process the following year. Also, in 1950, Congress strengthened the Anti-Deficiency Act to ensure that outlays (that is actual expenditures) did not exceed the appropriations it enacted. This was interpreted by the executive as permission to reserve funds not needed to accomplish legislative objectives—the device of "impoundment."

President Nixon went far beyond any previous chief executive in using impoundments to directly challenge Congress' constitutional power to establish spending priorities. The limits of presidential power in this area had been fuzzy; but Nixon claimed authority not merely to defer or delay spending for various programs, but to determine which programs should be continued and which eliminated altogether. By the early 1970s, impoundments were being vigorously challenged in the courts and within the Congress itself. Although almost all impoundments reviewed by the courts were reversed, the lack of a comprehensive and coherent budget process clearly placed Congress in a weakened position to contest the president's actions.

In addition to impoundments, there were three other elements which led to enactment of the Budget Act. The first was the problem of ''uncontrollable'' spending—expenditures mandated by law which could not be eliminated in any single year, such as social security benefits or payments on prior defense contracts. By the early 1970s, controllables had grown to encompass over 70 percent of all annual federal spending. Second, appropriations bills were seldom completed by the beginning of the fiscal year to which they applied, causing many federal agencies to operate on continuing resolutions for a portion, and in some cases, all of the year. This was because the necessary annual authorization bills for some programs took so long to be enacted. This was also because Congress was asked to enact 13 separate appropriations bills without any overall guidance. Third, by 1973, nearly half of all federal spending was approved outside the regular appropriations process—so-called backdoor spending—where it could not be weighed against the remaining expenditures reviewed annually by the Appropriations Committees.

Thus, the budgetary reforms which Congress studied in 1972, wrote in 1973, and enacted in July 1974 had two main features. One was a binding set of new rules, enforceable in the courts, greatly limiting the president's impoundment powers and establishing procedures by which Congress could block or approve any impoundments. The other was a new procedure for a comprehensive congressional budget system to give Congress the capacity to participate, on an equal footing with the president, in the formulation of national economic and fiscal policy.

A comprehensive analysis of the political climate and organizational reforms leading to the enactment of the 1974 Budget Act appeared in the January 1975 issue of *The Bureaucrat* (Vol. 3, No. 4). The article, ''A Congressional Budget: Will It Work This Time?'' written by Herbert N. Jasper, raised the serious question of whether Congress would be capable of adhering to the strict procedural and policy discipline required in the new law. During recent years, Congress has proven itself equal to the discipline the act demands. Let us examine what those requirements are and why they were successfully implemented this time.

The House and Senate Budget Committees

The Congressional Budget and Impoundment Control Act contains 10 titles which can be grouped into four categories: Titles I and II establish new Committees on the Budget in both the House and the Senate and a Congressional Budget Office to improve Congress' informational and analytical resources; Titles III and IV establish a timetable and new procedures for the adoption of authorizing legislation, budget targets, appropriations bills, and budget ceilings; Titles V through IX provide for a new fiscal year, improvements in budget materials in the president's submission including five-year economic and cost projections, and improved program evaluation procedures; and Title X establishes procedures for congressional review of presidential impoundment actions.

The act establishes a standing Committee on the Budget in each house. The House of Representatives committee is composed of 25 members including five from the Ways and Means Committee, five from the Appropriations Committee, 13 from other committees in the House and one member each from the Republican and Democratic leadership. This allocation rule was enacted not only for the obvious political reason of gaining support for the budget legislation from members of Ways and Means and Appropriations Committees, but also in recognition of the fact that success of any budget process in the House required coordination with and acceptance by members responsible for making taxation and expenditure decisions. Some contend that placing Ways and Means and Appropriations members on the House Budget Committee has made it more conservative than if all the members were selected at large, as is done in the Senate for the 16 members of its Budget Committee. While this contention may have some weight, it should be noted that the House Committee consistently reported larger (and by inference more liberal) budget deficits than the Senate committee during the first two years.

Where there are important political differences between the House and Senate committees is in the extent of bipartisan support each has received. In the Senate the senior Republican on the Budget Committee , Senator Henry Bellmon of Oklahoma, had regularly sided with Senator Muskie, chairman of the committee, rather than with President Ford on such significant budget issues as the veto of the fiscal year (FY) 1976 Labor-HEW Appropriations Bill and curtailment of military procurement expenditures. This bipartisan agreement on federal fiscal policies has resulted in Senate passage of the FY 1976 and FY 1977 budgets by wide vote margins. For example, the first time the Senate considered budget targets on the fiscal 1976 budget, it accepted the Senate committee recommendation by a vote of 69-22. In the spring of calendar year 1976, it passed an FY 1977 budget resolution by a vote of 62-22. These votes came despite Senator Muskie's open floor fights with Senator Stennis and the Armed Services Committee on military expenditures, and with Senator Long and the Finance Committee on tax reform.

By contrast in the House, Budget Committee Republicans, headed by Representative Delbert Latta of Ohio, have disagreed with the expenditure and tax policies developed through the congressional budget process. While praising the diligence of the committee's chairman, Brock Adams of Seattle, Washington, and while acknowledging the need for the process, Mr. Latta and his Republican colleagues consistently voted against all budget amounts above President Ford's recommendations, opposed the Committee budget resolution, and tried repeatedly on the House floor to gain adoption of sharply reduced federal spending.

In fact, solid Republican opposition, coupled with a large bloc of liberal Democrats, nearly defeated the whole budget process in the House in 1975. All but three Republicans voted against the Spring 1975 budget resolution which proposed a deficit of approximately $70 billion. They were joined by 20 liberal Democrats who felt the proposed budget did not do enough to reduce unemployment, then at 8.7 percent. Thus, the first budget resolution for fiscal 1976 passed the House on May 1, 1975 by only four votes (200-196) and the second passed on December 12 by only two votes (189-187).

As a result, Chairman Adams has had to work closely with the moderate Democrats in the House to ensure passage of the resolutions. He has, for example, enlisted the support of Chairman George Mahon and the House Appropriations Committee by faithfully enforcing the Budget Act's prohibitions against new "backdoor spending"—budget authority that is enacted without action by the Appropriations Committee. Mr. Adams and the Budget Committee have also endorsed in their recommended resolutions budget savings the Appropriations Committee has long sought, such as a ceiling on the highway construction trust fund. The Budget Committee has made it easier for other committees such as Veterans Affairs or Post Office and Civil Service to oppose big-spending legislation sought by special interest groups. Members are now able to declare that legislation for such things as higher benefits or larger salaries would "bust the budget" and therefore must be postponed.

As a further step in solidifying the support of moderate Democrats, Chairman Adams developed in early 1976 a five-year budget approach that balanced federal revenues and expenditures by 1981. In a February 18, 1976 statement on the floor of the House of Representatives, Mr. Adams called for holding overall spending on existing programs during the next five years to no more than current spending levels adjusted for inflation. Retaining existing tax laws, he projected a $26 billion surplus in 1980 and a $60 billion surplus in 1981 to be used for "additional tax reductions, new programs, welfare reform, and some expansion of existing worthwhile programs."

As a demonstration of intent, Mr. Adams ushered through the House an FY 1977 congressional budget with a deficit substantially less than the previous year. This budget also proposed to create one million more jobs by increasing spending for public works, housing and public service jobs—a realignment of spending which attracted the support of liberal Democrats. Although the deficit in this budget—$51 billion in total—was scarcely $7 billion higher than the deficit proposed by Ford, only 13 Republicans voted for the measure. Thus, the successful enactment of a congressional budget during the initial two years of this process was exclusively a Democratic achievement in the House.

The Staffs

Despite political differences, the House and Senate committees have similar staff arrangements. The House committee has a total staff of 63 while the Senate has 85 persons working for its Budget Committee. The largest portion of the House staff is composed of well-respected professionals who work with both the Republican and the Democratic members of the committees. The bulk of this staff consists of program analysts assigned to the various budget functions, such as defense, health, and veterans programs. In the House, more so than in the Senate, these people have tended to be program specialists who are called upon to analyze and discuss the pros and cons of specific federal programs. This trend can be traced to the fact that House members themselves tend to be program specialists since they are more numerous, have fewer committee and subcommittee assignments, and retain the constitutional responsibility for initiating all spending legislation. As such, the House Committee, with its staff capacity, has delved into program details that the Senate has avoided in building its budget resolutions.

Each Committee also has a smaller number of staffers assigned exclusively to either the Democrats or the Republicans to ensure that the partisan needs of particular members are adequately met. This dual staff arrangement of "nonpartisan and partisan" staffs is uncommon among congressional committees which typically have a majority and minority staff reporting to the Democrats and Republicans, respectively. This staff arrangement was chosen by the Budget Committees in recognition of the breadth of their subject matter, the lack of a functioning Congressional Budget Office during the first six months of the committee's existence and the need to get analytic, nonpartisan professional information to all members regardless of their party affiliation. While the Democratic members have tended to rely on the nonpartisan staff more than the Republicans, the arrangement has worked well in both committees and will likely be continued.

The CBO

In addition to their own staffs, the House and Senate Budget Committees have access to information and assistance from the Congressional Budget Office (CBO). This office, now about 200 strong, has been directed by Alice M. Rivlin who was appointed to a four-year term of office in February 1975. Unlike the Office of Management and Budget (to which it is too often compared) the CBO is by statute nonpartisan, and is barred from making any specific policy recommendations.

As such, it differs from the staffs of the committees which are responsible for reviewing CBO analyses and drawing up policy recommendations and suggestions thereon. Beyond its role of presenting Congress with respectable and realistic alternatives on taxation and spending, and providing forecasts on the economic outlook, CBO has exclusive responsibility for developing five-year cost estimates of all spending legislation reported in the House and Senate and for conducting the important "scorekeeping" function. This function involves monitoring Congress' numerous taxation and spending decisions and relating them to the budget authority, outlays and revenue levels in the Congressional budget resolution.

Dr. Rivlin and her staff aroused some discontent in the Ford administration and among members by testifying that to avoid a prolonged recession, the economy needed a more expansionary taxation policy and a higher expenditure level than Ford proposed in his FY 1977 budget. Dr. Rivlin's early popularity with the press also aroused the ire of some congressmen. Congress imposed a first-year staff ceiling of 193 rather than 259, as Director Rivlin had planned. This forced shifts in CBO staff resources away from the program analysis area into the budget analysis and scorekeeping functions where the greatest workload has fallen in the first two years. Despite some continuing workload problems and the need to augment its tax policy expertise, CBO has earned a reputation for professionalism. Perhaps its most important contribution in this early stage is its development of objective, open, and timely cost analysis data on congressional legislation. As such, CBO has helped to minimize much of the "budget numbers game" among the administration, agencies, lobbyists, and Hill staff that formerly accompanied legislative bargaining.

The Process

The heart of the new congressional budget system is found in Titles III and IV of the Budget Act which set forth a strict timetable for developing, implementing, and enforcing a congressional budget. Let us briefly review the major parts of this process before examining how well it worked and why.

The system begins with the November 10th submission by the president of a "current services budget." This new document is a projection of the cost of continuing all existing programs adjusted for inflation but without policy or legislative changes. It serves as a "benchmark" against which alternative budget proposals can be evaluated. The president's budget is submitted, as in the past, 15 days after Congress convenes in January. Shortly thereafter, the two Budget Committees begin hearings on budget alternatives, the state of the economy, and national priorities.

A critical step in the process is the submission of the views and recommendations of all standing committees of the House and Senate, due on March 15. They provide the Budget Committees with an early and comprehensive indication of the legislative and expenditure plans of the other committees. The CBO is required to submit its report on economic and fiscal policy and alternative budgets by April 1. However, since this date was found to be too close to the time when the Budget Committees must complete their work, CBO agreed in 1976 to move up their actual submission date to February 1.

April 15 is the deadline for both Budget Committees to report their budget recommendations, which are presented in the form of a concurrent resolution. This resolution, which does not require presidential signature, has two parts. The first sets targets for total budget authority and outlays, recommends a revenue level including any changes in taxes needed to achieve it, and identifies the resulting budget surplus or deficit and the total public debt. The second allocates total budget authority and outlays between 17 budget functions; that is, major programmatic categories such as defense, commerce and transportation, and health. The statute allows one month for floor consideration of the resolution in each House, a conference between the House and Senate to resolve any differences in the two resolutions, and adoption of the conference reports. It should be stressed that the amounts in the first budget resolution are targets, not ceilings, which serve to guide Congress in its subsequent spending and revenue decisions. No spending legislation can be enacted prior to the adoption by May 15 of this first budget resolution.

May 15 is also the deadline for the reporting of legislation authorizing new budget authority. Authorizations reported by a committee after that date may be considered in the House or Senate only if an emergency waiver is approved. Between the first resolution and seven days after Labor Day, Congress must enact all spending and appropriations bills.

In September, Congress completes work on the second budget resolution, this time placing a *binding ceiling* on budget authority and outlays and a *floor* on revenues. No legislation which would break the ceiling or cause taxes to go below the floor can be considered by Congress. Is should be noted that the allocations for each of the 17 functional categories are not binding. But in the event legislation comes up which would exceed the totals for a function, the Budget Committees will warn their respective Houses that enactment of the legislation will require Congress to cut spending in other functions or will "break the budget." Further, in order to ensure compliance with its spending ceilings and revenue floor, the second resolution may direct other committees to report legislation to rescind or amend appropriations and other spending legislation, raise or lower revenues, adjust the debt limit, or any combination of such actions. Congress theoretically may not adjourn until it has completed action on this reconciliation process.

Implementation

Almost from the outset, the new budget procedure has had to deal with two related questions: First, the issue of fiscal policy—what magnitude of federal spending, revenues, and deficit is best for the economy in the year ahead? And second, the issue of national spending and taxation priorities—where should expenditures be increased or decreased and from what sources should taxes be collected?

It has been the fiscal policy question which has dominated the budget process during its first two years. The deepening recession of early 1975 spurred Congress to implement the new Budget Act procedures that year, one year earlier than required by law. It was also the recession which led the Budget Committees to reject most of President Ford's FY 1977 budget and tax proposals and develop their own. In November 1975, the "current services" budget had estimated that it would cost $415 billion to operate existing federal programs in fiscal 1977 without any changes. In January 1976, President Ford called for a $394 billion spending level, with a deficit of $43 billion. This would have reduced projected federal spending from its current services level by nearly $21 billion. Mr. Ford also recommended permanent tax cuts totalling $28 billion including an accelerated depreciation rate, tax incentives for stock ownership, tax reductions for electric utilities, and changes in estate tax law. On the other hand, President Ford proposed increased payroll taxes for social security and unemployment insurance.

The Budget Committees concluded that the sharp restriction of federal spending in the national economy coupled with higher payroll taxes would result in a significant slowdown in the recovery. Major economic forecasters projected that the administration's policies would result in a real growth rate of only four percent, average unemployment of 7.5 percent in 1977 and inflation still hovering at six percent or more.

In contrast to Ford's budget, the March 15th views and estimates of the House Committees added up to a total spending estimate of $442 billion. Chairmen Adams and Muskie, with the help of the congressional leadership, had stressed the urgency of having these March 15th reports on time to act as a counterforce to the president's proposals. Most of the committees met the deadline and those that missed were only delayed a few days. Their compliance paid off since the staff and members of both Budget Committees made considerable use of these reports in developing the FY 1977 budget priorities, even though the total spending requests were regarded as too high.

Testimony received by the Budget Committees from numerous private economists, including conservatives such as Herbert Stein and Paul McCracken, suggested that the Ford proposal was too restrictive, but good fiscal policy required some reduction of the deficit from the FY 1976 level of $70 billion.

This clearly could not be done if all the proposals of the other congressional committees were followed.

It was in this environment that the House and Senate Budget Committees produced a congressional budget by April 15 and had it successfully approved by both Houses prior to May 15. The first resolution had an outlay target of $413.3 billion, a revenue target of $362.5 billion, and a deficit of $50.8 billion. While its totals were only slightly more expansionary than President Ford's, the fiscal policy it attempted to achieve through the targeting of federal spending was significantly different (see Tables 1 and 2). First, the congressional budget rejected Ford's $10 billion tax reduction package and went one step further—it called for raising $2 billion in new tax revenues through the closing of tax loopholes. Second, while sharing the new mood of caution about our defense readiness, the committees adopted a 14 percent, rather than 16 percent, real growth level in defense procurements, which shaved $2 billion from Ford's defense request of $115 billion.

Figure 8.1
FY 1977 Aggregate Levels (in Billions of Dollars)

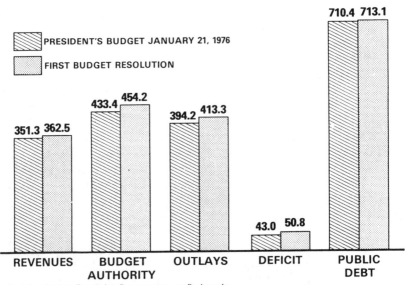

The First Budget Resolution figures represent final results of House-Senate Conference

Figure 8.2
FY 1977 Function Levels

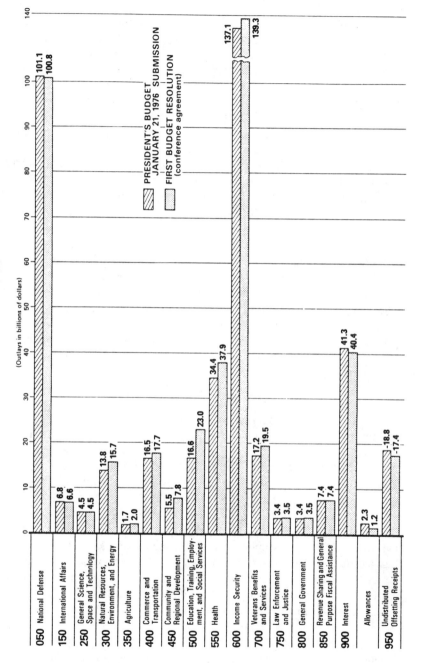

(Outlays in billions of dollars)

The Budget Committees then took the money made available by these actions, some $14 billion in budget authority, and redirected it towards job creation programs such as accelerated public works, public service jobs, countercyclical aid to states and localities, housing and highway construction. The committee estimated this allocation would create one million more jobs than Ford's budget had called for. They projected that this action could reduce unemployment to 6.5 percent in 1977 and still maintain inflation below 5.5 percent. The budget target allocations for most other federal programs which were not job-creating were kept to their FY 1976 levels. This means that nearly all other committee spending plans were restrained. As Chairman Adams expressed it, "We were tough but even-handed."

The presidential and congressional budget agreed on some expenditure and revenue issues. For example, both acknowledged the need to place cost controls on Medicare and Medicaid and the congressional budget reduced estimated outlays for these programs as a means of encouraging congressional action on cost savings legislation. The first resolution also assumed the sale of $750 million in military stockpile items which President Ford had been urging. In addition, the first budget resolution supported a "pay reform" package that called for the enactment of legislation eliminating the so-called "1 percent kicker"—the provision that gave retired federal workers an extra one percent increase in their pension benefits every time they received a cost-of-living increase.

Enforcement

The success of the budget process during the first two years depended to a sizeable degree on how well the Budget Committee monitored Congress' spending and revenue actions and tied these to the previously adopted targets and the 17 functional amounts. There are 22 standing committees in the House, 20 of which have jurisdiction over a portion of federal expenditures. There are 18 committees with spending jurisdiction in the Senate. To ensure that their spending decisions were in line with the budget targets Congress had enacted, it was necessary to develop a system that defined the relationship between the budget resolution and the money each spending committee controlled. To do this, the Budget Committees developed a "crosswalk" system that allocates money from each functional category in the resolution to the various commit-tees that have jurisdiction over the accounts and programs in each function. Under this system the Appropriations Committee received the largest allocation ($276.7 billion of the $413.3 billion in total outlays) and the Ways and Means Committee received the second largest amount ($162 billion). For those new entitlement programs included in the budget that required further authorization before funds could be appropriated, the responsible authorizing committee, as well as the Appropriations Committee, was given an allocation. Those committees expected to enact cost-saving legislation were given negative allocations. The committees in turn divided their allocations between their subcommittees or programs apportioning them essentially the way the Budget Committee did.

During the summer months these crosswalk allocations became the vehicle for tracking congressional actions against the resolution targets. The Budget Committees, aided by the Congressional Budget Office, produced weekly scorekeeping reports from June through September to inform the members of how each spending or revenue bill reported by each committee compared with the congressional budget targets. It was through this procedure that the Budget Committees were able to watch the 13 appropriations bills, ensure that the targets were closely adhered to, and protect the integrity of the budget resolution.

It was also through this procedure that the Congress was able to monitor tax revenues and achieve adherence to the budget resolution's revenue recommendations. Prior to the advent of the Budget Act, the size of the public debt, the magnitude of federal borrowings, and national tax policies were exclusively within the jurisdiction of the House Ways and Means and the Senate Finance Committees. The new act, however, vested in the Budget Committees the initial responsibility for determining total federal revenues, the deficit, and the debt level. Further, the Budget Committees were responsible for recommending how much federal revenues should be increased or decreased.

The first real test of the act came when Chairman Russell Long (D-Louisiana) and the Senate Finance Committee challenged this authority. The first budget resolution for FY 1977 had recommended a full year extension of the antirecession tax cut and had established a target of $2 billion in new tax revenues to be raised through tax reform legislation. The House Ways and Means Committee, chaired by Congressman Al Ullman (D-Oregon), who had served as the First Budget Committee chairman before Brock Adams, reported tax legislation that complied with the budget resolution. The Senate Finance Committee reported a tax bill that extended the antirecession tax cut for only nine months, and by the time it passed the Senate actually lost $300 million in FY 1977 through changes in the tax code. Furthermore, over a five-year period the House tax bill would have *raised* $9.9 billion while the Senate-passed bill would have *lost* $9.7 billion. This long-range revenue impact was calculated by the Budget Committees and CBO and had to accompany the report on the tax bill. This was because of the explicit Budget Act requirement that all bill reports must contain five-year cost data.

Armed with this information and with strong public calls for tax reform, particularly to meet the $2 billion tax reform goal of the first resolution, the Budget Committees and other members of Congress attacked the Senate tax bill. They argued that the Senate bill was a repudiation of the budget goals Congress itself had just endorsed. They strongly urged a "no" vote if the Senate version of the tax bill was adopted by the House and Senate conferees. The pressure mounted by this campaign was sufficient to cause the conferees to adopt the House bill instead—the version that complied with the budget resolution.

In addition to the "crosswalk" enforcement system, the Budget Committees have several procedural provisions in the Budget Act which they can use to enforce timely and orderly adherence to the new process. First, under section 303 of the act, except in an emergency, no spending legislation for a particular year can be adopted prior to the adoption by May 15 of the first budget resolution for that fiscal year. For example, when the House Ways and Means Committee reported out in January 1976 an unemployment insurance tax bill that would have raised $400 million in FY 1977 unemployment taxes and would have raised unemployment benefits, the bill was considered in violation of this section of the act. The House Rules Committee would not grant a waiver for this bill unless the House Budget Committee agreed. Seeing this as the first test of this part of the act and determining that no emergency existed, the House Budget Committee voted not to recommend a waiver. The Ways and Means bill was accommodated within the first resolution targets and the House did consider and pass the bill on July 20, 1976. This postponement was seen as a signal by other committees that unless they could demonstrate an emergency, votes on spending legislation would be delayed until after May 15.

May 15 is also the deadline by which legislation authorizing new budget authority must be reported. There is general agreement that the timetable in the Budget Act will work only if the authorizing committees comply with this date since it is a prerequisite for timely enactment of appropriations bills. In 1976 compliance was fairly widespread although some committees, including Muskie's own Public Works Subcommittee, reported legislation by May 15 in skeleton form, intending to fill in the details later. Again the House and Senate Budget Committees strictly enforced this provision recommending waivers only in a few isolated emergency cases such as the day care staffing funds bill and the Earthquake Hazards Reduction Act. Even a jobs-creating bill, the Young Adult Conservation Corps, which passed the House but had not been foreseen by the Senate Interior and Insular Affairs Committee in May, was not granted a waiver when that Committee reported similar legislation in July.

A third portion of the Budget Act which the House Budget Committee has regularly enforced is the prohibition against new "backdoor" spending—budget authority enacted without prior action by the Appropriations Committee. Specifically, section 401 of the act controls new borrowing, contract, or entitlement authority by making any bill subject to a point of order unless it provides that the authority is effective only to the extent provided in appropriations acts. Under this authority, Chairman Adams, this time with the support of the Republican committee members, opposed consideration of a series of bills, including the Energy Conservation and Oil Policy Act and the Nurses Training Act of 1975. Vigorous enforcement of this provision was supported by the House Appropriations Committee and its Chairman George Mahon, Democrat of Texas, and helped encourage cooperation between the Budget and Appropriations Committees during the past two years.

It was because of this cooperation, the stiff timetable and enforcement procedures in the Budget Act, the work of the congressional leadership, and the pressure of an impending adjournment that Congress enacted all 13 regular appropriations bills and a major tax bill before the fiscal year began on October 1—a feat Congress had not achieved since 1948.

Congress then was able to enact the Second Budget Resolution for FY 1977 on schedule in late September. It made only minor changes from the targets set in the first resolution. This was possible because the Budget Committees had kept careful vigilance on the size of appropriations and entitlement bills enacted during the Summer. It was also possible because there were some shifts in expenditures with lower spending for welfare, unemployment, and public service jobs than had been anticipated, offset by the failure to obtain legislative permission for the sale of military strategic materials, failure to enact Medicare-Medicaid cost controls, and the lack of action on related savings measures. Most important, there were few changes in the second resolution due to the fact that the Budget Committees heard no testimony that economic conditions warranted major changes in fiscal policy at that time. However, the committees made it clear in their report on the second resolution that they kept open the option of a third budget resolution in the Spring of 1977 if economic conditions warranted. Due to the persistence of the economic slowdown, a third resolution is now under consideration by both Congress and President Carter and could include the type of tax cut and spending increases the new Democratic administration has been considering.

Finally, because the second resolution for FY 1977 made few changes from the first and did not alter actions Congress had taken during the Summer, the Budget Committees did not invoke their "reconciliation" authority. Thus, this strictest part of the new process still awaits its first test.

Some Assessments

The success of this process during the past two years can be linked to at least six factors. The first was the recognition of the need for strong congressional fiscal policies and procedures to curb the Nixon budget abuses and stem the tide of budget impoundments. The second was the severe recession of 1974-1975 which pressured Congress into demonstrating that it could take the lead in guiding the nation out of the worst decline since the Great Depression. The third factor was the general public concern, heightened by a presidential election, over the growth in government spending. The fourth was the fact that the Budget Act was seen by Democrats as a mechanism which could be used to counter the power of the Republican White House during an election year. The fifth factor was the elaborate provisions of the Budget Act itself which ensured adequate staff assistance, enforcement mechanisms for the various deadlines, and coordination between all existing committees. Finally, success was due in large part to the diligence and foresight of House Chairman Brock Adams, the prominence and steadfastness of Chairman Muskie, the cooperation of his Republican colleague Senator Bellmon, and the hard work of many House and Senate Budget Committee members.

But these factors and the fact there is a budget resolution in place for FY 1977, may turn out to be President Carter's first major obstacle. Fiscal year 1977 began October 1, 1976 and runs through October 1, 1977. To make any impact on FY 1977 spending or revenues, President Carter must amend the 1977 budget immediately. This requires that he ask Congress to reopen the current budget resolution and amend the FY 1977 ceilings to fund additional antirecession jobs programs. The resolution revenue floor must also be amended to accommodate an immediate tax cut or tax rebate. To do this, he will have to work with a new congressional power structure. The new, but well established, bipartisan tradition of the Senate Budget Committee will require consultation and clearance with some Republicans as well as Democrats. Given the independence from the White House of the budget process and the new lineup of House and Senate Budget Committee members, new patterns of cooperation on budget matters will have to be established between Capitol Hill and the president. Senator Muskie, when asked in December to comment on Mr. Carter's hope of working out joint Carter/congressional Democratic budget amendments stated, "The Congressional budget process must have an integrity of its own . . . I cannot commit the Members of my own party, let alone the Republicans."

Beyond this, Mr. Carter faces the probability that tax cuts, jobs programs, and higher mandatory spending (i.e., for unemployment insurance and food stamps) may open the entire budget for revision under a third resolution and will likely lead to a protracted, partisan debate. This would open the door for sizable new federal spending demands from labor (for housing construction, for example), minorities, and Democratic liberals (for full employment funds) who view the current resolution as too little too late. If these groups are successful in adding program expenditures in FY 1977, President Carter will have little room to begin gradually phasing in new social programs.

Yet, it is clear that the congressional budget process has curbed Congress' propensity to spend. Absent a third budget resolution, in 1977 federal spending (budget authority and outlays) will rise 11 percent—a significant increase, but measurably less than the average of 17 percent a year in the three preceding fiscal years. Furthermore, despite rhetoric regarding Congress and inflation, the congressional budgets have established what many economists would regard as a moderate, if not restrictive, fiscal policy for the current state of the economy. To believers in ever-larger government expenditures, the process is a setback. The AFL-CIO, for example, has been very skeptical of the budget system, perceiving it as a method for curtailing federal growth in those labor-oriented programs they support. Yet even they would agree that the proper share of government spending in the total economy (now almost 38 percent if state and local spending is included), the tolerable level of taxation, and the "right" amount of budget deficits are all legitimate topics for orderly congressional review and debate.

The budget process is the only legislative forum for a comprehensive discussion of budget priorities and tradeoffs. Given its concentration over the past two years on fiscal policy goals, Congress is still a long way from formulating a truly alternative budget. The development of a genuine budget alternative will require better congressional control over existing federal expenditures. Congress has launched four important efforts to accomplish this: (1) elimination of "off-budget" agencies, (2) reducing the size of "uncontrollable" spending, (3) introduction of sunset legislation, and (4) new analytic techniques such as zero-base budgeting.

There are currently 23 government-owned or government-sponsored agencies whose spending and revenue activities do not appear in the unified federal budget. They are called "off-budget" agencies. They include such organizations as the U.S. Railway Association, the Rural Telephone Bank, the U.S. Postal Service, and the entire Federal Reserve System. While their expenditures do not appear in the budget, their spending and borrowing decisions do affect the national money markets, the availability of credit, and the size of the public debt. The House Budget Committee launched a year-long investigation of these agencies and issued a report in September 1976. It called for the inclusion of at least six of the agencies in the regular budget, further investigation of the remaining agencies and the initial inclusion in the budget of all future such organizations.

In FY 1977, about 75 percent of all federal outlays are mandatory under existing law. These are so-called "uncontrollable expenditures" and include such programs as food stamps, public assistance, farm price supports, and social security benefits. The House Budget Committee launched a two-year review of these expenditures in 1975 and 1976 under the direction of Congressman Butler Derrick, then a freshman from South Carolina. Mr. Derrick has stated that a zero-base budget system coupled with sunset legislation would implicitly provide for the elimination of mandatory uncontrollable spending.

By committing each federal program to a regular review procedure and by looking at each program *as if* it were a new proposal, its size, growth, and structure would be examined and its renewal made contingent upon the findings of regular reviews.

Sunset legislation, which is increasingly seen as a companion to the congressional budget process, has had Budget Chairman Muskie as its major proponent. It was cosponsored by 58 senators in 1976 and nearly came up for Senate floor action last year. Under this concept, each federal program would have a five-year authorization at the end of which it would come up for congressional review. Congress would have to specifically decide to extend, revamp, or eliminate it. Approximately 20 percent of all federal programs would expire each year. In the House of Representatives, sunset proposals have met with more skepticism. Opponents cite Congress' difficulty in reauthorizing those programs which already come up for periodic renewal. The House Budget Committee held exploratory hearings on ZBB and sunset proposals in June and July, 1976, but the measures were never brought up in the House Rules Committee (which has legislative jurisdiction). The House Appropriations Committee has launched a trial run of ZBB budget techniques for the FY 1978 budget justifications of NASA and the Consumer Project Safety Commission; and the Senate Appropriations Committee is doing the same with the Navy Department. However, it is likely that legislation to formally enact any government-wide ZBB effort or sunset provisions still has an uphill battle in the 95th Congress. This conclusion is reinforced by the fact that Congressman Jack Brooks, chairman of the House Government Operations Committee, whose cooperation is essential to the implementation of ZBB, urged President Carter as early as December to postpone an immediate introduction of zero-base budgeting for all federal agencies.

Turning to the FY 1978 budget and how specific programs will fare, it can be anticipated that Congress will continue to put the largest dollar increases in economic stimulus proposals, such as a new youth employment program, additional accelerated public works, or a revised investment tax credit. We can also look for small "set-asides" in the budget resolutions for welfare reform and national health insurance planning. Beyond this, given the balanced budget goal, fiscal restraint should be expected in all other federal programs and renewed cost savings are likely for health programs, and some mandatory benefit programs. Regarding the defense budget, it is still too early to judge at this writing whether Congress will continue a major spending effort to upgrade the nation's defenses or continue the pre-FY 1977 trend of lower real defense purchases.

While the new congressional budget process leaves the executive branch's budget responsibilities intact and vests a good deal of discretion in the regular standing committees of Congress, there is no escaping the extraordinary responsibility of the two Budget Committees. If the process continues to function as it has for the previous two years, the basic shape of our fiscal policy and the work of Congress—how much for defense, how much for the various domestic programs—will be significantly influenced by 25 Representatives and 16 Senators. The congressional budget resolutions will be the federal budget, accepting, revising, and replacing the president's. This point is perhaps best summed up by former Treasury Secretary Charles Walker who recently wrote: "Many 'instant historians' rate the forced resignation of Richard Nixon as the 93rd Congress' long term claim to fame. We disagree. Our nomination is the Budget Reform Act of 1974, which established an orderly and rational Congressional budget procedure."

More About the Impact of the Congressional Budget and Impoundment Control Act

Ernest C. Betts, Jr. and Richard E. Miller

While the Congressional Budget and Impoundment Control Act of 1974 was signed into law on July 12, 1974, its full effect on the procedures and budget systems of both the legislative and executive branches is still difficult to assess. It has neither been institutionalized to its ultimate nor has it completely deteriorated into gamesmanship on the part of either branch for cosmetic, public relations, or political purposes.

Before discussing the impact of this legislation, it would be well to take a brief look at the situations that produced a climate conducive to the enactment of such a wide-ranging and tightened congressional involvement in the budget process.

For years, critics had decried the lack of overall review of the budget by the Congress. When the president's budget was sent to the Hill, very little legislative attention was given to its total consideration even though the Joint Economic Committee, created by the Employment Act of 1946, held brief hearings on the budget as a part of its review of the total economy. Since, historically, it was presumed that revenue and appropriation matters must originate in the House of Representatives, the full Committee on Appropriations in the House usually was the first to start hearings on appropriation bills. Until the Act of 1974, the full standing Committee on Appropriations in the House (55 members) met shortly after the president's budget was sent to the Congress to consider the total budget. They asked the director of the Office of Management and Budget, the secretary of the treasury, and the chairman of the Council of Economic Advisors to appear before them. About a week later, the full Committee on Appropriations of the Senate (33 members) conducted a similar session. These hearings were relatively short and usually lasted about one day. The questioning tended toward broad, politically oriented, program matters with the members either trying to support the party in power in the executive branch or acting as adversary of the White House and critic of the budget. In fielding the questions from the Congress, the witnesses just mentioned attempted to divide their efforts along the lines of their expertise as follows: (1) the secretary of the treasury handled estimates of revenue, changes in the tax structure, or fiscal requirements; (2) the chairman of the Council of Economic Advisors handled economic assumptions, projects, and analyses; and (3) the director of the Office of Management and Budget handled program levels by function and by agency. Seniority among the members played a great part in the asking of questions since the 13 subcommittee chairmen had precedence in the order of asking specific questions, and in setting the general tone of the hearings. From observations, the individual member of the committee viewed the budget through his eyes as a member of a particular subcommittee, thus questioning specific program areas and not really examining the total budget.

These overall hearings did not result in any specific congressional actions such as those now required, since they were designed more to educate and inform the members of the two committees as to the scope of the president's budget than to achieve control.

Following the general hearings, the 13 subcommittees met and conducted their regular budget hearings over the ensuing months, examining the programs and agencies under their jurisdiction. There was little cooperation among the subcommittees in considering the total budget as they pursued their particular goals.

An outgrowth of this method of operation was a feeling on the part of the Congress of an inability to exert any real effort to control the budget process. Strong executive branch leadership with professional staff assistance from such agencies as OMB, CEA, and the Treasury, coupled with growing numbers of special interest groups, seemed to overpower the Congress and the staff of the Appropriations Committees. There was no place within itself to which the Congress could look for overseeing or guiding the financial management of the federal government. The substantive committees of Congress were writing more and more legislation that prescribed and gave explicit directions on federal programs and spending, leaving little discretion to the Appropriations Committees. Another frustration came with the development of many "unholy alliances"—also referred to as "cozy triangles"—when the program manager, the interested subcommittee chairman, and the outside pressure or special interest groups frequently united to thwart the will of the president and of the Congress as a whole.

Another element of frustration arose in the area of actual use of the funds once they were appropriated. For at least since the Antideficiency Act of the 1870s (31 USC665) and perhaps longer, the executive branch, with full knowledge and in many cases with the encouragement and approval of the Appropriations Committees, exercised its responsibilities for prudent management of governmental finances by establishing reserves or by administratively withholding budget authority from some programs. There were many reasons for establishing these reserves. These included changes in work plans, delays in contracting, delays in hiring staff, and redesign of material. Some of these reserves were volunteered by the agencies, but most were imposed by the Office of Management and Budget in its ongoing review of governmental operations. What made the situation critical in the early 1970s (beyond the general political climate) was the number and magnitude of the funds impounded on the orders of the chief executive, especially funds for those programs that had grown out of the Great Society of the Johnson years. The heavily Democratic Congress felt that the Republican president was usurping their power over the purse and thwarting the needs of their constituents. At the same time many program recipients thought that the impoundments were illegal, that the Congress was not acting in their best interests, and that they had no choice but to turn to the third branch of government, the judiciary, for redress. In numerous cases the courts upheld the program recipients, but, because of the lapse of time required for many of the court actions, the fiscal year had gone by and the funds were no longer available. Thus, in the short run, the president had achieved his goal of not spending the money in question.

Over the last decade or so the Congress had enacted an ever increasing number of items of legislation that required yearly reauthorizations for the programs before the appropriations could be enacted (military construction, foreign aid, State Department-USIA operating programs, to name but a very few). Because of this, and operating under the rule that no appropriation shall be made except in consequence of law, the Appropriations Committees were restrained from reporting many of their appropriations until the authorizing legislation was passed. In most cases this process went beyond the beginning of the fiscal year. More and more agencies were forced into starting their operations for the new fiscal year under a temporary appropriation called a Continuing Resolution, which permitted the agencies to continue their functions at the last year's level until a new appropriation bill could be enacted. In one year the Departments of Labor and Health, Education and Welfare operated for all 12 months of the year under a Continuing Resolution—a most devastating procedure for orderly and responsible program management.

The increased emphasis on outlays as a major part of budget considerations is another facet of federal financial management that has altered traditional management concepts and interest. With the ever greater stress by the economists on expenditures (or outlays) rather than budget authority as a measure of budgetary economic impact, program managers found themselves defending their budgets before the Office of Management and Budget and the Congress in terms of outlay as well as obligational levels. However, in many programs outlays had always been considered a byproduct of operations and therefore an item that didn't really require much thought or precision in developing estimates for the budget. The Congress also had difficulty in understanding the new emphasis. Congressman George Mahon, chairman of the House Committee on Appropriations, once stated in regard to the overall budget approximately the following:

> The Congress does not appropriate expenditures. It appropriates obligational authority—which in turn is used to acquire goods and services. After these are provided, a Treasury check is issued and the transactions result in an expenditure or outlay. Yet the overall budget is not discussed in terms of new obligational authorities but in terms of outlays compared with income or revenues. The deficit or surplus being the difference between the two. Some of us have difficulty in shifting from one basis to the other—especially to outlays which have prior years activity as well as the budget year. (This is a paraphrasing and not a direct quote.)

All of this led to the enactment of a far-reaching legislative reform that is having a noticeable effect on the work style of those federal employees most directly affected by the budget process. The impact basically and simply is this: more work. This impact will be examined in the areas of (1) more involvement with the Congress, (2) tighter time schedules, (3) more paper produced on deferrals, and (4) more frequent estimating.

Congressional Involvement

In "the good old days" the turf of agency staffers was, generally, well understood and easily practiced. The Appropriations Committees were the province of the budget officer, while the program managers and the legislative liaison staff worked the substantive committees. Many budget officers devoted a great deal of their time to the Appropriations subcommittees (both members and staff) and became a material force in the legislative consideration of their agency's budget. They, like the Appropriations Committee, tended to react to and to operate outside of the other parts of the legislative process, thus having a minimal involvement in the structure or impact of new programs. This is changing materially; now the situation is much more complex. No longer are the Appropriations Committees the primary decision-making point of the Congress insofar as providing operating funds for government programs. The two budget committees are also in the act with assistance from the Congressional Budget Office. Additionally there is a trend to move more and more programs from authorizations in perpetuity to yearly authorizations that involve another sort of annual re-examination of these items—and one that is much more involved with program costs.

The budget officer must now respond to all of these forces in order to keep the budget on track in the authorizing process while under the consideration of multiple congressional budgeteers. This is exacerbated by having to deal with congressional staff who are exercising an abundance of caution in avoiding an appearance of moving into another's territory, knowing all the while that some friction remains. Many budget officers have recently lamented that they need full time (or more) of oneself to deal with the Congress and of another self to handle the rest of the agency's budgetary management requirements. The answer to this problem does not necessarily lie in greater numbers of agency budget staff since the congressional parties involved do not like to deal with underlings. They all want the assurance which comes with dealing with the top budget person in an organization.

Time Schedules

There is a mixed reaction to the changes in timing that have come out of the new Act. The Congress, in changing the fiscal year from June 30 to September 30, allowed itself a bit more time to enact appropriations bills and brought a welcome discipline to the timing of the passage of substantive legislation in relation to subsequent appropriation requirements. However, there was no relief for the executive branch in its submission of the president's budget. Past year data that was available from the records in the summer months is not now ready until after mid-October. This not only squeezes production of the budget schedules that must be prepared, analyzed, and published in early January, it also delays availability of the benchmark data so necessary to full consideration of the estimates.

On the plus side, in the past many appropriations bills were still under consideratrion by the Congress in the late fall, causing last minute changes to the budget-in-process when they were finally enacted. If the Congress continues to meet the timing requirements that it has set for itself and passes all appropriation bills by September 30, this will be a big help. It will also alleviate a great deal of confusion throughout the government if the device of the Continuing Resolution is not required at the beginning of each fiscal year. It might be noted, though, that one former budget officer actually welcomed the advent of the Continuing Resolution, claiming that the very fact that it was universally misunderstood and inconsistently enforced allowed his agency to proceed as planning without undue "outside" interference.

Deferrals

Another area that seems to have caused additional workload, if not additional understanding, is in the handling of deferrals and rescissions. Many federal operators, either because they see a programmatic advantage or because they fear the consequences of the law, are rushing to spend in order to avoid becoming involved in notifications of deferrals. Those who interpret this part of the Act most stringently see the need to fully utilize their funds before the end of each quarterly allocation, thus moving the once famous "June buying" (to use up money prior to the end of the fiscal year by ordering marginal or unneeded items) to "December, March, June, and September buying".

Some Congressional staff call for deferral notices when they perceive a possible lag in a program, thus insuring that the delay either does not occur or that the Congress can examine the incident as it occurs. On the other hand, some executive branch staff prepare and forward deferrals "just in case" they misunderstood the law. All of this means more paper work, usually for small items. While this part of the Act is slowly being clarified by "case law," it is hoped that the designers of any amendment to the Act will clarify these particular requirements. Otherwise, we fear that the natural tendency of the total federal establishment to err on the side of conservative administration will make deferrals and rescissions ever more burdensome.

Estimating

Everything discussed so far, plus the advent of the current services budget in the Fall, have all worked to cause budget staff to conduct an increasing number of forays into the field of estimating for both budget authority and outlays. Each step of the way, each deviation from the original plan, each new change in the law, must all be "priced out" in accordance with accepted budgetary standards and shared with all of the other parties now enmeshed in the process.

Conclusion

Much has been written and spoken about this piece of legislation. More talk and writing will follow. Many analyses will be made. It seems to many that the Act that started out as a reform has resulted in a complication. It has added new bureaucracies on the legislative side. It has seemingly failed to clarify or establish criteria for setting national priorities, creating, instead, an almost predictable scramble to unscramble one set of priorities in order to set another—resulting only in more red tape. It has failed to address one of the major problems in budgeting a problem that continued to plague not only the government but the taxpayers as well. What to do about that part of the budget that is "uncontrollable"?

Of the $394.2 billion forecast as outlays in the president's budget in fiscal year 1977, $112.9 billion are from prior years' activities that must be paid. Even so, at the end of the fiscal year 1977 there will be available for expenditure in subsequent years, *without any further action by the Congress*, $554.8 billion or one-and-a-half times the total expenditures of the federal budget for 1977. In addition, of the $281.3 billion forecast as outlays from budget authority granted for 1977, more than half (some estimate it to be two-thirds to three-fourths) of the outlays are considered to be uncontrollable from the administrative point of view, i.e., outlays not dependent on further congressional action. These outlays often result from basic enabling legislation such as authority to spend from trust fund receipts, permanent appropriations, debt receipts, etc. Prime examples are interest on the public debt, payments from the Social Security System, Unemployment Insurance, Highway Trust fund, farm price support programs, payments from receipts from Customs, and revenue sharing. This is not a new problem resulting from the Act of 1974, rather it is a continuing problem of some duration which has puzzled both the executive and legislative branches for years. It is receiving further scrutiny as both branches now have to live within ceilings on total outlays. This may well be a point of friction between the Congressional Budget Office, the Budget Committees, and the Appropriations Committees just as it has been between the budget formulators (executive agencies) and the Troika (Treasury, OMB, and CEA). A similar basic conflict exists in the handling of funds appropriated on other than an annual basis. Since CBO and OMB seem to consider these funds as nondiscretionary in their management area, and thus inflexible, it follows that the yearly appropriated funds become the *manageable* part of the budget, and thus subject to more manipulation. The Act of 1974 does not address itself to this problem at all.

Perhaps the operations in connection with the 1978 budget will provide a better clue to the ultimate effectiveness of the new Act when staffs in both branches of government have had one more year of experience. The new administration is of the same political persuasion as the majority of the Congress. This will undoubtedly relieve some of the strains which have existed over recent years, allowing the president a better opportunity to rearrange some of the spending priorities. Thus the Act can be further tested as to whether it can accomplish its major objectives. If things go well enough between the president and the Congress there may well be less of the perceived need that fostered the Act and this could result in a lessening of its impact, since the major areas seem to be the establishment of congressional (as opposed to executive) program ceilings and priority setting, and the imposition of self-discipline by the Congress to assure control.

The budget process in the executive branch was often a game. Now the Congress has the resources and capabilities to play, too. It will be interesting to take another look at this law in five years to see if it is meeting its stated purposes, or to see if it exists in practice at all. Many Hill watchers are not optimistic about there being any outstanding achievements under the Act, but one thing is certain: As a result of the enactment of this law more people will have more knowledge about the federal budget process than before. That has to be a good thing.

10.

Sunset—A New Challenge*

James Davidson

It is a pleasure to be with you today to discuss what I believe is one of the most significant proposals before the Congress to reform the way the government conducts its business.

The use of labels to identify legislation has the potential of creating misunderstanding and confusion. Modern civilization, however, does not seem to have changed in its tendency to identify new ideas with old symbols. In ancient Egypt the sun was a common sign in religion and government. In the 94th Congress we adopted a new proposal requiring open meetings for multimembered agencies. It drew its name, the Sunshine Act, from laws developed by the state of its principal sponsor, Senator Lawton Chiles of Florida.

When our reform bill was first introduced in February, it was called the Government Economy and Spending Reform Act of 1976. That was too cumbersome for Washington jargon.

It soon became known as the zero-based budgeting bill, largely because many of the terms used in the legislation were borrowed from similar concepts employed by advocates of zero-based budgeting—a confusion of terms which I hope I will be able to clarify before the end of my remarks.

As the legislation moved forward, it increasingly became known as the "Sunset Bill." That title came out of Colorado, and I suppose it is appropriate that the western part of the country should originate the word "sunset" to deal with this subject.

One of the most common grievances against government which has been expressed by the American people in one public opinion survey after another is that they do not think they are getting their money's worth out of the tax dollars they pay.

Making the federal government more productive could well be one of the most difficult tasks any of us—either in Washington or outside—has ever undertaken. It demands not breezy promises which can never be met, but diligent, unexciting scrutiny of the nuts and bolts operation of Congress and the executive branch.

The sunset bill is designed to provide a process for applying such scrutiny to the operations of the federal government. It is intended to accomplish for the individual parts of the federal budget what budget reform has begun to do for the budget as a whole: lend discipline and cohesiveness to the way the federal government handles the taxpayers' money. In that, it is a logical follow-up to budget reform.

Let me briefly describe what the legislation would do.

First, it would put all government programs and activities on a five-year reauthorization schedule. All would have to be reauthorized every five years or be terminated. The sole exceptions to this provision would be payments of interest on the national debt and programs under which individuals make payments to the federal government in expectation of later compensation. For example, this would include railroad retirement, social security, civil service retirement, and Medicare.

Second, the bill would establish a schedule for the reauthorization of programs and activities on the basis of groupings by budget functions and subfunctions. Programs within the same function would terminate simultaneously; this would give Congress an opportunity to examine and compare federal programs in an entire functional area rather than to do so in bits and pieces. The schedule would be set up so that all of the functional areas would be dealt with within one five-year cycle.

Third, by establishing a termination date for each federal program, the bill does not presuppose that the Congress will simply allow large numbers of programs to die. Rather, it reverses the assumption which now exists that all existing programs and activities deserve to be continued simply because they existed in the previous year. In other words, it attempts to go beyond the mere incremental evaluations which presently are applied to most federal programs.

Fourth, the bill sets out a schedule for committee review of federal programs and for the reporting of the results of those reviews to the Congress. That schedule makes maximum use of the timetable for authorization bills already required by the Congressional Budget Act and it would encourage Congress to make use of the program review already undertaken by the General Accounting Office.

Fifth, the principle of periodic review and reenactment for federal programs also is extended to the area of tax expenditures. The concept of tax expenditures was borrowed from the Congressional Budget Act. It recognizes the importance, for example, for the Congress on one hand to examine the effectiveness of programs designed to stimulate housing development in the country, and on the other hand to give equal attention to tax incentives which have been created to achieve the same or similar purpose.

A number of factors led to the introduction of the sunset legislation.

I mentioned the public opinion polls which have told us that the American people have lost a measure of faith in their government. The only government worker getting high marks from the public is the local trash collector, because at least people know whether or not he is doing his job.

A second major factor has been the experience of working with the new congressional budget process. Under that process, Congress is beginning to reassert control over the federal budget—the most important statement of national priorities that we have.

If there is one point that has been brought home during our experience under the Budget Act, it is that we have only a limited amount of resources to commit to solving serious national problems.

There may have been a time when we could afford nearly a multiple of different legislative solutions to each of our national problems—when we didn't have to worry which programs were working and which programs were not—because we knew there was enough in the till for everyone.

Today we no longer have those options.

As the Congress began to work earlier this year on the fiscal 1977 budget, it was estimated that it would take approximately $45 to $50 billion more than last year to simply continue all of the 1976 programs in the 1977 budget.

Most of the growth was attributable to the increase in uncontrollable spending, which in 1967 accounted for about 59 percent of that years' budget, but which in 1977 will take up roughly 77 percent of all federal spending. Over the same period, taking inflation into account, discretionary or controllable spending has not increased.

As Edmund Muskie observed earlier this year, "At this rate, the much hailed congressional budget process could, in the not too distant future, become little more than the simple arithmetic sum of predetermined spending levels."

No matter how successful the new budget process is, the statement of national priorities embodied in the national budget as a whole will not be completed until Congress improves control over the individual parts and over services the budget is intended to buy.

S.2925 was offered as a framework in which we could begin to exert such control.

Another reason for the development of sunset legislation stems from our previous governmental efforts to solve what are truly serious national problems: hunger, poverty, ignorance, and disease. We have expended a considerable amount of energy in building a substantial federal structure for the purpose of attacking those problems.

Today, however, we find that many of the goals we have worked for have been thwarted by an unwieldy and unresponsive federal establishment.

On many occasions we have cited the example of the General Accounting Office study of outpatient health care facilities in the District of Columbia where several different federal programs funded eight separate clinics in one neighborhood. The result of this lack of coordination was that doctors in some of these clinics were seeing as few as four or five patients a day.

Edmund Muskie described this example as outrageous, not because he no longer believes in a major federal role to assure that Americans receive the health care they need, but because he believes so strongly in that federal role.

For if better use were made of those and other federal resources, more Americans could receive the services they need and which these resources were intended to provide.

The approach for program review embodied in S.2925 could offer a chance to gather together scarce resources that are not now used effectively and to redirect those resources where they are needed most.

In the short run, we can see how limited our capacity for innovation is by the fact that only 23 percent of the 1977 budget falls in the area of discretionary funding.

That presents a challenge for government to look beyond our year-to-year approach and install procedures by which we can examine the totality of federal expenditures over a longer range.

I would like to conclude with a few observations gained from nearly a year of attempting to develop a system of periodic program review.

First, sunset is essentially a congressional process. It was designed to complement the two-step authorization/appropriation process by which the Congress develops and funds federal program efforts.

In order to make the process manageable we do not terminate—and therefore require the re-enactment of—every provision in the Federal Code related to a program. Rather, we targeted only the provisions of law which serve as authorizations for appropriations. It is those which would become invalid if not re-enacted by the termination dates set forth in the bill.

This is not to say that the executive branch does not have a role in sunset. The executive agencies and the congressional support agencies, such as the General Accounting Office, the Congressional Budget Office, and others would play a significant role in assisting the Congress in its consideration of reauthorization proposals.

Second, we have attempted to respond at every point to concerns for the workload which this process could bring to the Congress and to the government. The schedule for review and termination has been structured to balance the workload on committees of Congress over the five-year period. In addition, we have attempted to build in an element of discretion which will allow committees to determine what programs deserve greater or lesser attention within any given review cycle.

Third, we have attempted, although admittedly with varying degrees of success, to separate this much needed periodic review process from the concepts associated with zero-based budgeting. Zero-based budgeting as it has been employed by private corporations and some state governments, is essentially an executive management tool for the development of decision options for program managers.

Sunset is a process by which Congress can begin to review federal programs as an integral and regular part of its authorization function. While there are references to procedures for review which parallel concepts drawn from zero-based budgeting, the similarity stops there.

Sunset is an attempt to offer a vehicle to Congress to respond constructively to criticism that it has not met its responsibility for program examination.

Earlier this year, a creative observer of the Washington scene likened Edmund Muskie's sunset bill and the Congress to the story of Archy and Mehitabel.

Archy, as readers may recall, was a poet returned to life as a cockroach. Mehitabel, was a fun-loving cat of easy virtue, perpetually producing kittens which she promptly forgot about.

Archy, with some social conscience, regularly inquired about the well-being of Mehitabel's offspring—only to be met by a blank stare and innocent query, "What kittens, Archy?"

Like Mehitabel, the Congress for a decade or so has been happily producing programs in a variety of shapes, sizes, and pieces. And like Mehitabel, Congress never checks up on its progeny.

Sunset offers a stronger congressional voice for setting national priorities—for taking responsibility for past actions out from under a suffocating system which now has the upper hand in controlling the fate of programs we have enacted.

Finally, it proposes a neutral process. It does not propose to judge the success or failure of any program.

Nor does it propose to make judgments as to what our national priorities should be. These judgments must continue to be made by the Congress and the executive branch together as they are now.

As Edmund Muskie states: "It does propose to open a dialogue on the important task of making government more productive. And I am convinced that this is an undertaking in which liberals and conservatives alike have a vital stake."

Note

*This speech was given to the National Capital Area Chapter of ASPA's annual (1976) conference.

11.

Evaluating Sunset
What Will it Mean?

Steve Charnovitz

During the past couple of years, there has been a renewed interest within the United States in improving the performance of government and the accountability of bureaucrats. While past rounds of such self-examination focused on management by objectives, decentralization, and reorganization, and before that on rational decison making and systematic planning, the current round focuses on resource allocation (through zero-base budgeting), legislative and program evaluation (through regulatory reform and sunset laws), and once again on reorganization. Of all the new reforms, it is the sunset laws which, although they have received the least attention, have the greatest potential for impact on public policy.

A sunset law is a special kind of law which automatically terminates government agencies, programs, regulations, or other laws after specified time periods unless the legislature first reviews and then decides to recreate them.[1] The idea behind sunset is that it is easier for a legislature to save the good programs than to discard the bad ones. Therefore, the sunset law attempts to facilitate legislative oversight by reversing the presumption of continuity.

At this time, it appears likely that the Congress, either this year or next, will enact a sunset law applying to the federal government. Last year, Senator Edmund Muskie introduced such a bill to terminate almost all federal programs every five years. The proposal, which was then called the Government Economy and Spending Reform Act, attracted extensive support and was modified and reintroduced this session with 42 cosponsors (since increased to 55) as the Sunset Act of 1977 (and given the low number of S.2). Support for the bill is bipartisan and includes both liberals and conservatives. For example, Senators Hatfield, Kennedy, and Goldwater were among the sponsors. The Senate Subcommittee on Intergovernmental Relations of the Governmental Affairs Committee held several days of hearings on the bill, at which time the director of the Office of Management and Budget voiced the support of the Carter administration for most of the bill.[2] In late April, the subcommittee made a few changes in the bill and referred it to the full committee for action.

The thesis of this article is that while all federal programs should be reviewed (and many do need detailed evaluations), applying the sunset process to the entire federal government is not likely to be workable and is very likely to do serious damage to both the substance of controversial programs and the process of policy making. (For a contrasting viewpoint, see Chapter 10, James Davidson's "Sunset—A New Challenge.") This article will discuss first, what sunset is and how it differs from the present system; second, the experience with sunset in the states; third, how the federal sunset process is designed to work; fourth, what sunset would do to the federal government; and fifth, how the sunset bill could be improved.

Is Sunset Anything New?

The essence of the sunset process is that it is action forcing. Because government agencies, programs, regulations, or other laws are automatically terminated after specified periods, no review or action by a legislature would mean the expiration of the program. Sunset is a legislative response to the perceptions of poor executive performance and lapse in congressional oversight. Sunset is not meant to replace the executive management and evaluation functions, but rather to supplement them with a rigorous congressional review. While zero-base budgeting and sunset laws could be complementary, they are by no means the same thing. The former is a system for program managers to examine the total budget through discrete decision packages and priority rankings, while the latter is a legislative tool to determine how programs have been working and whether they should be continued.

The argument has been made that sunset is not really anything new, that it exists now in the form of program authorizations for definite time periods.[3] Seen in this way, sunset is just the extension to every program of the present congressional oversight and reauthorization process. While this argument has some validity, it misses that which is very new about sunset.

First, while it is true that Congress could improve oversight without a sunset law, the passage of such a law would itself be a congressional commitment to perform the review and evaluation role in a much more comprehensive and conscientious fashion. An analogy to the congressional budget process is apt. While the Congress could have done all of what the budget committees are doing now through the regular appropriations committees and through a change in the floor rules, it took the passage of the congressional Budget and Impoundment Act both to signify and effectuate this new responsibility.

Second, a sunset law would facilitate the congressional review function by requiring detailed evaluations of programs during the examination year and by grouping similar programs together for sunset review. At present, program authorizations expire almost randomly, but under sunset they would expire by budget function (e.g., energy) which would make it easier for Congress to reduce overlap and duplication. For example, when a single agency comes up for review, as the Federal Energy Administration (FEA) did in 1976, it would be politically difficult to let the agency expire, but if all energy agencies (FEA, FPC, ERDA, NRC, and parts of Interior and Agriculture) came up for review simultaneously, it would be much easier for Congress to consolidate them into a logical organization.

Third, with respect to the federal budget, not that many programs have authorizations of definite time periods. While there is no complete catalog of federal program authorizations, a ballpark estimate (by the author) is that only about one-third of the authorizations are definite. An increase in oversight from one-third to nearly all federal programs is more a difference in kind than simply a difference in degree.

Sunset Legislation in the States

The impetus for sunset originated in Colorado where Common Cause proposed to "sunset" the state's Department of Regulatory Agencies. Colorado passed the first state sunset law last year and as of June 1977, 17 other states had enacted this type of legislation and every state legislature had considered sunset in some form. The state laws vary as to coverage, length of review cycle, and application. Some cover only the occupational licensing agencies (e.g., New Mexico), a few cover all the agencies in the state government (e.g., Louisiana), and the rest are somewhere in between. Some states have six-year cycles (e.g., Oklahoma) and the others have four-year cycles (e.g., Alabama). Most of the sunset laws apply to agencies, but a few (e.g., Georgia) terminate the law in question in addition to the agency that administers it. Many states provide for a terminated agency phase-out period of six months or one year.

At this time, it is too early to learn any lessons from the implementation of the state sunset laws because the provisions have only gone into effect in two states, Colorado and Alabama. The preliminary indications from these two states, however, are that the less extensive Colorado law was more successful.[4]

How Sunset Would Operate

The federal sunset bill calls for the automatic termination of spending authority for all programs (with the few exceptions of Medicare, Social Security, retirement and disability pay, and interest on the national debt) every five years.[5] Basically, there are three parts to the sunset mechanism. First, all government programs are divided into five groups according to government function (budget functional categories) and are evaluated and reviewed on a five-year cycle. The first review date of the cycle is September 30, 1979, which is the last day of fiscal year 1979. Second, the bill would prohibit the obigation or expenditure by an agency of any appropriation for a fiscal year beginning after the relevant review date unless the appropriation had been reauthorized by law. Third, any bill to authorize a new appropriation would be out of order unless the proper congressional committees had conducted a "sunset review" of the program and submitted the required report.[6] Unlike the state sunset laws, which would terminate agencies or laws, the federal bill would operate by starving programs through funding cutoffs. In other words, even though the law would remain on the books, no funds could be spent to enforce it.[7]

The best way to explain how the sunset process would work is by example. Consider the case of the Defense Department programs, most of which would expire on September 30, 1979. On or before October 1, 1978, the General Accounting Office would furnish to the House and Senate Armed Services committees the results of prior audits and reviews of all national defense programs. The committees would also be able to call on GAO, the Congressional Budget Office, and the Congressional Research Service for additional information and analyses and could seek information or assistance from the Defense Department.

During the next several months, both committees would conduct a sunset review of the defense programs "to determine if the merits of the program justify its continuation rather than termination, or its continuation at a level less than, equal to, or greater than the existing level." The committees would be allowed to determine the scope and detail needed in this systematic evaluation, but they would at least consider "the degree to which the original objectives of the programs have been achieved . . . expressed in terms of the performance, impact, or accomplishments of the program and of the problem it was intended to address, and an analysis of the costs of the program."

By May 15, 1979, both committees would have to submit the results of the sunset review. If either of the committees wanted to continue any of the defense programs, the report would have to include an "identification of the problem, needs, or mission," "the objectives of such a program," "an identification of any other programs having similar, conflicting, or duplicative objectives, and an explanation of the manner in which the program avoids duplication or conflict," "an assessment of the consequences of eliminating the program or consolidating it," and "a projection of the anticipated budget authority requirements for the program, including an estimate of when, and the conditions under which, the program will have fulfilled the objectives for which it was established."

Congress would have from May 15 to September 30 to decide whether to continue paying for a national defense system. No reauthorization would be in order unless the committees made the required reports and the Pentagon would sunset, unless reauthorized by September 30. If, because of scheduling problems or because of a filibuster, Congress is unable to take a vote on the question of reauthorization, a joint resolution (called an Extension Resolution) would be in order to allow the continuation of the spending authority for another year. There would be a strict limitation on debate of the Extension Resolution.

Life Under the Sunset Law

Sunset is being proposed as a partial answer to the problems of unaccountable bureaucracy, ineffective programs, and uncontrollable budgets. While these problems are, unfortunately, all too real in some cases, the Sunset Act would probably cause damaging systemic and behavioral changes in the way the federal government works without sufficient compensating advantages. Several of these potential changes are discussed below.

The Advantage Would Shift to the Opposition

Many new programs pass Congress by close votes and almost all of them are the result of painstaking compromises and coalition building. For example, one legislative strategy is to water down bills only as much as necessary in order to garner a majority of the votes. If each program sunsets every five years, the most controversial ones are likely to be eroded in the process of rebuilding the support necessary for repassage since those desiring to weaken a particular program would gain the tactical advantage.

This would happen for two reasons. First, Congress would be preoccupied with the whole mass of programs under reconsideration (one-fifth of the government) and therefore would not be able to focus on the most controversial of the group. Second, the sunset deadline of September 30 forces a vote to be taken at some point and thereby gives the opponents of the program an advantage that they did not have when the bill was passed originally. Proponents of a new bill have time on their side because they can choose the most opportune moment to press for enactment. Sunset would reverse this situation and therefore is not nearly as "neutral" as is suggested by the bill's statement of purposes which includes—"to provide a neutral procedure for the reexamination and reauthorization of all Federal programs."

Moreover, congressional consideration of issues might be unduly influenced by adverse publicity near reauthorization time or by temporary crises that jolt the public sentiment. For example, what if a large increase in car prices was announced just before a renewal of the Clean Air Act programs came up for a vote? Unfortunately, if such a coincidence appeared to influence policy, more coincidences would probably occur since the period of vulnerability for a program would be frequent and periodic.

Finally, when reauthorizations do get through Congress, they would still be subject to a presidential veto. Thus, a coalition to continue a controversial program might have to include two-thirds of Congress and therefore any president with the support of over one-third could completely reshape a large portion of the government every year. Of course, presidents can veto reauthorizations under the present system, but the difference is that Congress now has the capability to provide for a permanent authorization subject only to a congressional decision to review or repeal it. Under sunset, Congress would be giving up this capability.

Last Minute Decisions Would Cause Disorder

Under the timetable for sunset review, the review year coincides with the year in which the program authorization expires. In other words, if Congress does not reauthorize a program between May 15 and September 30, the program would terminate on October 1. This one-day notification (or even five months if the decision is made early) would severely disrupt congressional operations, federal program planning, state and local governments, and international agreements that require United States funding.

The congressional budget process now calls for a first budget target to be set by May 15 and a second by September 15. While the purpose of these targets is to adapt the budget to fiscal goals, the targets are composed of functional units which eventually must come down to judgments about the funding of individual programs. Under a sunset law, the setting of these targets by the budget committees would be greatly complicated since about one-fifth of the program authorizations would be in question each year. Moreover, with so many program authorizations subject to last minute changes, the appropriations committees would be forced either to rubber stamp the decisions made by the other committees or to delay the approval of new appropriations until they had been adequately studied. Such delays would mean the return of the old practice of government by continuing resolution.

Whatever sunset does to the congressional process would be doubled in its impact on the executive branch since authorizations for two fiscal years would be in doubt every summer during the time in which agencies draw up their budgets. The effect of this uncertainty would be to make any but the most short-term government planning impossible at federal, state, and local levels.

Not only would sunset interfere with government planning, but it would also directly interfere with day-to-day life, by constantly raising doubts about the continuation of basic federal programs. For instance, why make hospitalized veterans worry about whether the hospital will remain open? If the answer is that giving the ax to federal prosecutors, weather forecasters, or veterans' hospitals will never seriously be considered, then why write laws that are shams?[8]

Finally, any last minute lapses in program authority, while the substantive legislation is still on the books, would create controversies that would invite judicial intervention and the loss of public accountability that this entails. For example, even if no funds are appropriated by the Congress for unemployment insurance or food stamps, a person eligible for these benefits might be able to get a federal court to order the government to meet its legal obligation to carry out these programs.

Agencies Would Become Overly Self-Protective

While no one would deny that public administrators ought to feel accountable to the Congress, the sunset provisions could have the effect of making officials too timid to carry out their duties. During the year of congressional evaluation and review, how many officials would be brave enough to make a decision unpopular with any sizeable group? Under sunset, administrators would probably devote (and waste) quite some time to touching bases, assessing options, documenting decisions, and justifying for the record every decision taken. Moreover, agencies could be expected to spend additional funds for public relations efforts such as writing and distributing reports that extol their accomplishments.

Not only would sunset slow the pace of government action, but it would also inhibit administrators in setting proper objectives for their programs. Since agencies would be judged on the basis of how well they performed, administrators would be apt to set easy goals that they could be sure to attain and would avoid experimental programs out of a fear of failure. The one exception to this picture of agency malaise is the aggressive manner in which agency protectiveness would be manifested in interagency relationships. Because all agencies performing the same general function would be reviewed together under the sunset bill, agencies with similar missions may begin to see themselves in competition with each other for survival. While some ''creative confusion'' and competition may be desirable, sunset would hinder cooperation by causing agencies to downgrade the efforts and to publicize the mistakes of their rivals. Administrators would attribute program failures to organizational problems rather than to other underlying causes.

Executive or Congressional Administration?

The fundamental and continuing role of the Congress should be to determine the needs of the people and the priorities among various programs and then to embody these in legislation. While the oversight role is important and must be carried out if the appropriation power is to be executed responsibly, the level of effort expended upon it should depend on the extent of a program's problems. If Congress enacts the sunset bill, then a considerable amount of time will be needed for the detailed evaluation and review of every federal program and this will come at the expense of investigating new problems, making necessary trade-offs, and developing adequate legislation. This diversion of time would be a mistake because the legislative function is a full-time job and Congress is both the best and the only branch of government that can carry this out. Furthermore, Congress ought to be judged by the public, not by how many important programs have been reenacted, but by how Congress deals with new crises and responds to changing views.

If government programs are ineffective, which some are, then the president needs to be doing a better job of managing and evaluating them. This is true not only because the Constitution directs the president to "take care that laws be faithfully executed," and because the people look to the president to do this, but most importantly because the president, as chief executive, is best equipped to accomplish this difficult task. Regardless of any sunset law, the executive branch will have to do its own comprehensive program evaluation. If the president does this well, particularly in assuring standards of objectivity, then Congress should be able to rely on these results, together with some supplemental oversight of problem areas, to make legislative decisions. If the president does not do this well, then Congress should specifically direct improvement and watch carefully to make sure that it happens. Unfortunately, the president is not even mentioned in the sunset provisions of the Muskie bill, and the role of the agencies is only to provide information and assistance when requested. If the purpose of sunset is to prevent duplication and achieve the optimal use of resources, then something went wrong along the way.

Instead of a system of automatic expiration, why not a system of directed evaluation to examine unsatisfactory programs and then improve them through better management, controlled experimentation, adequate staffing and training, and clarification of program intent? The president should, of course, involve Congress and the public in program evaluation, but above all else he should involve himself (through his Cabinet).[9] For if the president won't take charge of administering the government, then Congress will be obliged to try. Finally, if the president is going to do a better job of management, then he must have several tools from Congress such as reorganization authority, program consolidation authority, timely budget decisions, and purview over some of the "independent commissions."

Sunset Bill Improvements

It is the contention of this article that the benefits of program evaluation can be obtained without the cumbersome and perhaps dangerous sunset process. If, as it now appears, Congress is going to sunset the government in some fashion, then several improvements in the current bill should be considered.

First, the review year for programs should be changed so that it precedes the year in which the program authorization expires. For example, the military defense programs, which would expire on September 30, 1979, should be brought to a reauthorization vote before September 30, 1978. If the programs are reauthorized, then both the budget and military planning for fiscal year 1980 would go much smoother. If the programs are not reauthorized, then the Pentagon would have one year to close down its bases and Congress would have one year to reconsider its decision.

In most cases, it is not the termination of programs that will be desired, but rather the improvement of programs attained through organizational reform, efficient administration, and revised goals. The one-year period would allow the president to work with Congress to reform the program in accordance with congressional direction. Along these lines, Congress should require itself to issue a report explaining what needs to be corrected.

Second, the agency head should be given the chance to testify before the review committee after the committee has reached a preliminary decision on the reauthorization of the program. In addition to examining any relevant GAO reports, the committee should also examine any relevant evaluations done by the agency or by outside groups. Moreover, the agency head should be directed to work together with Congress in designing needed program evaluations.

Third, if the sunset procedures are rewritten so as to rely more upon the executive for the detailed program evaluations, then Congress could focus on a function which is in need of much more attention, that of reviewing legislation to see if it is being carried out. Too often, the problem with a program is not that it has failed to work, but rather that it has not been seriously tried (and Congress has done little about it).

Fourth, if Congress allows an authorization to expire, then it should repeal the substantive law to which the authorization relates. Otherwise, the government will be left open to intervention by the courts and charges of hypocrisy by various affected groups.

Fifth, the method of cataloging programs for sunset review should be reconsidered as the use of budget functional categories, which are generally input rather than output (or mission) oriented, does not appear to be the most appropriate way either to determine the proper level of resources for a particular purpose, or to make the necessary trade-offs among various programs. For example, programs relating to social services, public assistance and other income supplements, and training and employment are reviewed in three different years, rather than all together. In addition, there seems to be a contradiction between grouping similar programs and spacing out committee workload over the five-year period. Health programs, for example, are considered in three different years.

Sixth, careful planning and evaluation should precede the introduction of reforms as it should precede the introduction of new programs. Before implementing sunset, Congress should either await its results in several states or experiment with it on a small group of programs at the federal level.

Seventh, to be consistent with its own theory, any sunset law should be subjected to sunset review after its first round of operation.

Conclusion

If government is going to succeed in solving some of the difficult problems of society, then government programs must be made more effective and efficient. This must happen because ineffective programs shatter expectations and thereby cause contempt for government, because inefficient programs unnecessarily raise government spending and thereby cause adverse economic and political effects, and because the implementation of one set of actions often precludes doing another. Moreover, if the public is going to continue to ask its government to take on very difficult problems, then it is important that a thorough housecleaning be conducted soon. Otherwise, the perception of some that government causes more problems than it solves will be reinforced.

It is the conclusion of this article that the enactment of the sunset bill would probably not lead to the kind of program evaluation that is urgently needed, that the sunset process would be likely to have harmful side effects, and that its adoption would postpone the implementation of more constructive reforms. At this point, sunset is a virtually untried procedure. If it succeeds, then some government programs would be improved and some useless programs would be discontinued. If it fails, then governments at all levels would be handicapped, some useful programs would be gutted, and considerable time and effort would be wasted. Only those favoring less government activity have nothing to lose from the enactment of the federal Sunset Act.

Later Developments

On July 1, 1977 the sunset bill was reported in the Senate following the unanimous approval of the Governmental Affairs Committee. The sunset bill now has 60 cosponsors and will probably come up for a Senate vote later this year. No action has yet been taken in the House.

Several significant changes have been made in the bill, the most important of which are: (1) the title of the bill was changed to the "Program Evaluation Act;" (2) the first review date was postponed from September 30, 1979 to September 30, 1982; (3) the five-year review cycle was changed to a six-year cycle composed of three review periods, each covering most of the two years of a Congress (for example, the first review period would extend from March 1981 to September 1982); (4) a procedure was set up whereby changes in the review schedule could be made through 1980; (5) programs funding civil litigation, criminal litigation, and the enforcement of court actions relating to civil rights guaranteed by the Constitution are no longer automatically terminated; (6) the bill totally exempts the Federal Judiciary Agency and exempts for the first complete cycle 21 regulatory agencies (including both independent agencies such as the FTC and executive agencies such as OSHA) and the regulatory activities of three agencies (EPA, FHA, and the Federal Reserve); (7) provision was made for the review of the substantive law related to any program authorization that is not reenacted; and (8) a title dealing with Tax Expenditures was stricken.

The most important change, however, was that a two-track approach was established to distinguish between periodic reconsideration (a streamlined "sunset review" that would be done for all programs) and formal evaluation (a comprehensive examination of selected programs). Programs to be evaluated would be selected by the House and Senate following recommendations by the authorizing committees and by the president. The president would be required to submit his evaluation of these programs by December 31 of the first year of the review period and the committee's report on its evaluation would be due by May 15 of the second year. Both the president's and the Committee's evaluations are required to cover the 12 topics listed in the bill, one of which is "an assessment of the effect of the program on the national economy, including, but not limited to, the effects on competition, economic stability, employment, unemployment, productivity, and price inflation, including costs to consumers and to business."

Many of these changes are significant improvements over the original bill. The postponement of the first review date will give Congress more time to learn from the state experiences and to regroup the programs for review. Lengthening the review period will allow more time for evidence collection and analysis. Examination of the substantive laws underlying any terminated authorization will avoid dangerous inconsistencies. The two-track approach is a recognition that the president needs to be more involved in program evaluation and that a major evaluation is not needed and cannot be accomplished for every program.

The original thesis of this article was that sunset was not likely to be workable but was likely to cause damage to certain programs and to the policymaking process. While the changes made in the bill by the Committee would go a long way toward making the sunset process workable, sunset would still place important programs in jeopardy, disrupt government planning and operations, and inhibit agencies from carrying out their duties. Nevertheless, the Committee is moving in the right direction by requiring the president to carry out comprehensive evaluations of designated programs. Perhaps further emendation will permit the benefits of congressional review without the disadvantages of the sunset mechanism.

Notes

1. The sunset concept is generally traced to Theodore J. Lowi's *The End of Liberalism* in which Lowi advocated a "Tenure-of-Statutes" Act to set a limit of from five to ten

years on the life of every organic act. Lowi suggested that "[a]s the end of its tenure approaches, an agency is likely to find its established relations with its clientele beginning to shake from exposure, new awareness, and competition." (Lowi, *The End of Liberalism*. New York: W.W. Norton & Company, Inc., 1969, p. 309.) The first sunset law was probably the Federal Advisory Committee Act of 1972 (USCA 5 App. I) which terminates all advisory committees (whose duration is not fixed by statute) every two years, unless specifically extended by the president, the department head, or Congress, as appropriate.

2. Testimony before the Subcommittee on Intergovernmental Relations of the Senate Committee on Government Affairs by Bert Lance, the then director of the Office of Management and Budget, on March 22, 1977.

3. Program authorizations are the parts of laws that give Congress the authority to pass appropriations for a specific use. Appropriations can be three types—permanent, multiyear, or annual. Both Houses of Congress require that appropriations be authorized by law (House Rule XXI and Senate Rule XVI) and any appropriation bill not so authorized can be stopped by a point of order. The Muskie sunset bill also declares out of order any appropriation (for any year following the review date) that does not have an authorization in law except in cases of emergency or, for the first year following the review date, in cases in which either the House or the Senate committee had reported a reauthorization bill.

4. Neal R. Peirce and Jerry Hagstrom, "Is it Time for the Sun to Set on Some State Sunset Proposals?" *National Journal*, June 18, 1977, pp. 937-939.

5. The Subcommittee mark-up of S.2 on April 28, 1977 added another section to the bill excluding independent regulatory agencies (e.g., FPC, CAB, ICC, FCC, and FTC) from the sunset process. This was a compromise with the sponsors of the Regulatory Reform Act of 1977 (principally Senators Percy and Byrd) whereby certain regulatory agencies would be reviewed under the provisions of the Regulatory Reform Act rather than the Sunset Act. It remains to be seen how long this compromise will remain in effect.

6. The requirement for a sunset review also applies to the programs exempt from automatic termination (Medicare, Social Security, retirement and disability pay, and interest on the national debt) if the appropriations for these programs would change for any year following the review date. The appropriations for these programs are uncontrollable and will almost certainly change from year to year.

7. In addition to establishing this sunset process, the sunset bill (as approved by the Subcommittee) also includes several other provisions worth noting. First, CBO, in cooperation with GAO and CRS, is required to submit a comprehensive inventory of all federal programs. Second, the bill establishes a Citizens' Commission on the Organization and Operation of the Government to study and make recommendations on ways to improve the effectiveness of the federal government. The commission would have 18 members and would submit a final report by September 1980. Third, the House Ways and Means and Senate Finance committees are directed to prepare a five-year reauthorization schedule for all tax expenditures, in line with the reauthorization schedule for program authorizations. Finally, following the submission of the president's budget, all agencies are required to send a copy of their OMB submission to Congress.

8. Edmund Muskie was correct when he stated that "there is no program so important that it should not be reviewed on a regular basis." (Hearings before the Senate Committee on Rules and Administration, September 8, 1976, page 7.) But the issue is not *whether* basic programs should be reviewed (of course they should); it's *how*

they should be reviewed. The sunset method would hamstring Congress into an inflexible review schedule that may prove impossible to meet.

9. Congress and the executive branch should collaborate in deciding the priorities for evaluation, in determining the proper measures of success, in designing and carrying out the study, and in interpreting the results. This is not done nearly enough at the present time.

PART III

OTHER DEVELOPMENTS

In this portion of *Contemporary Public Budgeting*, three separate topics are explored: a budget information system; productivity; and tax revolt.

Governments are complex undertakings involving large sums of money, many people, numerous programs, and hopefully, several interrelated management systems. Dean Silverman explains to us New York City's integrated financial information system developed to help resolve some of the City's financial problems. In 1975, the city was faced with a crisis that state and federal governments eventually helped the city resolve. One of the mandated reforms by the state was to improve the financial records of a city, whose budget was larger than most of the nations in the world. Although New York City's information problems are complex, they are reflective of the budget problems found in many other moderate to large budget systems. Thus, this article is instructive to those interested in the contemporary complex interrelationships between budgeting and other management functions.

In an era when the worth of government is questioned, government productivity, or the lack of it, is a common topic. Harry P. Hatry, in an article first published in the *Public Administration Review*, helps us understand that topic. He tells us what productivity measurement is, the current status of productivity measurement, the emerging measurement methods, measuring output/input ratios, effectiveness measurement procedures, and the status of comprehensive measurement systems. Dr. Hatry gives us a status report on productivity as a tool of public management.

In the last chapter, this editor and Sydney Duncombe examine the tax revolt, most commonly associated with California's Proposition 13. The chapter explains the reform, the motivation causing it, its effect on California, and the spreading tax reform movement, The chapter then focuses upon a case study of tax reform in the state of Idaho. The study allows one to see how the reform came about, and the effects of more radical tax reform on a small state.

12.

New York City's New Integrated Financial System

Eli B. Silverman

Introduction

In the spring of 1975, New York City could not market its bonds, service its debt, and faced the prospect of service curtailment and nonpayment of employee salaries and moneys owed vendors and suppliers.[1] This fiscal crisis spotlighted financial management issues that have become increasingly relevant to all levels of government.[2] State and local governments throughout the United States are faced with complex financial management issues due to the scarcity of resources, the increased level of intergovernmental fund transfers, and subsequent dependency upon higher levels of government.

New York's problems led to the imposition of city, state, and federal financial management mandates. New York State had already created a Charter Revision Commission for New York City in 1972 with a broad directive to provide for "structural [governmental] reform, . . . citizen participation, . . . and effective local government." In the intervening three years before the commission issued its 1975 report, however, financial issues emerged as preeminent, prompting the commission to focus on the city's financial management. Therefore the first, and probably most important, of the commission's six governmental recommendations read: "Shall the fiscal, budget, audit and accounting changes proposed as amendments to the City Charter be adopted."

These financial changes (presented in the spring and approved by the voters in November, 1975) sought to rectify financial inadequacies, and shaped some of the provisions embodied in the June 1975 State legislation establishing the Municipal Assistance Corporation (MAC)[3] and the September 1975 legislation creating the Emergency Financial Control Board (EFCB).[4] These acts required a balanced city budget by fiscal year 1978 and, in addition to the federal legislation providing seasonal loans, mandated that the city have auditable financial records maintained in accordance with generally accepted accounting principles for municipalities. The December 1975 federal loan legislation also required that the city demonstrate real and measurable progress toward these objectives.

The achievement of these goals required substantial changes in the city's financial management system. These involved financial management concepts and practices, which are of great concern to all governments. They include budgetary planning, cash planning and management, resource allocation, expenditure control, budget management, revenue and grant management, and relationships between expenditures and revenues. The enormous task of designing and installing a comprehensive integrated financial information and control system was intensified by the fact that IFMS (Integrated Financial Management System) was first installed in July 1977, spanning an eighteen month period. This period compares favorably with similar but less complex efforts commonly requiring five year implementation periods.[5]

This paper examines IFMS's fundamental features directed at the city's major financial management weaknesses and other salient IFMS uses. These features are discussed under the topics of accounting, budget preparation and organization, budget management and control, purchasing, and payroll. Finally, the major processes of system design, training, implementation, and maintenance will be reviewed.

Accounting

Accounting weaknesses have generated the greatest amount of state directives and subsequent city changes. The city's exemption from the State General Municipal Law, requiring every municipality to prepare its budget and control its finances according to the state comptroller's Uniform System of Accounts for Municipalities (a system based on generally accepted principles and practices), bred inconsistency and nonuniformity in the city's accounting system. Concerned with their own individual needs, the city's Office of Management and Budget, comptroller, and Finance Administration each maintained their own system of accounts, yielding varying budget account and employee data. This diversity was compounded by the divergence between the comptroller's accounts designed for aggregate central control and the preaudit of payrolls and vouchers, on the one hand, and individual agency data, on the other, entered on the comptroller's account—further maximizing error and disagreement.

Revenue and Expenditure Recognition

Absence of uniform and standard accounting principles was also manifested in inconsistent yearly recognition of revenues and expenditures. Revenues were created or expenses postponed in order to end a fiscal year with a paper-balanced budget. These revenues were generally recorded as soon as identified, even if cash receipt was later, while expenditures were not recorded until cash was actually spent. Besides violating generally accepted accounting standards, the mixed system facilitated budgetary imbalance and hastened the growth of short-term debt required to finance expenses while awaiting anticipated revenue.

The Charter Commission, the MAC, and the EFCB legislation all required the city to follow a system of uniform accounting and reporting, based on the principles set forth in the state comptroller's uniform system of accounts for municipalities as modified by the state comptroller in consultation with the city comptroller. These principles included accounting for all expenses, excluding debt service and pension fund contributions, on an accrual basis (when they are incurred rather than when paid), and recognizing all revenue when they are received (cash) except for those recognized on an accrual basis only if they are both measurable and available (primarily federal and state grants).[6]

Table 12.1 illustrates these changes in the city's accounting policies.

Table 12.1
Comparison of New York City Accounting Policies

Bases of Accounting

	Pre-IFMS	IFMS
Recognition of Revenues		
Federal and State Grants	Accrual	Accrual
Real Estate Taxes	Accrual	Cash
Other Revenues	Accrual or Cash	Cash
Recognition of Expenses		
Personal Services (PS)	Cash	Accrual
Other Than Personal Service (OTPS)	Accrual or Cash	Accrual
Debt Service, Pension Contribution	Cash	Cash

Encumbrance Accounting for OTPS

	Pre-IFMS	IFMS
Requisitions	--	Preencumber
Purchase Orders	--	Encumber
Contracts	Encumber	Encumber

Source: Management Accounting for New York City's Integrated Financial Management System. New York: Urban Academy, April 22, 1977, p. III-5.

Fund Structure

The adoption of state-approved standard municipal accounting principles required changes in the city's chart of account's definition of the manner in which financial transactions were categorized, recorded, summarized, and reported. A chart of account's important fund classes is supposed to comprise a complete set of independent, self-balancing accounts comprising revenue and expenditure entries. The diverse nature of governmental operations precludes a single, unified set of accounts for recording and summarizing all of a governmental unit's financial transactions.

The city's existing fund structure, however, did not comply with these municipal accounting principles. The expenditure side of each fund class was subdivided by agency, then by program within an agency, and finally by object of expense. The revenue side was subdivided on a different basis, by service and type of revenue. Over 60 fund classes were maintained but most transactions were recorded in four classes. Most expenses were charged against one fund class ("expense budget accounts"), while most revenues were entered into one of three fund classes ("general fund," "real estate taxes," and "miscellaneous revenue"). The latter three were primarily used to collect and transfer revenues to the expense budget account before money was expended. *Contrary to municipal accounting principles, there was no clear relationship between particular revenues and particular uses.* Increased dependency upon, and transfer of, federal aid into an undifferentiated miscellaneous revenue account led to the use of these earmarked funds for nonpermissable purposes causing subsequent disallowances by the grantor agency. In addition, the city's ability to legitimately borrow through the issuance of revenue anticipation notes was restricted through the mingling of federal and city-generated revenue.

Under IFMS, several existing funds oriented toward revenue sources (such as real estate taxes, supplementary revenues, and special and miscellaneous revenues), which should have been listed as assets within a fund class, are now consolidated in a new general fund. In other areas, additional funds have been created to segregate certain enterprises' activities, intergovernmental service activities, long-term debt actions, and other items not previously recognized as separate funds.[7]

The above accounting changes were necessary to provide timely, accurate information on city finances to the investment community and city residents. To accomplish this, the restructured accounting system is geared to provide general information and reports that service the needs of budget control and financial management. Indeed, the MAC legislation mandated that these accounting changes govern budget preparation and presentation as well as the return of expense budget items, previously included in the capital budget, to the expense budget.[8] Subsequently, the EFCB legislation's requirement of a three-year financial plan, capped by a balanced Fiscal Year 1978 budget, was based on this new accounting system. As designed in IFMS, the interface of accounting and budgeting systems is very essential.

Budget Organization and Presentation

Under IFMS, budgeting and other system components (purchasing and payroll) are integrally tied to accounting in a number of ways. As a basic dictionary characterizing system transactions, the chart of accounts (held in common by all IFMS components), ensures uniform system classification and permits users to translate descriptions of various types of activities to numeric codes and vice-versa. Subsystems also have common access to master tables that permit cross-referencing of IFMS's organizationally based budget data and nonorganizationally structured data. The tables store information about these data elements' relationships and aid in data selection and generation of IFMS's wide variety of financial reports.

Basic to IFMS's major thrust, therefore, is the replacement of separate fragmented financial management systems by one system unified not only by the chart of accounts and master table but also by the standardized formats for most types of transaction, all stored in one integrated data base. Citywide accounting, budgeting, purchasing and payroll data are, for the first time, brought together in a single computer facility at the newly created Financial Information Services Agency (FISA).[9]

The restructuring and reorganization of the data base supports IFMS's major budgetary changes. These are organizationally based budgets, separate revenue and expense budgets, and plans for revenue and obligations.

Organizationally Based Budgets

Organizationally based budgets replace the previous arrangement under which the expense budget was organized by agencies, then subdivided into personal services (PS), other than personal services (OTPS) and, lastly, into programs and subprograms. The subprograms contained supporting schedules of budget lines. Many of these programmatic budgets lacked conformance to true municipal program structures and, perhaps more importantly, precluded financial control since they lacked designated managers accountable for budgeting resources.

Under IFMS, agencies must budget by responsibility centers, which are units that are part of an agency's organizational hierarchy under the control of a specific manager. Every budgeted expense and revenue dollar is associated with a responsibility center whose manager is responsible for monitoring and managing its expeditures and revenues.

Separate Revenue and Expense Budgets

In a departure from previous structure, IFMS provides for separate expense and revenue budgets. The latter, organized by revenue source, assigns revenue monitoring and collecting responsibility by indicating the organizational unit(s) responsible for earning and/or collecting the revenue. While the city's expense and revenue budgets should be equal, agency revenue budgets only contain those revenues that the agency is responsible for estimating and generating. Consequently, agency revenue and expense budget totals often differ. IFMS revenue budgets include greater detail of revenue sources (including state and federal aid) than previously available in order to further pinpoint revenue managerial responsibility.

Planning for Revenue and Obligations

Central to budget organization and presentation is the preparation of monthly agency plans for obligations, revenue recognition by budget source, and cash collection by revenue sources. These monthly plans are indispensable to agency budget management and control.

Budget Management and Control

IFMS enhances agency budgetary management and control through a variety of mechanisms. IFMS generates monthly reports on actual spending, revenue recognition, and cash collection versus the plans. These reports compare the previous month's activity to the plan; they also compare the current annual forecast to the budget for each item. Exception reports identify cases in which: (1) the current spending forecast exceeds the budget; and/or (2) the current revenue forecast is less than the budget. A state of exception signals the need for management action, either to adjust activity in remaining months or to modify the budget to bring it in line with current projections. This ability to monitor agency fiscal situations and make adjustments during the ongoing year contrasts favorably to the previous inability to adjust to seasonal spending and revenue variations due to limited periodic revenue and expenditure information.

Other reports useful to budget management and control include: reports that keep track of budget modifications; and monthly reports on the current modified PS (personal service) and OTPS (other than personal service) expense and revenue budgets, by responsibility center, by revenue source for each agency, and cityside. In addition, monthly reports are generated by attributes that transcend IFMS's organizational budgetary format. For example, agency summaries of budgeted expenses are reported by organizational level, by program, and eventually, as a future IFMS feature, by community service districts.

The procedures utilized to modify and update the budget have significantly changed under charter revision and IFMS provisions. Within overall appropriation limits and certain OMB controls, the charter gives agencies the authority to adjust their PS and OTPS supporting schedules. Thus, within those specified limits, agencies are granted greater resource allocation flexibility through the creation of new position lines, changes in their titles, and shifts within OTPS object funding. IFMS, then, can accommodate the charter's thrust toward increased agency authority for financial management commensurate with greater accountability for financial management decisions.

Purchasing

The purchasing component participates in IFMS's financial control and management by establishing controls over OTPS expenditures which refer to the purchase of supplies, materials, equipment, and services that are procured through purchase orders and contracts.

Some of the city's previous purchasing controls were developed by individual agencies while others were instituted under the central control of the Department of Purchase. Further fragmentation of purchasing records occurred, moreover, as the result of agencies adopting a variety of systems to keep track of their purchases. The pre-IFMS purchasing system also required comptroller control of and responsibility for some OTPS appropriations, and expenditures.

Under IFMS, this responsibility rests primarily with agency managers as charter revisions require delegations of detailed preaudit responsibility. Agency managers must also be able to ensure that no purchasing commitments be made unless sufficient funds are available. This requires that managers have adequate data on purchasing activities. In turn, this requires an integrated system of data on all purchasing transactions as a means of preventing overobligation of available funds. The purchasing subsystem provides timely and accurate information in the form of management and control reports. These are extracted from a unified purchasing data base that is fully integrated with the budgeting and accounting subsystems.

Payroll

A multiplicity of agencies and departments and a variety of forms and procedures complicated the city's pre-IFMS payroll system. IFMS provides information on the flow of payroll documents and transactions at a detailed level of control. The payroll, as with the purchasing subsystem, is integrated with budgeting and accounting to ensure that payroll expenditures do not exceed budgeted PS expense appropriations. Thus payroll expenditures are preaudited by verification for availability of funds against the budgeting and accounting subsystems. This integration also enables the cost accounting features of the system to provide agencies with improved PS cost allocation information.

In addition, the creation of a single payroll data base obviates the necessity of agencies maintaining separate records. Again, eliminating multiple records removes the need for difficult reconciliation and discrepancies between disparate records. Finally, automated routine processing, by preventing large transaction delays and backlogs, allows payroll personnel to monitor the payroll process and make appropriate managerial decisions.

IFMS as an Aid to Agency Heads

In the process of providing a more comprehensive, integrated, swift, and timely financial management information and control system, IFMS offers agency heads numerous options for improved financial operations. It is appropriate to briefly discuss some of these.

Securing Revenue from Federal and State Grants

Since many agency programs are partially reimbursable by federal and/or state aid, agencies need expenditure data on their programs and operations that are reimbursable (called expenditure driven revenue).

In order to claim the aid, agencies require rapidly assembled detailed proof of expenditures charged against these programs. IFMS provides this ability (through reporting categories) to tag, collect, and report such actual expenditures incurred by personal lines or goods and services expended by such a claimable program. In addition, IFMS produces a record of the transaction in order to ensure the auditability of claims and lessen the chances of disallowances.

Increasing Agency Earned Revenue

The Mayor's Management Plan (mandated by the new City Charter) requires agencies to maximize their revenues. This is often difficult without information to evaluate different uses of scarce agency funds. IFMS codes (reporting categories) provide agencies with a means to relate the cost of personnel to their revenue collection. If the Parking Violations Bureau, for example, wants to assess the revenue gathering impact of increasing the number of meter maids, then all meter maids can be tagged with the same tag (reporting category code) as the fees they collect from parking violations. This determines the impact of specific personnel increases or decreases on revenue from parking violations.

Analyzing the Costs of Agency Programs and Operations

Either on their own initiative or at the request of the mayor, agencies may wish to assess the costs of particular programs or "missions." Agencies can restructure their budgets to parallel IFMS organizational units (responsibility centers) with programs or missions. For example, the organizational unit, prison health services, could parallel delivery of health services.

In instances where programs or missions cut across more than one organizational unit (responsibility center), IFMS easily and readily provides a means of identifying and associating (through program codes) up to five of these programs or missions for each IFMS organizational unit. This information is more easily and readily provided than prior to IFMS.

Analyze and Plan for Maximizing Service Delivery and Performance

Given scarce city dollars, agencies can associate responsibility centers to service delivery units (i.e., precincts in the police department and borough command level in the fire department). This enables comparison of similar crime statistics-precincts with their respective staff levels, performances, and expenditures. This type of information will become increasingly important due to the new charter's requirements for reporting to community boards and the need to report productivity information to the financial community.

Meeting Charter Requirements for Geographic Reporting

By 1981, the city must completely implement new charter requirements on local service districts. In the future, IFMS will be able to sort and collect data by defined geographic areas. This feature, when implemented, will provide resource allocation data by geographic reporting areas.

Improving Monitoring and Control of Agency Purchasing and Budget Modification Transactions

Programs and services are sometimes impeded because of delays in securing purchase or in processing personnel assignment changes. IFMS enables agencies to retrieve updated, instantly accessible information as to the status of purchase orders, contracts, and vouchers. In addition, a pending modification file efficiently tracks the status of budget modifications entered into the system and "in process," and, most importantly, indicates how long they have been pending.

As indicated above, IFMS's time schedule was extremely tight. It is appropriate to summarize the city's approach to designing, training, implementing and maintaining this new financial management system.

System Design

In December 1975 New York contracted with American Management Systems, Inc. (AMS) and Touche Ross (TR) to assist in defining new budgeting and accounting principles in conformance with state comptroller prescriptions, developing new public and management financial reports, and developing a systems concept for new budgeting and accounting systems. The January 1976 contractor reports, "City of New York Financial Management Policies, Procedures and Systems," provided the preliminary design concept and framework for the city's new financial management system and its implementation. The documents addressed the previously discussed subsystems of budgeting, accounting, purchasing, and payroll.

In February 1976 additional contracts awarded to AMS, TR, and Ernst and Ernst (E and E) required assistance in establishing financial management policies, defining reporting requirements, and strengthening organization structures and personnel skills. Specific assignments included: AMS-general subsystems design and automatic data processing support; TR-subsystem design assistance, development of a general implementation plan, and procedures for improving control over federal and state aid revenues and certain types of encumbrances; E and E-implementation plan for system installation and necessary documentation for agency conversion to the new system.

In June 1976 the assistance of two other contractors, Bradford National Corporation and the Urban Academy, was also enlisted. Bradford was contracted to assist in the automatic data processing aspects of the new system and the specific payroll subsystem design. The Urban Academy was responsible for development of training requirements, training manual preparation, and training classes.

By October 1976, except for the payroll subsystem, the overall design specification and documentation, requirements for agency subsystem implementation, and implementation plans were completed. In addition, several features were being developed. These included design of the new payroll subsystem, improvement of the city comptroller's present accounting system, improved interim encumberance system, and interim federal and state aid revenue systems.

Training

Since training had to be geared to analyses of current financial management weaknesses and new system requirements, it was addressed in conjunction with system design. By July 1976 agency procedures for "converting" current agency expense budgets to IFMS's organizationally based budgets and development of IFMS revenue budgets were published. Six hundred city personnel received training in budget conversion procedures.

By September 1976 a needs analysis of city agency employees was completed. This analysis, which helped shape training approaches, assessed the impact of IFMS on personnel tasks and the extent and nature of city personnel affected by IFMS. Between November 1976 and June 1977 training manuals, curricula, and training materials were developed. Numerous and varied training courses were provided for over 6,000 city employees during this period.

Project Management

IFMS's design, training, and implementation was organized through a project management approach. The mayor and comptroller each appointed a codirector, both of whom shared responsibility with a project manager. These individuals managed a task force that consisted of the five consultant groups and key city agency personnel. Project management required a continuous, high degree, and largely successful flow of interaction, cooperation, and delivery of IFMS products (reports, manuals, etc.), within agreed upon time schedules. While some city personnel were actively involved in such activities as advising and reacting to design and implementation and serving as pilot implementors, etc., IFMS's tight schedule necessitated a basically top-down approach with little opportunity for significant agency conceptualization.

System Maintenance

When IFMS was installed on July 1, 1977, the new Financial Service Information Agency (FISA) began processing 5,000 daily documents involving over 10,000 transactions. While a full assessment of its success is premature, there are notable signs of progress. By September 1977 purchasing was the most advanced subsystem, processing between 3,000 and 4,000 documents a week, with 80 percent going through error-free on the first pass, 17 percent on the second pass, and 3 percent on the third pass. In addition, 1,700 accounting documents were processed weekly with few significant problems. The most troublesome problems centered on delays in the budget modification process. From July to September 1977, 150 weekly mods consumed up to 15 days as compared to IFMS's proclaimed goal of five to seven days. This situation is being addressed.

System maintenance is closely geared to continuation of the arrangement of an IFMS coordinator designated for each agency and a consultant attached to each agency. Current plans call for continued system improvement and refinement, updated and individualized training, and eventual inclusion of the capital budget.

Notes

1. The consequences would, of course, be immense. In the words of the state legislation creating the Emergency Financial Control Board: "If such failures and defaults were to occur, the effect on the City and its inhabitants would be devastating: (1) unpaid employees might refuse to work; (2) unpaid vendors and suppliers might refuse to sell their goods and render services to the City; (3) unpaid recipients of public assistance would be unable to provide themselves with the basic necessities of life; and (4) unpaid holders of City obligations would seek judicial enforcement of their legal rights as to City revenues. These events would effectively force the City to stop operating as a viable governmental entity and create a clear and present danger to the health, safety and welfare of its inhabitants."

2. To be sure, the causes of the City's fiscal crisis are complex and multifactored. Some explanations have focused on externally induced socioeconomic and demographic factors such as employment decline, a continual outflow of middle income, highly educated residents, and an inflow of poorer, less educated, and more service-consuming groups. These and other factors, it is contended, have contributed to the rapid expansion of city services, expenditures, employment, and borrowing.

   Still others have focused on state and federal politics that have benefited suburban and sunbelt areas at the expense of urban and northeastern areas. Federal policies include: subsidies supporting southern agricultural mechanization, hastening the migration of previously employed poor tenant farmers to northern cities; G.I. Bill of Rights, supplying veterans with four percent home loans with no required down payments, helping to vacate city neighborhoods; the tax deduction allowance on home mortgage, stimulating suburban development; transportation programs, which earmarked gasoline taxes for highway construction, laying down a vast network of roads among suburban areas, encouraging transportation at the expense of the railroads and facilitating commuting from suburb to city; and discriminatory federal assistance programs. The state is also accused of contributing to the city's plight through its urban renewal and road building projects that have devastated older stable neighborhoods. In addition, state and federal policies also partially establish the level of contribution the city must make to the public programs it administers.

   For a collection of divergent perspectives, see Roger Alcaly, and David Mermelstein. *The Fiscal Crisis of American Cities*. New York: Vintage Books, 1977.

3. The June 11, 1975, Municipal Assistance Corporation (MAC) legislation was an attempt to avert New York City from pending default by injecting state control over city borrowing practices and budget and accounting systems.

   MAC was empowered to convert the city's pressing short-term debt into long-term bond obligations by selling bonds backed by a corporate reserve fund containing city sales and stock transfer tax revenue. MAC would oversee the city's budget process, examine financial records, and limit short-term borrowing.

4. The Emergency Financial Control Board (EFCB) was created as a second state attempt to avoid city default of its debt obligations when it became clear that the available MAC credit was not restoring investor confidence. The EFCB, dominated by state appointed members, oversees city financial operations and administers additional state aid and loans.

5. In an April 1977 progress implementation review of the city's new financial management system, the General Accounting Office observed: " . . . American Management Systems, Inc., indicates that developing a complex system such as this one requires 31 to 88 months, depending on whether certain phases are performed

sequentially or concurrently. We believe that these estimates are reasonably accurate.'' Comptroller General of the United States, *New York City's Efforts to Improve its Accounting Systems*, April 4, 1977, p. 5.

6. Both the Charter Commission and MAC legislation also required annual audits of the city books by the state comptroller or an independent public accountant, a state requirement from which the city was previously exempt.

7. Currently, however, IFMS fully supports only the general fund, debt service fund, and trust and agency fund. As a step toward a full-scale implementation of the intragovernmental service fund, the Municipal Service Administration bills agencies for its services using the intracity sales and purchase feature of IFMS. This represents an initial support of this fund.

   The intracity sales and purchase feature separates the accounting for these activities, thus permitting adoption of such accounting conventions as inventory accounting and depreciation that are not appropriate to the general fund.

8. Transfer of expense-budget items from the capital to the expense budget was also addressed in the Charter revisions, EFCB legislation, and the December 1975 federal legislation providing for up to $2.3 billion a year in federal loans through July 1978 to assist the city in meeting seasonal cash needs.

   This federal legislation also required an increase in city taxes, balanced budget by Fiscal Year 1978, adoption of EFCB approved accounting procedures, and General Accounting Office audits.

9. FISA uses an IBM 370/158 computer with an IBM 370/145 computer for backup and load leveling. IFMS uses IMB's Information Management Systems for data base management and teleprocessing control.

13.

The Status of Productivity Measurement in the Public Sector

Harry P. Hatry

Unless you are keeping score, it is difficult to know whether you are winning or losing. This applies to ball games, card games, and no less to government productivity for specific services and activities. Productivity measurements permit governments to identify problem areas and, as corrective actions are taken, to detect the extent to which improvements have occurred.

This status report deals first with what productivity measurement is, then presents a viewpoint on the current status of productivity measurement in government in the United States, and—finally—briefly examines the likely prospects for the future, including consideration of facilitating and inhibiting factors.

What is Productivity Measurement?

Productivity is most often defined as the ratio of output to input for a particular activity. To apply that definition to any particular government service, however, is a complex task and subject to controversy. Productivity measurement general y has been defined in the public sector as encompassing both *efficiency* and *effectiveness*. *Efficiency* indicates the extent to which the government produces a given output with the least possible use of resources. *Effectiveness* indicates the amount of end product, the real service to the public, that the government is providing. Effectiveness encompasses the concept of quality and level of service provided.

The difficulty with measuring most government services is that the measures of the amount of work being done do not adequately reflect the "real" service being provided. Output indicators such as number of tons of paving materials used—or number of potholes patched—are useful measures of work accomplishment, but they indicate nothing about the effectiveness of the service, i.e., the resulting rideability of the streets. Similarly, the "number of clients treated" in a health or rehabilitation program does not indicate how many people are actually helped.

The measurement of *efficiency* also requires that product quality be considered. How meaningful can the "cost per ton of waste collected" be unless it pays attention to the quality of the output? A reduction in unit cost achieved at the expense of a reduction in service quality is not a true efficiency improvement. Has the service degraded, through excessive spillage, for instance, or a shift from backdoor to curb collection? Another example: Increases in the "number of arrests per police officer" may not mean increased efficiency if the percentage of arrests failing to lead to conviction because of police error (i.e., the quality of arrest) is worsening.

Measures of efficiency can take various forms. These include the following.

The ratio of number of units of work accomplished per unit of input. This is the classic efficiency measurement. The output is expressed in work units such as tons of garbage collected, number of arrests, square yards of street patched, gallons of water treated, etc. The input units can be expressed in terms of the number of employee-hours allocated to that activity (to measure labor productivity), or in terms of dollars, adjusted for inflation over the relevant period of time (to act as a substitute for all resources applied—"total factor" productivity). The ratios can be expressed as output divided by input or input divided by output.

Utilization-availability measures. Also often used in some government activities are measures of "downtime" for vehicles and equipments and "productive hours" for personnel. In the latter case, employee time is logged to distinguish the amount of time spent on activities defined as productive (doing maintenance; being on patrol for police) as opposed to other activities defined as nonproductive (a maintenance crew waiting for materials to work with, or a police officer waiting in a courtroom to testify). This type of measure should be considered as only a proxy measure of efficiency, since shifts in downtime or productive time will not necessarily result in improvements in output or costs. These changes will occur only if personnel are reduced or if additional output results from the extra available time. (For example, added time released for police officers to permit them to patrol streets leads to increased productivity only if that extra patrol time leads to fewer crimes or more successful arrests.)

Ratio measures that consider the quality of the output. Examples would include "number of clients *helped* per employee-hour" (rather than "number of clients *treated* per employee-hour") and "number of arrests that survive the initial judicial screening per police officer" (rather than "number of arrests per police officer").[1] These measures are rarely used today by state or local governments, in part because of the current lack of precedent and the need to revise data-collection procedures to obtain them.

Productivity indices. These are used to measure the percent of change from one year to the next. They measure relative rather than absolute efficiency. A productivity index can be constructed for any of the types of measures described above, but thus far they have been constructed primarily from ratios of output to input. The level of efficiency in a base year (or base period of perhaps two to three years) is given the value of 100, and performance in future years is then expressed as a percentage of the performance in the base period times 100. An over-all index of the efficiency of all government activities can be computed as a weighted sum of the indices for different activities (such as by weighting each activity by the number of employee-hours it used in the base year).[2]

Current Status of Productivity Measurement

The federal government is conducting annual productivity measurement using the traditional output divided by input type of measures. This will be discussed further below.

At the state or local government level, there is currently little regular productivity measurement of any kind. A review in early 1976 by Hughes, Heiss, and associates for the public sector committee of the National Center for Productivity and Quality of Working Life reported few major operational efforts in place in local governments. A 1976 Urban Institute examination of the budget documents of 247 cities and counties found that only a small proportion contained either efficiency or effectiveness measures to any extent: Only 25 percent displayed at least one effectiveness measure; 10 percent listed at least one efficiency measure. Only a very small number of those jurisdictions presenting measures went beyond such familiar ones as the number of crimes, number of fires, number of traffic accidents, and number of illnesses (which have been collected largely because of strong federal impetus).[3] Of course, many local governments do not put all their performance measurement information into their budget document. However, the author's observations of a number of governments suggest that these findings are typical of the degree of productivity measurement in the United States.

At the state government level, the Urban Institute and the National Asssociation of State Budget Officers conducted a mail survey in 1975 to obtain perceptions of state budget offices as to the adequacy of existing efficiency and effectiveness measures.[4] Results of the responses from 32 states are presented in Table 13.1. They can be summarized as follows:

- 15 of the 32 responding states, or 47 percent, rated existing *efficiency* measures as only barely adequate or inadequate; only 10 states, or 31 percent, rated their measures as adequate or quite adequate.
- 29 of the 32 responding states, or 91 percent, rated current *effectiveness* measures as barely adequate or inadequate; none rated these measures as adequate or quite adequate (the other three had no opinion).

Table 13.1
How 32 State Budget Offices Rate the Adequacy of Available Efficiency and Effectiveness Measurements

	Economic and Manpower Development		Corrections		Transportation		Physical and Mental Health	
	Efficiency Measures	Effectiveness Measures	Efficiency Measures	Effectiveness Measures	Efficiency Measures	Effectiveness Measures	Efficiency Measures	Effectiveness Measures
Excellent	1	1	1	—	1	—	—	—
Good	8	5	4	2	14	7	8	4
Fair	7	9	13	14	9	9	16	12
Poor	10	11	9	11	3	10	1	10
No opinion	6	6	5	5	5	6	7	6
	32	32	32	32	32	32	32	32

	Public Assistance		Other Social Services		Parks and Recreation		Licensing and Regulation	
	Efficiency Measures	Effectiveness Measures	Efficiency Measures	Effectiveness Measures	Efficiency Measures	Effectiveness Measures	Efficiency Measures	Effectiveness Measures
Excellent	1	—	—	—	1	1	1	—
Good	11	8	4	2	10	4	6	4
Fair	7	10	9	10	10	9	7	5
Poor	9	8	15	14	6	11	11	14
No opinion	4	6	4	6	5	7	7	9
	32	32	32	32	32	32	32	32

	ALL STATE PROGRAMS	
	Efficiency Measures	Effectiveness Measures
Quite adequate	3	—
Adequate	7	—
Barely adequate	7	11
Inadequate	8	18
No rating given	7	3
	32	32

SOURCE: The Urban Institute, *The Status of Productivity Measurement in State Government: An Initial Examination* (September 1975).

A separate examination of state budgets and other public documents found very few states had a significant number of efficiency and effectiveness measures.[5] As with local governments, a very small number of states accounted for a large percentage of the measures.

Emerging Measurement Methods

Despite the paucity of productivity measurement, four potentially significant developments are emerging:

1. Renewed efforts at efficiency measurement involving the calculation of ratios of work accomplished to inputs, with the latter defined in terms of numbers of employee-hours or dollars.
2. Greatly increased use of engineered work standards.
3. Development of effectiveness-measurement procedures. This development appears to have two directions, one using citizen or client ratings of various service characteristics, and the other using more systematic data-collection procedures such as predeveloped rating scales and trained observer procedures to systematize ratings of service characteristics (e.g., street cleanliness).
4. Increased interest in comprehensive measurement systems. These may involve the use of more than one, and perhaps all, of the foregoing approaches.

Each of these will be discussed in turn.

Measuring Output/Input Ratios

The use of measures expressed as ratios of the amount of work accomplished to the amount of employee-hours (or dollars) goes back decades (including the enthusiasm for performance budgeting in the 1950s). However, their use has been relatively rare in recent years.

The foremost example of current use of these indicators is the federal government. Since Fiscal Year 1972 it has annually collected such measures for many federal activities. The 1976 federal effort included more than 1,320 output indicators from 53 agencies. A total of 1.8 million employee-years of federal civilian employment representing 67 percent of total civilian employment was covered.[6] Table 13.2 displays a sample of the output indicators provided by the agencies. The Bureau of Labor Statistics uses these output data, together with agency-provided data on the number of employee-years, to compute productivity indices. The focus is entirely on labor productivity—that is, output related to the number of *employee-years* (and not to dollars expended).

Based on these data, the Joint Financial Management Improvement Program reported in 1976: ''Since the base year, Fiscal Year 1967 [the federal government retroactively obtained data for prior fiscal years], productivity has increased 10.7 percent, or an average annual increase of 1.3 percent. As might be

Table 13.2
Sample Federal Output Indicators

Function	Sample Output Indicator
Citizens' records	Claims processed
Reference services	Reports issued
Transportation	Millions of long-tons shipped
Power	Kilowatt hours sold
Medical services	Outpatient visits
Education and training	Student-years trained
Agriculture and natural resources	Planning & application services provided
Library services	Items loaned
Military base services	Millions of meals served
Internal audit	Investigations completed
Regulation: Rulemaking & Licensing	Applications approved

Source: Extracted from "Annual Report to the President and Congress on the Joint Financial Management Improvement Program, July 1976, Productivity Programs in the Federal Government: Supplement to Volume I, The Measurement Data Base." One indicator has been selected from 11 of a total of 25 functions.

expected, there are substantial variations in the rates of change for individual organizations and for the 25 functions for which productivity indices have been developed. Average annual rates of change for the different functions range from −2.4 percent to +6.5 percent." [7]

It is important to note that the output measures illustrated in Table 13.2 do not reflect the true end products of federal services. As the earlier discussion of workload outputs stressed, these measures by no means reflect the effectiveness in delivering quality health care, education, defense, economic well being, and the like. Also, it is not clear whether agencies providing the output data consider the quality of these products, or define these products sufficiently tightly to assure consistency—often difficult for government activities.

At this time, it is not clear whether Congress or the agencies have used these productivity data. In addition to the question of meaningfulness of such data, it also appears that the data presented publicly are too aggregative; they are presented for each of 25 functions but not for specific agencies or activities. The Bureau of Labor Statistics, however, *does* provide output-input ratios and productivity indices on each indicator of the individual agencies for their analysis and use. Some of the output indicators are shown in Table 13.2 for a sample of the 25 functions.

Nevertheless, despite these failings, the federal government has made a reasonable beginning. It can be argued that even such limited data can provide government managers with information for spurring productivity improvements.

At the local government level, there have been a few attempts at such efficiency measurement—perhaps most notably by the city of Sunnyvale, California. Sunnyvale, as does the federal government, has stressed productivity indices based on ratios of amount of work accomplished to input.[8] Along with each program, however, Sunnyvale also includes quality goals such as (for patrol services): "the achievement of no more than 5 percent growth rate in crimes against persons or property" and "maintain an average response time of 3.5 minutes to all emergencies, 90 percent within five minutes."

Engineered Work Standards

Local, state, and federal governments have rediscovered the industrial engineer. In recent years there has been a rapid increase in the number of government agencies using engineered work standards.

In engineered work standards, individual work activities are examined systematically to determine the amount of time that the activity *should* require— the "standards." Subsequently, workers report on the actual time used. The actual times can then be compared to the standard times to indicate the efficiency of the work force. Work standards are employed primarily for relatively routine operations such as clerical activities and street maintenance.[9]

A 1973 survey of state and local governments found that 61 of 509 responding cities and counties (12 percent) had made use of work standards.[10] Most of these were established since the late 1960s. Of the state governments, 10 of 42 responding governments, or 24 percent, indicated that they used work standards in at least one agency.

It seems quite likely that the usage at both the state and local levels has increased substantially since then. A 1976 International City Management Association survey found that 50 percent of the responding 456 local governments reported some form of work standard/work measurement activity, but this figure very likely includes many jurisdictions without "engineered" standards.

There also has been a growth in the range of activities to which work

Table 13.3
Examples of Applications of Work Standards in Phoenix, Arizona

Police:
  Communications Bureau
    Clerical positions
    Police service/information
      center
    Police telephones
    Radio dispatchers
  Information Bureau (Records)
    Clerical positions

Water:
  Water distribution
    Meter repair shop
    Field repair/service crews
  Water production
    Treatment plant operators
    well sites/pump stations
  Water accounting
    Service orders
    Meter reading

Sewers:
  Sewer field repair/service
    crews
  Treatment plant operators

Library:
  Clerical positions
  Overdue book notifications
  Circulation desk
  Orders & processing
  Cataloging-clerical positions
  Book mending

Street Maintenance:
  Preventive maintenance
    (sealing, etc.)
  General Maintenance
    (patch crews, etc.)

Traffic Engineering:
  Sign maintenance
  Paint striping

Computer Services:
  Keypunch operators

Housing Inspections:

Real Estate:
  Title searches

Parks and Recreation:
  District parks
    Grounds maintenance
    Facility maintenance

Public Housing:
  Grounds maintenance
  Facility maintenance

Building Safety:
  Plans review
  Inspections
  Landfill compaction
  Inspections

Maintenance Services:
  Building maintenance
    Custodial services
    Remodeling Crews
  Equipment management
    maintenance

Source: "Employee Incentives to Improve State and Local Government pro-
    ductivity," Greiner, Bell, and Hatry, NationalCommission on Pro-
    ductivity and Work Quality (March 1975), Table 14, pp. 114-115.

standards have been applied. Table 13.3 illustrates some applications for such standards. (Note that ratios such as the ''number of cases per caseworker'' are not work standards but rather are indications of the incoming workload per employee; such ratios say nothing about the output of the work effort.)

Effectiveness-Measurement Procedures

A small number of jurisdictions have begun to introduce effectiveness-measurement procedures on a regular basis. An example is the use of inspectors to assess the cleanliness of city streets by means of a preconstructed photographic rating scale. The cities of Washington, D.C., New York, and Savannah, Georgia, for example, have made periodic ratings of this kind. Table 13.4 illustrates one way in which such effectiveness-rating data is being used by the New York City Department of Sanitation. As illustrated, such performance data can be used to make comparisons among areas of the jurisdiction, from one time period to another, and to compare actual results to targets. Other local governments, including Dayton, Ohio; Fort Worth, Texas; Lakewood, Colorado; Nashville, Tennessee; St. Petersburg, Florida; and Sunnyvale, California, along with states such as Pennsylvania and North Carolina, have also recently undertaken multiservice effectiveness-measurement efforts.

The use of regular ratings by citizens of various characteristics of local government services appears to be growing. Surveys of random samples of citizens (such as of 500 to 1000 households) have been undertaken both to obtain citizen ratings of service characteristics and to obtain ''factual'' information related to service quality such as extent of citizen use of various government programs (e.g., recreation, libraries, and transit), extent of crime victimization, and frequency of rat sightings. The cities of St. Petersburg, Nashville, Dallas, and Dayton have been unusual, thus far, in undertaking such citizen surveys for these purposes on an annual basis (since about 1973-74), thereby permitting progress to be identified. A number of other jurisdictions (small and large) have recently begun to try such surveys, though thus far primarily on a one-time basis. (These include such cities as Palo Alto, California; Randolph Township, New Jersey; Sioux City, Iowa; Sunnyvale, California; and Zeeland, Michigan.) Examples of regular use of such surveys by state governments are as yet rare or nonexistent. However, North Carolina and Wisconsin have recently undertaken initial tests of such surveys of their citizens.

Comprehensive Measurement Systems

It is becoming apparent that the complexities of government services require multiple productivity measurements for each service in order to provide a comprehensive perspective on how productivity is progressing. Seldom does a single measure capture enough information to provide government officials or

Table 13.4

Illustration of Use of Effectiveness-Measurement Information: New York City Citywide Street Cleanliness—December 1976**

Sanitation* Command	Rank This Month	Per Cent Better (+) or Below (−) Target	Dec. 1976 Target	Dec. 1976 Rating	Dec. 1975 Rating	Per Cent of Streets Acceptable (1.5 or Cleaner)		
						Dec. 1975	Dec. 1976	Change Dec. 1975 to Dec. 1976
Brooklyn North	1	+5.2	1.55	1.47	1.52	45.1	48.6	+3.5
Bronx West	2	+3.8	1.56	1.50	1.54	53.8	46.4	−7.4
Manhattan West	3	+2.7	1.50	1.46	1.49	53.6	50.4	−3.2
...	...	...	...	...	...	...	...	...
Richmond	10	0.0	1.22	1.22	1.24	86.3	89.5	+3.2
Queens North	11	−0.8	1.22	1.23	1.20	93.1	89.5	−3.6
Citywide		+1.5	1.36	1.34	1.34	73.1	71.7	−1.4

*Five of a total of eleven Sanitation Command areas are shown.
**New York City rates cleanliness on a scale of 1.0 to 3.0. The lower the rating, the cleaner the street.

the public with a satisfactory perspective. One particular effort is the recent "total performance measurement system" (TPMS) approach that the U.S. General Accounting Office, the National Center for productivity and Quality of Working Life, and the Office of Policy Development and Research of the U.S. Department of Housing and Urban Development are exploring. Initial test sites include the State of Washington's Department of General Administration; Los Angeles County's Patient Financial Services Division of the Department of Public Health; Sunnyvale, California; and the Office of Housing Production and Mortgage Credit of the Region IX Office of HUD. Just beginning are efforts by the State of New Jersey (in its water resources agency) and the City of Cincinnati (in its highway maintenance division).

In TPMS, performance data are collected on both output per unit of input and client perceptions of service quality. However, two additional ingredients are included in the TPMS concept: employee attitude surveys, and an attempt to integrate the data from all three sources (customers, "hard" data, and employees) in an analysis aimed at suggesting productivity improvements. Thus, TPMS is intended not only as a measurement tool but also includes a productivity-analysis component. The employee-attitude information is used to identify productivity problems and is not itself productivity-measurement information.

The initial round of tests recently has been completed. Although the General Accounting Office feels the initial work is encouraging, it is too early to tell whether such an integrated effort will be continued by the participating agencies or introduced by other state and local governments without federal assistance. Nevertheless, the concept of using a variety of information on efficiency, effectiveness (including client feedback), and employee attitudes is provocative and merits careful evaluation.

Prospects For the Future: Facilitating and Inhibiting Factors

What are the prospects for the future of productivity measurement? A number of pressures have come together, including recent state and local government fiscal crises (or near crises) which are encouraging more intensive efforts at improving productivity as a way to decrease or contain expenditures, and recent pushes to tighten up on all programs through more careful budgeting and evaluation, performance auditing, accountability, sunset laws with the requirement for periodic review of government activities, management by objectives, and zero base budgeting. Each of these processes appears to require adequate measurement of productivity on a regular basis, encompassing both efficiency and effectiveness.

In addition, there has been a development of the state-of-the-art of measurements, as in citizen and client survey techniques, systematic trained observer approaches, and the like.

Adding to all this is the trend for schools of public administration and similar professional graduate schools to expose students to a wide variety of quantitative tools so that the managers and public officials of the future will be familiar with, and presumably less resistant to, such approaches.

Despite all these favorable factors, however, there are constraints on the widespread emergence of productivity measurement. The analytical capabilities of state and local governments are still highly limited and are likely to be so for many years. The measurement effort discussed here can require considerable data collection and analysis. The data-collection procedures themselves may not be very expensive; however, the data require considerable in-depth analysis to obtain the full benefits from such regular measurement. The smaller governments certainly will not be able to apply much in the way of new resources to such new procedures. Unless they receive assistance (perhaps from their region or state, or the federal government), their ability to make substantial efforts (such as to undertake an annual citizen survey) will continue to be highly limited. The larger governments, however, including most states, should be able to undertake at least some such data collection and analysis.

An underlying issue at all levels of government is the problem of setting up regular uses for performance measures that are sufficiently attractive to make agency people wish to cooperate in the measurement effort and use. Improvements in governmental management incentive systems are needed to encourage administrators to analyze productivity and implement change.

An emerging question concerns the value and availability of standards, norms, or targets for productivity measures. Annual samples of local government performance on various measures, collected using standardized procedures, might, for example, be undertaken nationally or regionally. Individual governments, if they collect the same data themselves, then could compare themselves against these ''norms''—as a spur, where appropriate, to corrective actions. State and local government representatives and the federal government need to consider whether such comparative data will be more constructive than troublesome. However, even without these, an individual government can still compare its own performance from one year to the next and from one geographic area within the jurisdiction to the next, at least for some measures.

Governments have just begun to consider the various range of productivity-measurement options. There is likely to be a considerable amount of experimentation in future years. If help is forthcoming, including training by universities and others, along with some limited technical assistance (perhaps provided by state or regional agencies), substantial albeit slow progress seems likely to occur over the forthcoming decade.

Notes

1. This measure of "arrests surviving the initial screening" is discussed in: *Oppor-*

tunities for Improving Productivity in Police Services, The Urban Institute, *The Challenge of Productivity Diversity: Improving Local Government Productivity Measurement and Evaluation,* for the National Commission on Productivity, Part 3 (June 1972: available from the National Technical Information Service, order number PB 223117).

2. In addition, a more technical approach sometimes proposed is to utilize statistical analysis to relate outputs simultaneously to a number of input factors. Such procedures have thus far been applied mostly by universities and research organizations rather than by governments themselves, and therefore are not discussed in the body of this paper. For discussions of this approach see: John P. Ross and Jesse Burkhead, *Productivity in the Local Government Sector* (Massachusetts: Lexington Books, 1974); Bruce R. Neumann, "Hospital Productivity: An Evaluation of Proposed Measurement Methods," *Public Productivity Review,* Vol. 1, No. 5 (summer 1976), pp. 23-26; and Urban Institute, *Challenge of Productivity Diversity,* op. cit.

3. The U.S. Bureau of the Census annual reports on state and local government finances provide calculations of per-capita costs for selected expenditure categories for individual governments, but population counts should not be confused with output indicators appropriate to measure efficiency.

4. *The Status of Productivity Measurement in State Government: An Initial Examination,* The Urban Institute with the National Association of State Budget Officers (September 1975).

5. A listing of the measures found in these budget documents and the frequency with which they were found is provided in *Status of Productivity Measurement,* op. cit.

6. *1976 Annual Report to the President and Congress,* National Center for Productivity and Quality of Working Life (Washington, D.C.: U.S. Government Printing Office).

7. *Annual Report to the President and Congress, Productivity Programs in the Federal Government,* Vol. I: "Productivity Trends and Current Efforts," Joint Financial Management Improvement Program (Washington, D.C.: U.S. General Accounting Office, July 1976).

8. *Improving the Quality of Life: Resource Allocation Plan, 1976-1977 to 1983-1984 Fiscal Years,* City of Sunnyvale, California (1976).

9. Recent widely disseminated publications on work standards for government include: "Work Measurement in Local Governments," *Management Information Service Report,* International City Management Association, Vol. 6, No. 10 (October 1974); and *Improving Municipal Productivity: Work Measurement For Better Management,* The National Commission on Productivity and Work Quality (November 1975).

10. John M. Greiner, et al., *Employee Incentives to Improve State and Local Government Productivity,* National Commission on Productivity and Work Quality (March 1975), p. 112.

14.

Taxpayer Revolt

Sydney Duncombe and Thomas D. Lynch

In the United States, taxpayers are voting for and demanding smaller budgets for government. The trend to stop the increase in taxes and actually reduce taxes was not started with California's Proposition 13, but it greatly stimulated the movement. The following is the actual wording of the now famous Proposition 13 referendum:

> Tax Limitation—Initiative Constitutional Amendment. Limits realty tax to 1%; increases to 2%. Imposes 2/3 voting requirement on new taxes. Financial impact: Commencing with fiscal year beginning July 1, 1978, would result in annual losses of local government property tax revenues (approximately $7 billion in 1978–79 fiscal year), reduction in annual state costs (approximately $600 million in 1978–79 fiscal year), and restriction on future ability of local governments to finance capital construction by sale of general obligation bonds.

This chapter will examine California'a Proposition 13 and its effects, tax reduction in another state (Idaho), and the national character of the tax revolt.

Proposition 13

The June 6, 1978 California constitutional amendment received 4.2 million votes, with a voter approval rate of two to one. The Jarvis-Gann initiative became effective on July 1, 1978 and it:

1. set the maximum property tax rate in the state at one percent of market value;
2. "froze" the county assessor's valuation of real property at 1975–1976 levels with a two percent maximum increase per year allowable;
3. prohibited the legislature from levying a new state ad valorem property tax or property transfer tax;
4. required a two-thirds vote of the legislature to increase any state tax;
5. prohibited any increase in property tax, even by public vote; and
6. required a two-thirds approval of qualified voters for any special taxes levied by local governments or special districts.[1]

The Effect

If you were a California property taxpayer, you noticed a radical decrease in taxes due to Proposition 13. An average 57 percent statewide tax reduction occurred. Some renters received a rent reduction when their landlords received a tax cut, but that decrease did not always occur. Thus, one of the post–Proposition 13 events in California was a demand for rent control or other action to reduce or hold down rent charges. Prior to Proposition 13, California's property tax burden was the fourth highest. It has now dropped to about 37th among the states.[2]

If you were a school district or county official, you also noticed a revenue loss for your government. Revenue reductions constituted 22 percent of the total of California's local government funds. Figures on expenditure cuts are difficult to determine because a surplus from the state government was used in the first post–Proposition 13 year to cushion the loss of local government revenue. On a more permanent basis, the state government has acted to lessen the severity of the local government's lost revenue by increasing state transfer payments to them, and local user charges and fees, e.g., garbage collection, have been increased. The net effect seems to be a small decrease in local government employment, the curtailment of some programs, especially school summer programs and cultural enrichment activities, delay of capital improvement projects, and higher bond interest charges. Counties gained 1.9 percent, cities lost 6.5 percent, enterprise special districts gained 9.5 percent, nonenterprise special districts lost 11.5 percent, elementary schools gained 2.7 percent, and community colleges dropped 11.5 percent from the previous fiscal year.[3]

Why Revolt?

The strong support for tax reductions can probably be attributed to: an increasingly large share of a family's expenditures which must go for taxes, frustration with inflation, and frustration with government as an effective and efficient social agent.

Taxpayers react to their general condition. Proposition 13 was addressed to local property taxes, but it was a part of, and came to represent, all forms of taxes at all levels of government. In 1948 the average family paid 7.03 percent of their expenses for state and local taxes, and by 1977 the percentage was 12.87. This very real increase has meant that family resources have been reduced, relatively speaking, for other normal living expenses.[4]

In California the price of property has been going up rapidly, and property taxes have been rising radically. For example, a house worth $40,000 could easily have jumped in market value to $100,000 in three or four years. Property tax is based on market value; thus the taxes would also jump up. Families do not see a difference in their living standard because their house increases in value, but they are aware that more of their yearly income must go to paying their property taxes. Thus Californians saw their property value and corresponding taxes rise rapidly. In some cases, the tax increase forced families, especially those on fixed incomes, to sell their homes and move to smaller owned or even rented dwellings. In those cases, the tax increase meant their standard of living dropped.[5]

Another reason for the tax revolt is inflation. With inflation your dollar is buying you less than in the past. If you earn $15,000 a year without any salary increases for several years, inflation erodes your standard of living. One obvious plus for families in such circumstances is to cut expenses such as taxes. In prosperous periods, taxes are not liked; but in inflationary times, taxes become an expense item that many people are quite willing to cut by voting for reductions.

The image of bureaucracy is negative, and there is strong concern about the effective and efficient use of our tax dollar. In a 1978 Harris poll, a decline in the confidence of the people in government was noted. People believe they are not getting their money's worth in the taxes they pay. They are not against taxes; often not even the rate of taxes. They are against tax money being wasted, and that is their perception of government.[6]

Another Look at Effects

Who profited and lost from Proposition 13? It benefited the homeowner who did not sell his or her home or business. It especially hurt youth, minorities, and new property owners.[7]

Obviously the homeowner benefited. Taxes were reduced, but more significantly, taxes now can be raised only two percent per year, which is well below the inflation rate. Thus property taxes should become a decreasing burden for those families with incomes which keep pace with inflation. If the homeowner does not sell his or her house, then the valuation stays at the 1975–1976 level. Thus, the house value for tax purposes by which the one percent is multiplied to determine the tax is significantly lower than the real market value of the house. The result is continued low property tax in spite of rapidly rising house prices.

Homeowners who do not sell their homes benefit, especially with relationship to new property owners. Normally, property tax law stipulates that property be valued at market value or a uniform percentage of that value. The reason for that provision is to treat all people in a similar manner—tax all people on the basis of the value of their property. The California constitution now treats people unequally, i.e., new owners of property will be taxed at market value at the time of purchase, but old owners will be taxed at the artificially adjusted 1975–1976 value. In time this will mean significantly higher taxes for new owners.

A less obvious group that benefited was business. Business owners received cuts in their taxes and benefited like homeowners. Businesses own a great deal of California property, and many of these businesses are corporations. Corporations, for legal purposes, are treated like individuals; but unlike people, corporations need not die, and thus property need not be transferred. Therefore, less business property over time will be adjusted upward to market value than individually owned property. The result will be less taxes paid by business as compared to individual property owners.

Minorities and young people have been disadvantaged more than other citizens because the services cut in California disproportionately benefitted them. Summer educational and work programs were among the first programs to be cut. The last hired—usually the youngest and minority employees—were cut first. The significance of this loss of benefits is difficult to determine because it has only been observed and not been calculated yet.

The Idaho Experience

Idaho's experience with a one percent property tax limitation is significant in two respects. It provides insight on why the electorate supported a one percent tax limitation in a state which had almost no surplus. It also shows the problems the legislature and local governments have in implementing a one percent limitation on property taxes.

Initiative No. 1 in Idaho

The Idaho One Percent Initiative was modeled so closely after California's Proposition 13 that some people thought it was sired by a Xerox machine. Idaho's Initiative No 1:[8]

1. limited property taxes on any parcel of property to one percent of the actual market value of the property;
2. exempted from the limitation only the interest and redemption charges of debt incurred prior to the passage of the initiative;
3. allowed the market value base of property to increase no more than two percent per year for most property but permitted an increase to actual market value for property that was newly constructed or sold;
4. prohibited the legislature from imposing any new property tax and permitted the legislature to increase other taxes only by a two-thirds or greater vote of both houses;
5. permitted cities, counties and other taxing districts to impose "special taxes" by a two-thirds or greater vote of the qualified electors in such districts; and
6. became effective October 1, 1979, except for the section on the Idaho Legislature, which was to become effective in November, 1978.

The most significant difference between California's Proposition 13 and Idaho's Initiative #1 was that Proposition 13 was a constitutional amendment and Initiative #1 was a law which could be amended by the Idaho Legislature.

Why Idaho?

To those unfamiliar with Idaho politics, it may seem strange that a one percent property tax limitation would be proposed and passed in Idaho. California had a large state surplus which was a factor in passing Proposition 13 and a cushion to ease the shock of implementation. Idaho had almost no state surplus.[9] Idaho's tax levels were low in comparison with California and most other states. Idaho's per capita state and local taxes stood 35th in the nation and lowest in the eleven western states.[10] Idaho property taxes were 34th in the nation and ninth among the eleven western states.[11] According to one report, Idaho had the lowest increase in state and local taxes in the nation between 1966 and 1976.[12] Furthermore, the Initiative was opposed by the Idaho Education Association, key city officials, the Idaho Innkeepers' Association, and even an official of the Idaho Taxpayers' Association.[13] Why then did Idaho's Initiative #1 pass with a resounding 58.3 percent of the total vote?

To understand the success of the One Percent Initiative in Idaho, it is first necessary to understand the Idaho voter. Robert Blank has extensively studied Idaho political culture and has concluded that Idahoans "strongly favor limiting the role of government and perceive big government as a threat to their individualistic values."[14] It is not surprising, Blank comments, that Idaho citizens would be favorably disposed toward any "highly visible and direct means of limiting . . . government."[15] Western voters tend to have the strongest antiproperty tax sentiments in the nation, according to a 1978 Advisory Commission on Intergovernmental Relations poll,[16] and the individualistic Idahoan may be among the most avid property tax citizens in the nation.

Idaho voters had reason in 1978 to be concerned about property taxes. The Idaho Legislature in the mid–1960s passed an act requiring a ratio to assessed value to market value of 20 percent by 1982. For years little change in this ratio occurred, as it increased only from 11.9 percent in 1968 to 13.4 percent in 1976.[17] Suddenly county assessors were faced with the need to substantially increase the ratio to meet the 20 percent requirement by 1982. Massive reevaluations took place in 1977 and 1978, particularly in residential property in such predominantly urban counties as Ada, Kootenai, Nez Perce and Bannock. Homeowners were particularly affected by the change as the residential percentage of all assessed valuation increased from 18.1 percent in 1965 to 41.5 percent in 1977.[18] Moreover, the ratio of assessed value to market value varied greatly from county to county and even within counties. The massive reevaluations and inequities provided the tinder for the Idaho tax revolt.

The spark that began the tax revolt was supplied by the Idaho Property Owners' Association. The association was a diverse group of realtors, developers, farmers, landowners, and others who opposed both increases in property taxation and land use plans adopted without a public vote. During the 1978 legislative session the Idaho Property Owners' Association lobbied for property tax relief and unsuccessfully backed a bill that was nearly a carbon copy of California's Proposition 13.[19] The legislature adjourned without passing the IPOA bill. It provided only about $17 million in property tax relief. The Idaho Property Owners' Association then launched their initiative campaign. The people who launched the campaign were not looking at the size of the state surplus or how Idaho stood in relation to other states in terms of tax burdens. They were concerned with substantial increases in assessed valuation (particularly on homes and farms) during 1977 and 1978.

The Initiative Campaign and Election

The proponents of the Initiative had three significant obstacles to overcome: lack of public awareness, opposition of local government officials, and flaws in the wording of the Initiative. In April 1978 only 48 percent of the Idaho public was aware of the Initiative and only 30 percent of those aware of it were in favor.[20] The process of gathering 90,000 signatures—in a state in which about 300,000 voters normally go to the polls—increased public awareness of the Initiative. A month before the deadline for submission of the Initiative petitions, the campaign received a boost from the news that Proposition 13 had passed by a large margin in California. In July 1978, 80 percent of the people were aware of the Initiative, and suport had increased to 46 percent.[21]

The supporters of the Initiative acted to nullify their opposition through open attack. Don Chance, president of the Idaho Property Owners' Association, claimed that a group opposing the Initiative, Citizens for Responsible Government, was "a coalition of associations made up of greedy tax spenders whose only purpose is to suck the last drop of blood from the taxpayers . . . ."[22] This tended to nullify statements from opponents that the Initiative would cause a 66 percent reduction in property tax revenues to local government with drastic consequences for school and other local government services.

The imperfections in the drafting of the Initiative also might have caused its defeat. The Initiative had an incomplete sentence, at least one clearly unconstitutional provision, and a serious misconception about the beginning of the property tax year. When it became apparent that the Initiative would be placed on the ballot, a leading supporter was successful in expanding the work of the legislative interim committee he chaired to consider clarifications and modifications of the Initiative. Working closely with the Idaho Property Owners' Association, the committee drafted a bill by October that removed the unconstitutional provisions and most of the poorly drafted language.[23] The proponents blunted the attacks on the Initiative by describing the much better drafted alternative they intended to introduce in the next legislative session.

The major reason for the passage of the Initiative was, however, the concerns of the property taxpayer. Their fears were enhanced by statements supporting the Initiative such as the following:

> Your taxes will double or triple by the end of 1981, if we remain under the present ad valorem system.[24]
>
> Do you want to continue to force our retiring citizens out of their homes by ever increasing taxes? If not, vote for the 1 percent limit.[25]

The concern about the possibility of future increases in property taxes causing the loss of one's home was widespread. When asked, ''Do you feel that rising property taxes are threatening your 'freedom and right' to own real property, 78 percent of those interviewed responded affirmatively.''[26]

The Election Results

The election results did not follow the anticipated urban-rural, liberal-conservative pattern. The highest margins for the Initiative were in predominantly urban counties where massive reevaluations had occurred. Thirteen of the fifteen counties in Idaho which voted against the Initiative were predominantly rural counties without a city of 10,000 or more people.[27] Many farmers in those counties were concerned that farm land would be valued for assessment purposes at actual market value (as the Initiative stated) rather than at a lower valuation based on capitalization of farm income.

Predominantly Republican counties were expected to vote for the Initiative and predominantly Democratic counties to vote against it. This trend did not occur. The county with the largest margin for the Initiative (Kootenai) is a predominantly urban, Democratic county in which a substantial reappraisal had occurred. The three most strongly Democratic counties in the state all voted with a 56 percent or greater margin for the Initiative, as did many other Republican and Democratic counties. The fifteen counties opposing the Initiative included eleven that normally vote Republican.[28] The county with the largest margin against the Initiative was a rural county (Jerome) which is usually among the most conservative in Idaho. The Initiative had widespread support in all areas of the state and received 58.3 percent of the vote.

Messages of the Idaho Property Tax Revolt

To learn why Idaho voters supported Initiative #1, the University of Idaho chapter of Phi Delta Kappa sponsored a statewide telephone poll a month after the election. The sample provided a good cross section of voting sentiment.[29] The interviewers asked the open-ended question, ''What were the most important reasons why you voted as you did on the Initiative?'' Of those who voted for the Initiative, 83 percent said the most important reason was to reduce taxes, five percent wanted fair taxes, four percent wanted stable taxes, two percent wanted to cut red tape, and two percent wanted to reduce spending. ''Cutting government expenditures'' was much less emphasized than cutting taxes in the minds of those who voted for the Initiative.[30]

A surprise in the poll was not that Idaho residents wanted their property taxes cut, but they were not deeply committed to the One Percent Initiative as a means of reducing property taxes. When asked if they agreed or disagreed with six specific tax reform proposals, the most popular reform was taxation of residential and farm property at lower rates than business and utility property. Limiting property taxes to one percent of actual market value ranked fourth of the six proposals.

The Phi Delta Kappa poll attempted to get the views of the voter on how the Initiative should be implemented at the local level. The respondents were asked the open-ended question, ''If state and local expenditures must be cut, what expenditures do you think should be cut the most?'' Significantly, 39 percent of those interviewed declined to name any area of reduction, and the most often named target (welfare) was named by only 18 percent. The other areas cited were : salaries (10%), all government agencies (8%), school waste (5%), politicians' expenses (4%), administration (3%), overlapping services (2%), highway construction (2%), unnecessary projects (2%), and a miscellany of other choices (7%).

When asked to name the state and local expenditures which they thought should be cut the least, the respondents were much more definite. Their responses were: schools (47%), law enforcement (11%), fire protection (6%), public services (3%), health (3%), senior citizen benefits (3%), roads (2%), and a series of other choices that added to two percent. Twenty-three percent of those asked the question did not respond.

The respondents were asked further questions designed to learn what advice they would give the legislature in implementing the Initiative without making major reductions in such favored programs as schools and law enforcement. One option was for state government to make up the loss in local revenues. When asked, ''Do you think that money from state taxes should be distributed to local governments to replace property tax revenue lost due to the passing of the 1 percent initiative?'' 51 percent agreed, 22 percent were opposed, and 27 percent were undecided. When asked where these funds were to come from, 47 percent felt they should come from reduced state expenses, 6 percent from increased taxes, 21 percent from a combination of reduced expenses and increased taxes, 4 percent gave other responses, and 22 percent did not respond. The message was clear. The respondents wanted state government to somehow replace most of the property tax revenues which schools and other local governments were to lose. They wanted to cut property taxes, not school programs.

Implementation Dilemmas Faced by the 1979 Idaho Legislature

Legislators were getting two messages as the 1979 legislative session began in Idaho. The people had unmistakably spoken for substantial reductions in property taxes, and some legislators heard the message as implementation of the One Percent Initiative with few modifications at the earliest possible time. There was also strong sentiment for preserving school programs and such other vital local services as police and fire protection. How do you implement both mandates in a state with almost no surplus?

The most pressing problem was when to implement the Initiative. The October 1, 1979 implementation date in the Initiative was impractical because the Idaho property tax year begins on January 1. Idaho legislators could implement the Initiative on January 1, 1979, causing a drastic reduction in property taxes in a single year. Or the legislature could delay implementation until January 1, 1980 to allow time for local governments to make adjustments. However, this would delay the first property tax relief until December 1980—a month after the state's next general election. Legislators did not relish explaining to angry voters why they had received no property tax relief two years after the One Percent Initiative was passed.

The Idaho Legislature steered a middle course. It set January 1, 1980 as the effective date of the one percent limitation, thus giving local government an additional year to adjust to lower property tax revenues.[31] At the same time, the legislature reduced school district tax levies by eleven mills and provided schools with an additional $26 million to make up the loss through the school foundation formula. Property owners were to receive tax relief not only from the eleven mill reduction in property taxes but also through a freeze imposed by the legislature in the total dollar amount of property taxes that each unit of local government could receive in the 1979–80 fiscal year for operating purposes.[32]

The freeze for the 1979–80 fiscal year will mean that cities, counties, and other units of local government may not certify anymore in property taxes for operating purposes in 1979 than they certified in 1978. Although the freeze will not apply to bond redemption levies and nonproperty tax revenues, it will apply to property tax levies that provide nearly half of all city and county government funds. Cities that annex new areas and local governments in rapidly growing areas will be particularly hard hit because they will receive no additional property tax funds as a result of annexation or growth.

The freeze will continue in the 1980–81 fiscal year, and local governments will receive the lower of the two figures: (1) the amount of property taxes they certified in 1978, or (2) the amount they would receive under the one percent limitation.[33]

The extent to which local government revenues will decline in 1980–81 when the one percent limitation goes into effect was not known. It depended, in part, on what happened to market valuations during the 1979 and 1980 tax years. The 1979 legislature recognized that there was a great variation in assessment practices between counties and within counties, and that all property needed to be brought to the same base before the one percent limitation was imposed. County asssessors were ordered to revalue all property under their jurisdiction by May 15, 1980, and the State Tax Commission was given powers to insure compliance with these procedures.[34] The increase of market valuation as a result of the reappraisal alleviated the effect of the One Percent Initiative by about $27 million with another $20–25 million relief coming as a result of new residential and other construction in 1978 and 1979.[35]

The impact of the One Percent Initiative on local government when it is fully implemented depends also on what method the Idaho Legislature chooses to distribute funds under the one percent limitation. The Initiative did not address the question of a distribution formula and the 1979 Idaho legislature left this question for the 1980 legislature to decide. There were five main alternatives under consideration.[36]

1. The one percent county-wide tax. Under this alternative all existing local government operating levies would be eliminated and replaced with a one percent county-wide tax. This approach would raise the property taxes of many rural residents who would otherwise pay less than one percent of the value of their property taxes. Moreover, the system would mean that rural residents would pay the same tax as urban residents even though many of them receive less in services. To partially meet these objections, a rebate system might be used so that persons having their taxes raised to one percent of the market value of their property would receive a rebate from the State Tax Commission of the amount that the one percent tax exceeded the amount they would otherwise have paid.
2. The fixed levy approach. With this approach, tax limits would be revised downward so that all of the tax limits for operating purposes do not exceed in total ten mills (or one percent) of market evaluation. The tax limits would be greatly reduced under this approach, and a very significant reduction in local revenue would result.
3. The full scale-down. Under this system, some official would be given the authority to find the parcel of property with the highest tax rate in the county and scale this rate down to one percent. All other property in the county would then be scaled down by exactly the same percentage. For example, if the highest taxed piece of property in the county was taxed at two percent of its market value, its taxes would be scaled down to one percent—a 50 percent reduction. All other taxpayers in the county would also have their property taxes scaled down 50 percent. This method would also lead to a very substantial reduction in local revenues.
4. The modified-scale down. This is a variation of the full scale-down system in which property taxes would not be scaled down as much in most areas of the state as in the full scale-down approach.
5. The priority levy approach. This approach would provide full property tax funding to certain functions of local government such as education, law enforcement, and fire protection. Funds for other local government functions would be scaled down greatly.

The impact of the One Percent Initiative on local government depends also on the method or methods used by the state—if any—to provide financial assistance to cities, counties, and other local units. The 1980 legislature might take one or more of the following actions which would ease the financial problems of local government.[37]

1. Permit local governments to levy one or more optional nonproperty taxes. Except for allowing a hotel-motel and liquor-by-the-drink tax in certain resort cities, the legis-

lature has thus far not approved optional nonproperty taxes for local government.

2. Shift more of the financing of city streets, county roads, and highway district roads from the property tax to gasoline taxes and/or motor vehicle registration fees. This shift would enable a greater proportion of nonhighway local government expenditures to be financed from the property tax under the one percent limitation.

3. Shift more of the financing of public schools from the property tax to the school foundation formula. This would free the property tax to fund more nonschool local functions. The Idaho legislature used this approach in 1979 when it reduced school tax levies by eleven mills and compensated schools with an additional $26 million of state funds.

4. Increase the percent of sales tax funds distributed to local government. Currently, 20 percent of the sales tax is distributed to cities, counties, school districts, and special districts.

5. Establish a state revenue-sharing plan. The plan might distribute a portion of the state income tax to local governments on a per capita and/or tax effort basis.

Effect on Local Government

In June 1979 most city and county governments in Idaho were beginning to formulate their budgets. Local government officials knew that the amount of property taxes they would receive was frozen at the 1978 level. They also knew that there would be increases during the year in state retirement system costs (16%), gasoline (15%-30%), and other supplies and equipment (5%-15%). Most city officials surveyed felt they would have to increase employee salaries four to seven percent to retain competent employees.[38] City officials in six regions of Idaho were interviewed during May and June 1979 and asked what they would do to meet the inflationary increases in property tax revenues for operating purposes. Their answers were:

1. use up any remaining fund balances first;
2. defer purchase of expensive capital outlay items;
3. defer some large maintenance items such as street resurfacing;
4. not fill some positions when vacancies occur;
5. raise some fees and charges that are not paying the full cost of services. For example, swimming pool charges and building inspection fees; and
6. charge the enterprise funds (particularly the water and sewer funds) with their proper share of the cost of administration paid out of the general fund. This would relieve the general fund (the most hardpressed city fund), but would probably require increases in water and sewer rates.

City officials recognized the problems with deferring large capital outlay purchases and needed maintenance, but they felt that results would not be too serious for one year. They also recognized that they would lose some CETA positions, in comparable categories, by not filling vacancies. They say their problems are serious but surmountable in 1979–80, but they will be critical in 1980–81.

Table 14.1
State General Fund Revenue Growth

Fiscal Year	Revenues	Dollar Increase Since Previous Year	Percentage Increase Since Previous Year
1976–77 actual	$253,059,301		
1977–78 actual	282,778,986	$29,716,685	11.7%
1978–79 estimate	320,300,000	37,520,014	13.3
1979–80 estimate	357,825,000	37,525,000	11.2

Source: Legislative Fiscal Office, The 1979 Legislative Report (Boise, Idaho: Legislative Fiscal Office, May, 1979), pp. 4,5. The estimates shown are those of the Legislative Fiscal Office.

Effect on State Government

The One Percent Initiative has had a greater immediate effect on state government than local government. The general fund of the state has been growing at a rate of 11 percent to 13 percent a year as shown in Table 14.1.

An 11 percent increase in the state general fund would normally provide enough revenue to meet inflationary cost increases and the needs of increased work load. The 1979 Idaho legislature felt, however, that there should be a two-year phase-in to implement the One Percent Initiative, and that state government should share in this austerity program. The governor proposed that there be a nine-mill reduction in school property taxes with the state general fund compensating schools for their losses. Ultimately the 1979 Idaho legislature reduced school property taxes by eleven mills and funneled $26 million of general fund money to public schools through the school foundation formula to compensate them for their losses. The legislature provided an additional $10 million to schools through the school foundation formula to meet inflationary cost increases and salary raises. The result, as the following table shows, was that state agencies, other than public schools, received only a $2.6 million increase.

The Idaho legislature did not make a specific appropriation for salary increases. As a result, state agencies had to absorb salary increases, which averaged seven percent, from their own appropriations. The net effect for many agencies was the need to reduce the number of positions to meet salary and other cost increases. The Human Rights Commission, for example, found itself $6,700 short of the amount needed to pay its seven-member staff. One of its four investigators was cut from full-time to half-time work as a result.[39] If a

Table 14.2

Comparison of Idaho General Fund Appropriations for 1978-1979 and 1979-1980 (in Millions of Dollars)

	1978-79	1979-80	Dollar Increase	Percentage Increase
Office of the Governor	4.6	4.6	.0	.0
Legislative Branch	2.5	2.5	.0	.0
Judicial Branch	5.5	5.8	.3	5.5
Health and Welfare	48.5	49.5	1.0	2.1
Higher Education	67.4	68.5	1.1	1.6
Vocational Education	11.6	11.9	.3	2.6
Research and Extension	7.5	7.5	.0	.0
Other Education	3.1	2.9	(.2)	(6.5)
All Other Departments	36.5	36.6	.1	.3
Sub-Total	187.2	189.8	2.6	1.4
Public Schools	131.8	167.8	36.0	27.3
Total General Fund Appropriations	$319.0	$357.6	$38.6	12.1

Source: Data provided by the Idaho Legislative Fiscal Office, June 25, 1979.

reduction in completed cases occurs, as it probably will, a further reduction in federal funds could result. The Division of Budget, Policy Planning and Coordination had to cut back five positions, including its regional planning staff in the north and southeast, with the result that its technical assistance to local governments in these areas was sharply curtailed.

Colleges and universities in Idaho were also faced with the need to fund salary and other cost increases with less than a two percent increase in general fund appropriations. More than one hundred positions were eliminated at the University of Idaho alone.[40] There was a 40 percent reduction in the funding of the summer session at the University of Idaho, an elimination of a number of faculty and graduate assistant positions, significant reductions in student services, and elimination of the funds for short-term applied research. The cooperative extension program at the University of Idaho received no increases in appropriations, and the university abolished the expanded food and nutrition program, eliminated the resource development program, and made substantial reductions in other programs.

The Idaho Department of Health and Welfare found that the rising costs of medical care, salary increases, and other cost increases far exceeded the 2.1% general fund appropriation increases provided by the legislature. Moreover, there were some federal fund cut-backs, including the cancellation of a $400,000 grant for state health-planning. The result was that a number of specific actions were taken that eliminated 67 positions and substantially curbed certain other costs. Some of the curtailments were:[41]

- eliminating two program managers in each of the state's seven regions, resulting in a reduction in program supervision.
- reducing by one-half the 24-member staff of the Bureau of Support Enforcement, thus reducing the funds this staff collects from absent fathers who are not supporting their children on aid to families with dependent children; and
- eliminating almost all capital expenditure funds in the budget with the resulting danger that department-managed buildings will fall into disrepair.

The One Percent Initiative has had a significant indirect impact on most state agencies for the state fiscal year, beginning July 1, 1979. Because most of the 12 percent increase in state general fund appropriations was channeled to public schools, most other state agencies have had to absorb salary and other cost increases from appropriations that increased less than two percent. The additional funds were provided for schools primarily because school property taxes were reduced as a means of phasing in the One Percent Initiative.

Future Impact of the One Percent Initiative in Idaho

The impact of the Initiative on state government during the fiscal year, beginning July 1, 1979, is known and has been described previously. City, county, and special district budgets were unknown at the time this was written, so the exact impact of the Initiative is also unknown until that time. However, local government property tax revenues for operating purposes will be frozen at the 1978 levels, so we have been able to make some reasonably accurate predictions of the impact of the measures taken to implement the Initiative in 1979-80.

The impact of the implementation of the Initiative in 1980-81 is much more difficult to predict. State agencies can expect another year of one to three percent increases in appropriations, and the result will probably be a second round of elimination of existing positions and deferral of capital outlay and maintenance. The legislature will probably again take some of the state general fund growth and funnel it back to local government.

The most difficult impact to predict is the effect of the Initiative on local government in 1980-81. The full effect of the Initiative will be felt in that year, and the reduction in property tax revenues will depend on the extent that property taxes in each local area now exceed one percent of the value of property in that area. The amount of revenues each local government receives will also depend on the property tax distribution formula adopted by the legislature during its 1980 session and the amount of state funds funneled back to local government. It depends also on whether the legislature allows local government authority to levy nonproperty taxes, such as a county income or sales tax, and the extent to which local units raise fees and charges.

Adoption of the One Percent Initiative seemed to many voters a clear cut issue—tax relief vs. local government services. In retrospect, it appears that neither the supporters nor the opponents of the Initiative appreciated the immense number of ramifications of the brief one and one-half page initiative petition.

A National Movement

State Action

In November 1978 the voters in 13 states other than California voted on measures designed to either cut taxes or slow the growth rate of government. Two states, Idaho and Nevada, passed Jarvis-Gann types of rollback measures. Eleven states either rejected or passed mild versions. The decisions, state by state, are as follows.[42]

Alabama. Approved a measure to restrict the increase of all property taxes in the county to 20 percent of market value. However, taxes would not be lowered.

Arizona. Approved an amendment to the state constitution limiting state spending to seven percent of total personal income.

Colorado. Defeated a measure to link spending increases to the national consumer price index and to increases in the state's population.

Hawaii. Approved amendments holding spending to the rate of the state's economic growth, limiting the state's debts, and providing for a tax rebate if the state has over a five-percent surplus in two consecutive years.

Idaho. Rolled property tax back to one percent of market value from the previous 1.7 percent.

Illinois. Approved an advisory measure to limit spending and property tax increases.

Michigan. Approved a state limit, based on 9.5 percent of the state's personal income, but rejected a 43 percent property tax cut. Future increases in property tax were tied to the level of inflation. Voter approval on all new taxes was required.

Nebraska. Rejected holding local spending to a five-percent annual increase.

Nevada. Approved the first phase of a two-phase vote to have a proposition 13-type reform.

North Dakota. Approved cutting state taxes for individuals and raising them for corporations.

Oregon. Rejected a proposition 13-type reform.

South Dakota. Approved the requirement of a two-thirds legislative vote to raise sales or real property taxes.

Texas. Approved measures that increased the homestead exemption, eased taxes on the elderly, and linked government-spending increases to economic growth.

Of note is that Paul Gann was able to get another tax reform initiative on the 1980 California ballot. That proposition places expenditure limits on all California governments.

Obviously, there is voter support for tax cuts that range from radical to moderate in size. The strength of the reform movement is strong, but the desire for large significant cuts by voters does not appear to be present in most states. Tax cut reforms, such as the following, do have appeal:

- restrict the rate of increase of property tax;
- limiting state spending to the current levels or slightly below current levels;
- linking spending to the state's economic growth;
- tax rebates for state surpluses;
- impose stricter requirements on increasing the state debt;
- increase the vote requirement needed for a legislature to vote for a tax increase; and
- increasing homestead and elderly exemptions.

National Action

Thirty-four state legislatures can vote to call a constitutional convention for the purpose of approving a balanced federal budget amendment.[43]

In March 1979 the Senate Judiciary Subcommittee on the Constitution held hearings on a constitutional amendment requiring a balanced federal budget. At that time 28 states had requested a federal balanced-budget amendment. The matter is complicated by the fact that no one can be certain that a constitutional convention need limit itself only to the one amendment. Thus the fear exists that the whole constitution may be rewritten. Also, the states did not pass identical "calls," so legal challenges could be raised about the validity, if the magic number of 34 were reached.

Senator Birch Bayh labeled the hearings a "serious business" and stressed that the government tax-revolt effort throughout the nation is a serious political question.[44] Persons such as Senator Harry F. Byrd, Jr. believe there is no other way to achieve fiscal responsibility in the federal government than a constitutional amendment. Conservative groups point out that the average debt per citizen is $3,528.28.[45] This, they believe, is wrong, and the debt should be retired. Senator Strom Thurmond says voluntary restraint by Congress has failed and will continue to fail from preventing Congress to increase the debt. Senator John C. Stennis supported the measure and argued for a special tax surcharge to guarantee federal receipts equal expenditures. Scholars of the high caliber of Aaron Wildavsky—a professor at the University of California at Berkeley—have, and do, argue for a balanced-budget amendment.[46]

The argument against the amendment stresses that such a constitutional change is not needed and is foolish. Such an amendment, the opponents stress, would prevent the federal government from responding quickly and flexibly to changing economic conditions. Also, they say a balanced budget might be impossible to achieve in recession periods. If a surcharge, as recommended by Senator Stennis, were imposed, a terrible economic burden would exist on the taxpayers in periods of recession.[47]

Senator Muskie and others arguing against the amendment point out the debt situation of the federal government is not that serious a problem.[48] It requires only about nine percent of the operating budget to pay the interest charges.[49] Since World War II, the federal debt has grown more slowly than the GNP, as well as the debt held by state and local governments and private corporations. Also, the new congressional budget process has brought "an unprecedented level of disciplines to the Hill's budgeting procedure."[50]

The federal government does not have a capital budget financed by bonded indebtedness. Another argument against the amendment is that the federal government would have a balanced operating budget if it had a capital budget similar to the ones of many nations, as well as many state and local governments. The financed capital items transferred to a federal capital budget would allow the operating budget to be "balanced." Other nations, state and local governments, corporations, and private citizens have capital budgets. The present nonuse of a capital budget distorts the debt situation, and a more conventional approach would permit more reasonable comparisons and judgments. Therefore, the concern about an unbalanced budget is misplaced. The federal government can easily pay the yearly interest charge, the debt is not a national burden, and the nonuse of a capital budget distorts the deficit situation facing the nation.[51]

The national debate for a balanced federal budget will continue with strong emotion.

Conclusion

A tax revolt does exist. Where the voters believe that taxes are particularly threatening to their pocket book, more sweeping tax reductions do occur. Although there does not seem to be widespread support for large tax reductions, there is national support for modest tax reduction reforms. The movement should continue with the probable result of a slow down in government growth and possibly a relative decline in the size of government.

Notes

1. Sara Fitzgerald and Patricia Meisol, "The 'Tax Payers' Revolt' Takes to the States," *National Journal* No. 22 (June 3, 1978): 873–874. Also, *Proposition 13: Employment, Cities, and Services* (Washington, D.C.: National Institute of Public Management, 1979). For further information see, *Final Report* (Sacramento: Commission on Government Reform, 1979), pp. 17–19.
2. *California Tax Study: An Analysis of Taxes and Expenditures of State and Local*

Government in California (Burlingame, California: The California Roundtable Taxation Task Force, 1979), p. 1.

3. Jerry McCaffery and John H. Bowman,"Participatory Democracy and Budgeting: The Effects of Proposition 13,"*Public Administration Review* (November/December,1978): 533. See also, John J. Kirline,"More Income Cuts Threaten California Budgets," *Public Administration Times* (June 15, 1979): 1, 3.

4. L. Laszlo Ecker-Racz, "Coping With Proposition 13," *Today's Education* (September–October, 1978): 42.

5. *Ibid.*

6. Louis Harris, "Confidence in Government," *The Bureaucrat* (Spring, 1979): 23–24.

7. See the National Institute for Public Management report for more detail.

8. The full, official title, "Initiative Petition Number 1," will be shortened to the popular titles, "Initiative #1" and the "One Percent Initiative" in this chapter. For an expansion of the summary of the Initiative used here, see Sydney Duncombe, Charles Holden, Neil McFeeley, and James Weatherby, *Local Government Implementation of the One Percent Initiative* (Moscow, Idaho: Bureau of Public Affairs Research, University of Idaho, 1979), p. 1.

9. The governor estimated in December 1978 that there would be a general fund balance of only $2.6 million at the end of the 1979–80 fiscal year. The July 1, 1979 general fund balance was not known at the time of writing, but it is estimated to be less than $2.6 million. A surplus of $2.6 million is too small to provide any significant allocation of funds to local government.

10. C.A. Hoffman, "Idaho Taxes: Comparative Analysis, Evaluation and Recommendation, A Technical Appendix to the Report of the Governor's Committee on Taxation." Report delivered to Governor John V. Evans, September, 1978, pp. 7–11, 18.

11. *Ibid.*

12. "Sound and Fury Over Taxes," *Time* (June 19, 1978).

13. For a more extensive description of the groups supporting and opposing the Initiative see, Roger Snider, Sydney Duncombe, and James Weatherby, "Tax Limitation—Idaho Style." Presented at the American Society for Public Administration 1979 Regional Conference, San Francisco, California, February 8, 1979, pp. 13–16.

14. Robert H. Blank, "Idaho Political Culture and the Passage of the One Percent Initiative." Presented at the Idaho Political Science Association Meeting, February, 1979, p. 22.

15. *Ibid.* p. 1.

16. *Changing Public Attitudes on Government and Taxes* (Washington, D.C.: Advisory Commission on Intergovernmental Relations, 1978), p. 1. When asked "Which do you think is the worst tax?" 44 percent of western voters said the property tax as compared to 35 percent in the north-central states, 27 percent in the north-eastern states, and 27 percent in the southern states.

17. Hoffman, p. 94.

18. Data supplied by the Idaho State Tax Commission.

19. H.B. 555 was introduced late in the Idaho legislative session and contained language some legislators felt was more appropriate for a constitutional amendment than for a law.

20. *Idaho Poll*, ·Boise (July, 1978), Boise, Idaho, p. 1.

21. *Ibid.*

22. *Weiser American* (October 16, 1978), Weiser, Idaho, p. 1.

23. The work of Representative Gary Ingram's committee on improving the language of the Initiative is described more fully in Sydney Duncome and Roger Snider, "Implementation of the One Percent Initiative in Idaho." Presented at the Idaho Political Science Association Meeting, February 9, 1978, pp. 5–6.

24. *Weiser American.*

25. Quoted from an advertisement placed by the Shafer Lumber Company in the *Lewiston Morning Tribune* (October 28, 1978).

26. *Idaho Poll*, p. 2.

27. The two urban counties with a majority against the Initiative were Latah and Twin Falls Counties. The University of Idaho is located in Latah County, and a number of University of Idaho employees thought that passage of the Initiative would lead to severe reductions in state appropriations as state government provided increased fiscal assistance to local government. In Twin Falls, the local chapter of the Idaho Property Owners Association disagreed with the statewide organization on the Initiative.

28. Seven of the ten counties in south-central Idaho, the most conservative area in the state, voted against the Initiative. There was widespread fear in many rural areas of those counties that farm land would be taxed at one percent of market valuation. Farm income is now taken into consideration in setting farm assessed valuations, and many farmers feared that a tax at one percent of their market valuations would increase their taxes.

29. A total of 430 people were interviewed by telephone in late November and early December 1978. The sample was drawn from a list of randomly selected numbers from each telephone exchange in the state. The poll showed a 48.6% majority voting for the Initiative as compared to 58.3% majority in the general election. The poll was sponsored by the University of Idaho Chapter of Phi Delta Kappa. The findings are reported in Eldon Archambault, Robert Blank, and Sydney Duncombe, "Message of the One Percent Initiative," a paper printed by the University of Idaho Chapter of Phi Delta Kappa and distributed to the Idaho legislature in January 1979.

30. The respondents were given a list of potential messages the voters intended to send to the legislature by their vote. Fifty-seven percent of all respondents thought one message was to reduce taxes and fifty-six percent thought one of the messages was to reduce government spending. "While many respondents had picked 'cutting government expenditures' as a 'message' they thought OTHER VOTERS intended to send to the legislature, few of them thought it was very important IN THEIR OWN VOTES." In Eldon Archambault, Robert Blank, and Sydney Duncome, "Message of the One Percent Initiative," a paper printed by the University of Idaho Chapter of Phi Delta Kappa and distributed to the Idaho legislature in January, 1979, p. 2.

31. The 1980 property tax year begins January 1, 1980, and property taxes for 1980 will be paid by most people in two installments—December 1980 and June 1981. If the legislature had set January 1, 1979 as the implementation date, the first impact of the Initiative on property tax payments would have been in December 1979.

32. The amounts which local governments could receive for taxes to pay the principal, interest, and redemption charges on bonds is exempt from the freeze. The language in House Bill 166, passed by the Idaho legislature, has not been tested by the courts so there is still some uncertainty as to exactly how the freeze affects operating fund levies.

33. The amount that most local governments will receive under the one percent limitation is expected to be less than the amount they certified in 1978.

34. If the State Tax Commission finds that a county is failing to meet the required

procedures, it may conduct the indexing or reappraisal itself and pay the cost of the program from sales tax funds the county would otherwise receive.

35. The estimate was received by telephone from Alan Dornfest, Research Analyst, State Tax Commission, in June 1979.
36. The alternatives are described in greater detail in Duncombe, Holden, McFeeley, and Weatherby, pp. 34–35.
37. *Ibid.*, pp. 54–55. This provides more details on these alternatives.
38. The author attended city meetings in six areas of Idaho in May and June 1979 to conduct workshops on austerity budgeting and implementation of the One Percent Initiative.
39. The example in this paragraph was provided by Mr. La.,y Schlict, Idaho Division of Budget, Policy Planning and Coordination, by telephone on June 26, 1979.
40. The examples in this paragraph were supplied by Mr. Jerry Wallace, Budget Officer of the University of Idaho, Moscow, Idaho, in June 1979).
41. "Klien Assesses Impact of 1979 Legislative Session on Department," *Serving* (April, 1979): 1–4. *Serving* is published by the Idaho Department of Health and Welfare.
42. "Voters Reject Heavy Tax Cuts," *Public Administration Times* (December, 1978): 1. Also, *National Journal* (June 3, 1978): see note 1. Also, Patricia Meisol, "Searching for a Cure for the Proposition 13 Epidemic," *National Journal* (August 28, 1978): 1362. Also, Susanna McBee, "Prop. 13 Aftermath: A Tax Revolt That Didn't Happen," *Washington Post* (Thursday, November 9, 1978), p. A-5.
43. "States Urge Limit to Federal Spending," *Public Administration Times* (December, 1978): 1.
44. Elizabeth Fletcher, "Congress Opens Debate on Budget Amendment," *Public Administration Times* (March 15, 1979): 1.
45. "U.S. Indebtedness Profiled," *Monthly Tax Features*, Vol. 23, No. 5 (May 1979): 1–2.
46. Fletcher, p. 1. See also, Aaron Wildavsky, "Why Amending the Constitution is Essential to Achieving Self-Control Through Self-Limitation of Expenditure," *The Bureaucrat*, Vol. 9, No. 1 (Spring 1980): 48.
47. *Ibid.*
48. *Ibid.*
49. *U.S. Budget, FY 1980* (Washington, D.C.: Government Printing Office, 1979).
50. Fletcher, p. 1.
51. *Ibid.*

Appendix

Study Questions for Part I

Chapter 1

1. What was the history of ZBB prior to its use in Georgia?
2. What are the distinctive and essential hallmarks of ZBB? The three basic elements?
3. What are decision units and how are they determined?
4. How is a decision package put together?
5. How does the ranking process work?
6. What factors should be carefully weighed before embarking on ZBB?
7. What types of benefits are expected to be achieved from ZBB?
8. Why are implementation strategies significant?
9. Why is determining linkage to existing management systems important?
10. What technical and procedural aspects of ZBB are particularly important?
11. Explain the difference between budgeting in the private and public sectors. Where are they the most similar?
12. What purposes can be served by ZBB in the executive branch?
13. Why isn't ZBB equally appropriate for all types of expenditures?
14. What government programs are best suited for ZBB?
15. How should ZBB relate to the overall budget process?
16. Why does Taylor argue for a "middle ground scenario"?
17. Taylor says it would be difficult for a President to submit his ZBB rank order list to Congress. Why?

Chapter 2

18. How long did it take the federal government to implement ZBB after Carter took office?
19. Explain the HUD transition process.
20. Explain the Ford-Carter transition difficulties as they related to the 1978 budget.
21. Explain how the April 1977 OMB issues were a carry over from the PPB era.
22. Explain how the HUD budget staff prepared to implement ZBB. The use of training?
23. What was ths significance of the May 1977 "Call?"
24. Explain ZBB in HUD.
25. Explain the significances of the secretary's retreat to the ZBB process.
26. What was an issue paper?
27. How long did it take to pull together the decision packages?
28. Explain the difficulty of establishing minimum levels.
29. Explain the significance of the July OMB "planning letter." Note the defining of issues.

30. Note the demand for SAS by OMB.
31. Explain why HUD staff work based on OMB guidance was impossible. Is this significant? Why?
32. Why did the late receipt of materials bother the MBRC?
33. Why was the MBRC week significant for ZBB?
34. Explain how the computer was used. Explain the scoring process.
35. Explain "gate control."
36. Explain the learning value of the MBRC.
37. Explain the tight deadline for the secretary and its significance.
38. What was in the HUD submittal to OMB?
39. Why were mock OMB hearings used? What was accomplished? Did the mock hearings pay off?
40. What did OMB then do?
41. Why is the "Z" impossible?
42. Why is heavy program manager involvement critical?
43. Why is ranking difficult?
44. Why will ZBB require more paper work?
45. Explain why ZBB is time and staff consuming.
46. Why is staff attitude toward ZBB important?
47. Why is top management attitude important?
48. Explain the significance of time demand on management.
49. Why is the origin and sponsorship of ZBB important?

Chapter 3

50. Did OMB interrank agency and department programs?
51. Why did ACTION wish to use several rankings? What result?
52. Why did ACTION wish its domestic and foreign program treated separately?
53. Explain the pro-rating strategy?
54. What problems, associated with ZBB, did ACTION have?
55. What are mark-ups and reclama?

Chapter 4

56. Explain the implications of Miles' lead paragraph.
57. According to Miles, what are the five fundamentals of a good budget system?
58. Explain the two types of authorizations and their significance to budgeting?
59. What does Miles mean by "ZBB is not the endless summer. We are not looking for the perfect wave"?
60. What does the tenure of an assistant secretary have to do with the ZBB procedure?
61. Explain the significance of the crosswalk.
62. Why are high level bureaucrats not likely to be risk-takers and be slow to change? How does this effect consideration of alternatives.
63. Why don't bureaucrats seriously consider reductions in program levels?
64. Why doesn't it make sense to rank programs in the minimum band?

Chapter 5

65. What was OMB's role in ZBB?
66. How did OMB react to ZBB's place in the budget process?
67. What were the ZBB weaknesses in the first year?

68. What was the "aggregated decision packages" problem? What other problems existed?
69. Why was ranking difficult? How did OMB use the rankings?
70. Did ZBB lay out the budget issues? Obscure budget issues?
71. Explain how ZBB helped in interdepartment communication.
72. What problems or negative effects resulted from ZBB?

Chapter 6

73. Did ZBB bring an end to incrementalism in Georgia?
74. What was the research method used by the South?
75. Was the Georgia budget built from zero?
76. If budgeters work in an environment of conflicting values and goals, then does a rational based budget approach such as ZBB make sense as a viable tool?
77. How was the minimum level determined in Georgia?
78. Explain how ranking in Georgia equals incrementalism.
79. Were services cut back or programs eliminated due to ZBB in Georgia?
80. Why did incrementalism continue in Georgia in spite of ZBB?
81. Does the Georgia Legislative Budget Office use ZBB?
82. What are the achievements of ZBB in Georgia? Does it raise the level of debate?

Chapter 7

83. What problems do small local governments face in upgrading their management processes?

Part I Review Questions

1. What are the distinctive and essential hallmarks of ZBB?
2. According to Taylor, what should be considered before an organization embarks on ZBB? To the extent possible, compare Graeme Taylor's advice to what occurred at HUD.
3. Would you say that ZBB was a success? Why or why not?
4. What "implicit problems" exist with ZBB? Based upon the reading (and citing those readings), explain those "problems" and why they are "implicit."
5. What are the implications of Wanamaker's article in terms of (a) applying the ZBB reform to local government, (b) the need for greater professionalism in local government, and (c) potential strategies for upgrading the quality of public budgeting at the local level?

Study Questions for Part II

Chapter 8

1. Explain the significance of the following: "Congress has a proven mechanism to challenge the President's budget policies and priorities and establish its own."
2. Explain the genesis of the 1974 Act.
3. What is the role of the House and Senate budget committees?
4. Explain the overlapping membership provision in the House Budget Committee.

5. Contrast the bipartisan support found in the House and Senate Budget Committees. Why is that significant?
6. Explain the role of staff on the budget committees.
7. What is the CBO? What does it do?
8. Explain the congressional budget timetable. Why is it the heart of the 1974 Act?
9. Why is fiscal policy important to federal budgeting? How does it affect decisions?
10. How does the Budget Committee monitor Congress' spending and revenue actions as well as tie them to the budget resolutions? Explain the crosswalk. Explain the importance of the score keeping reports.
11. Explain why the Budget Committee needed to and did challenge Senator Long over the first FY1977 budget resolution.
12. Explain each procedural provision of the 1974 Act.
13. What six factors help explain the success of the new congressional budget process?
14. Do you agree that the 1974 Act was historically more significant than the Nixon resignation? Why or why not?

Chapter 9

15. Why was the lack of a congressional overall budget review a subject of criticism?
16. Explain the use of reserves by OMB prior to 1974. Why did it become an issue in the Nixon administration?
17. Why does a "continuing resolution" lead to bad administration? Why was it a common situation prior to 1974?
18. Explain why budget people and program managers must think in terms of both obligation and outlay levels.
19. In what ways are there more involvements between the agency budget officer and Congress today?
20. Why are time schedules more difficult today for the agency budget officer?
21. Why does the handling of deferrals and recession constitute more work for the agency budget officer?
22. Why is estimating more important today?

Chapter 10

23. What is the purpose of sunset legislation?
24. What prompted introducing sunset legislation? Why was the uncontrollable program factor important?
25. Explain the significance of sunset being essentially a congressional process.
26. Why are programs not terminated with sunset legislation?
27. Explain the work load problem associated with sunset legislation.

Chapter 11

28. What is new about sunset?
29. Why are the most controversial programs likely to be hurt more by sunset?
30. Explain the significance of "doubt" upon a program.
31. What is the problem with agencies becoming more self-protective?
32. Why would sunset interfere with the president's ability to manage?

Part II Review Questions

1. Explain how, citing Smith's chapter, the power of the Congress was strengthened in contrast to the president's power by the 1974 Act?
2. Budget offices were growth areas in the federal government due to the 1974 Act and ZBB. Citing the Betts and Miller article as well as others in this book, explain why. What more must be done by the agency budget office due to the reforms of the 1970s?
3. Summarize the pro and con arguments for sunset legislation. Do you believe this legislation will make much difference in federal programs? Why or why not?

Study Questions for Part III

Chapter 12

1. Explain some of the activities associated with a financial management system.
2. Explain the role of MAC in the New York City fiscal crisis.
3. Explain the accounting problem in New York City and the reform adopted. What problems arose? Explain the problem with the fund structure. Why was reform essential?
4. Why is an integration of budgeting and other system components important?
5. Why is it wise to have organizationally based budgets?
6. Explain the use of monthly plans for obligations, revenue recognition by budget source, and cash collection by revenue sources.
7. Explain the usefulness of monthly reports compared to plans and exception reports.
8. What reports are useful?
9. Explain the advantage of having agency managers primarily responsible for purchasing. How does the system help the manager?
10. Why is it important for the IFMS to provide a flow of payroll documents and transactions at a detailed level of control?
11. Why should the payroll be integrated with the budget system?
12. Explain the advantage of an automatic system.
13. Explain how an IFMS helps secure federal and state grants.
14. Explain how an IFMS can help an agency maximize its revenue.
15. Explain how an IFMS can help an agency analyze its costs and plan better.
16. Explain how New York City used consultants to develop its IFMS.

Chapter 13

17. Explain the difference between efficiency and effectiveness.
18. What are output indicators?
19. Explain how one describes efficiency through measurement.
20. Is productivity a major concern of state and local government?
21. Explain the use of output/input ratios by the federal government.
22. Why are engineered work standards important to productivity?
23. Explain how effectiveness measurement procedures work.

24. Why is a comprehensive measurement system important for a sophisticated productivity understanding?
25. What is the likelihood of sophisticated productivity work being done at the local level of government?

Chapter 14

26. What are the major aspects of California's proposition 13?
27. What results can be attributed to proposition 13's passage?
28. What prompted the positive vote for the initiative?
29. In what ways do homeowners benefit from proposition 13?
30. In what way are new property owners treated unequally from old property owners?
31. In what way did business benefit?
32. Why are minorities and young people more likely to be disadvantaged by the initiative?
33. What are the major aspects of Idaho's proposition 13?
34. Why did Idaho's initiative #1 pass?
35. What implementation dilemmas existed for the 1979 Idaho legislature?
36. How could the legislature ease the local financial problems caused by the iniative?
37. What effect did the initiative have on local government? What cutback measures were used?
38. What effect did the initiative have on state government?
39. What future impacts seem likely?
40. How widespread is the tax revolt?
41. What reforms seem to have widespread appeal?
42. Explain the controversy surrounding the national balanced budget movement.
43. What are the pro and con arguments?

Part III Review Questions

1. Explain what clumsy administrative practices one should anticipate that would be associated with integrating financial management systems. Why do they tend to exist? What are their consequences?
2. Why is it difficult to measure government productivity? What type of skill and knowledge is useful to achieve increased productivity?
3. What "caused" the tax revolt? What factors tend to mitigate against the movement?

Contributors

ERNEST C. BETTS, JR. is principal associate of Executive Management Service and was formerly the budget officer and assistant secretary for administration of the U. S. Department of the Treasury.

NANETTE M. BLANDIN was a budget examiner in the Intelligence Division of the U. S. Office of Management and Budget.

RALPH C. BLEDSOE is professor of political science at the Federal Executive Institute.

STEVE CHARNOVITZ is a policy analyst in the U. S. Department of Labor.

JAMES DAVIDSON was staff counsel for the U. S. Senate Committee on Government Operations' subcommittee on Intergovernmental Relations.

ARNOLD E. DONAHUE is the director of the Intelligence Division of the U. S. Office of Management and Budget.

SYDNEY DUNCOMBE is professor of political science at the University of Idaho.

HARRY P. HATRY is director of the State and Local Government Research Program of the Urban Institute.

THOMAS P. LAUTH is assistant professor of political science at Georgia State University.

THOMAS D. LYNCH is associate professor of political science at Mississippi State University.

EMERSON MARKHAM was director of the Budget Division of ACTION.

JEROME A. MILES wa a comptroller at the Department of Energy as well as a budget officer for the Department of Agriculture.

RICHARD E. MILLER is vice-president of the Executive Management Service and was formerly comptroller of the U. S. Department of Labor.

ELI B. SILVERMAN is associate dean of John Jay College of Criminal Justice, City University of New York.

LINDA L. SMITH served on the majority professional staff of the U. S. House Committee on the Budget.

GRAEME M. TAYLOR is senior vice-president of Management Analysis Center, Inc.

DANIEL K. WANAMAKER was director of Title I programs (Higher Education Act of 1965) and assistant professor at the Public Service Institute, Western Kentucky University.

Index